WITHDRAWN

THE AMERICAN CORPORATION

Its Power, Its Money, Its Politics

THE
AMERICAN
CORPORATION

Its Power, Its Money, Its Politics

By Richard J. Barber

E. P. Dutton & Co., Inc.
NEW YORK   1970

Second Printing March 1971

Published simultaneously in Canada by
Clarke, Irwin & Company Limited, Toronto and Vancouver

Library of Congress Catalog Card Number: 77-93749

Printed in the U.S.A. by Vail-Ballou Press, Inc.

SBN 0-525-05324-7

For Bets

Contents

viii   Contents

Tables and Charts

Introduction

CHAPTER 1

Politics and
the New Worlds of Business

"When faced with a totally new situation, we tend always to attach ourselves to the objects, to the flavor of the most recent past. We look at the present through a rear-view mirror."
—*Marshall McLuhan*

Most people are overly accustomed to using the term "revolution" to characterize all sorts of social adjustments and are even more prone to confining its application to the harsh, violent symptoms of change. As a consequence, the quieter, often more powerful forces that fundamentally reshape our world—like those in business—are commonly overlooked. Today the American business system is quite literally being torn apart and reassembled in a radically different form, with an even more pronounced change in its ingredients. But this is a silent revolution and most people—in government, journalism, on the campuses, and in industry itself—have failed to appreciate, in any comprehensive manner, what is actually taking place. Yet the implications—for the political no less than the economic order—are truly massive in scale, though complex and subtle in character.

To be ignorant of these forces of change in business is to acquiesce passively in the kind of society they will resolutely mold, one that is likely to be acceptable only to the comparative handful of people who will comprise an elite of affluent technocrats holding strategic places of power in corporations, universities, "nonprofit" institutions, and government. It is time for us to remove the blinders and take a hard look at the realities of the new worlds of business. That is the aim of this book and this chapter offers something of a preview of what is to follow. You will remember from Lewis Carroll's *Through the Looking-Glass:* "the first thing to do was to make a grand survey of the country she was going to travel through. 'It's something very like learning geography,' thought Alice as she stood on tiptoe in hopes of being able to see a little further." Well, this chapter is that "grand survey."

Whatever one's political or ideological outlook, it is imperative to recognize that the American economy *is* dominated by business, that it will continue to be so for the foreseeable future, and that, as a result, the decisions of U.S. companies and their officers will play a vital role in shaping the future of our economic and social order. One does not have to be a Chamber of Commerce tub-thumper to recognize that business accounts for more than four out of five jobs and that just about the entire national output is attributable to business activity. Of the more than $130 billion invested annually in fixed capital, about three fourths consists of outlays for new plant and equipment.

Business—whether the global billion-dollar auto corporation or the corner service establishment—is itself changing through its own activities, but it is also being changed by outside forces in a way and to a degree far different from ever before. In the process new alliances are emerging and old concepts are losing their relevance. Government, once accepted as the regulator of business, is now its willing partner. Indeed, privately owned corporations are becoming so deeply immersed in functions which historically have been regarded as "public" that the old demarcation of "public" and "private" no longer has meaning. Not so long ago Calvin Coolidge said that "the business of government is business." As recent as 1957 Charles E. Wilson conveyed much the same thought with his famous remark that "what's good for General Motors is good for America." Ridiculous, it was said at the time and so it seemed. Today both comments have substantial accuracy, for government and business have embarked on a new partnership that is drawing together what once were regarded as deeply rooted foes.

Our worlds of business are changing in many other ways of no less public consequence. It now makes no more sense to think of corporations as American, or English, or Dutch, than to attach significance to a company's state of incorporation. (Where is General Motors legally incorporated? What difference does it make?) Many "U.S." companies earn more from their foreign sales than they do "at home." Corporations are not only sprawling out all over the industrialized world, but they are losing their product identity, too. Primarily through mergers, corporations are shrugging off their old forms and diversifying wildly throughout American industry. For dozens of conglomerate firms—like Litton Industries, Gulf & Western, Ling-Temco-Vought, and Textron—any effort at categorization by product or industry is futile. For those of us who grew up in a simpler world—when Ford meant cars, Pet was synonymous with milk, when Standard Oil was just a giant petroleum company (rather than also a builder of new cities and a maker of chemicals and synthetic food), and the New York Central was a railroad (rather than a mate in a goliath enterprise that goes under the name Penn Central and disavows any exclusive interest in railroading or even transportation)—these radical shifts in the nature of corporation operations pose baffling issues of policy.

The old landmarks are gone, but the fundamental issue remains: how can we be sure that large, diversified, geographically diffused, and immensely powerful corporations serve rather than frustrate the public interest? The search for the answer to that central question is no less important to business than to the public, for corporate executives too are embarking on a sea that is largely uncharted. Business today is being urged, from within and outside its ranks, to get "involved" in the toughest, most sensitive problems of the society—in the cities, housing, job training, civil rights, education, and the elimination of air and water pollution and generally in the improvement of the human environment. With the payoff only partly in profits, companies are thus being asked to participate in the solution of social problems for which no one has sound answers and which lie well outside the accepted, known bounds of their experience.

Business is at the very center of the confluence of forces that are transforming the society. It is the nation's primary instrument of technological change—performing most of our research and putting the discoveries of science to use. Its planning for the future—a function of increasing importance and sophistication—promises to shape and be shaped by the contours and composition of the American economy. The development and expansion of financial institutions—like pension funds, bank-managed trusts, and mutual funds—are altering the patterns of control of the country's biggest corporations. Although business itself is a major source of this change, it is also caught in the currents that emanate from other social and economic forces. Business's constituency is being transformed in its ideological orientation. Nonprofit organizations are competing with profit-seeking corporations. At the same time that trade unions are losing much of their significance, the growing presence within the contemporary corporation of scientists and highly trained young management specialists introduces new pressures and distinctive tensions within the firm. From outside, consumers, suppliers, and universities are subjecting the modern company to a unique set of forces that inevitably shape its behavior and condition its role in the society. Finally, whether they will acknowledge it or not, most corporate executives have become Keynesians, accepting the essential role of government as stabilizer and energizer of the economy. Here, though, it is not enough to recognize government's critical role in the economy, for the economy's rate of growth can be assured only through careful management and the broad-gauged cooperation of both government and business. This fact—this emerging interdependence—is still another reason for their new partnership and for the near-disappearance of their old hostility.

A convulsion of change has clearly swept through the American business community since the end of World War II and particularly since the mid-1950s, but it has been largely masked by the fantastic growth of the economy. Most public attention has been focused on the large contours of growth rather than on the more refined, less immediately apparent changes that have taken place in the business sector. Since 1946 Gross National Product (GNP) of the United States has grown two and a half times (in real terms), soaring to a level well above $900 billion—an amount not far from being equal to the output of the rest of the world. U.S. manufacturers added as much to their output in these two-plus decades of growth as they had in all the prior years since the industrial revolution of the nineteenth century. While our population rose by a third—more than sixty million people—Americans have 50 percent more money to spend per capita in 1970 than in 1946, after making allowance for inflation. And they are spending it by the billions—for cars, housing, appliances, and clothes, but increasingly for services and for education. Nearly twenty million more people are employed and more than thirty million homes and apartments have been built. It has truly been a sparkling record of economic achievement, but the demands and opportunities will continue unabated.

What will happen between now and 2000? By the end of the century another 125 million Americans will be sharing the bounty of an economy four times bigger than that we now have. An additional 50 million people will be employed—working fewer hours yet producing goods and services with a value two and a half times as much as a third of a century earlier. With average annual family incomes near $15,000, it will be an era of superaffluence.

With all of this economic thunder and lightning, it is not surprising that most people have not looked closely at the transformation of business that has taken place. And yet these changes in the worlds of business are of incalculable importance—for corporations and citizens alike. Take the matter of corporate size. Bigness in American business is not new, but it has accelerated at such a pace in the postwar period that it has taken on what amounts to a distinctive character. Carried forward by a massive wave of mergers, the biggest firms have gotten bigger—much bigger—and have acquired such a large position in the economy that for all practical purposes they have become major sovereigns—rich empires with their own barons, emissaries, and constituencies.

General Motors is an example of this modern feudalism. With its 1,300,000 stockholders (of whom a substantial number are citizens of other countries), its 700,00 foreign and American employees, its hundreds of suppliers, plants in virtually every state, and facilities in twenty-four countries, General Motors—to take just one example—is a political "state" except to those who are interested in formalities. Like most political entities the big U.S. corporations have shown a marked tendency to expand and to diversify in recent years, shrugging off their established product and industrial identities. Oil companies have acquired coal mining companies and embarked on major real estate ventures, dairy corporations have merged with chemical producers, railroads now make steel products and manage new towns, auto makers have added electronics subsidiaries, and electronics specialists have plunged into publishing and education. As a consequence many well-known firms have disappeared from the business scene, swallowed up into the bellies of gargantuan corporations that resemble Insull's holding companies of the twenties or the Zaibatsu of prewar Japan.

Industrial diversification is only one aspect of this new corporate diffusion. Another is geographic, for American companies have gone global. In a billion-dollar international invasion on European shores, they made their initial large-scale landings in the 1950s. From there they went on to gain a primary position in computers, electronics, petroleum, autos, and heavy machinery, among other industries, much to the chagrin of many Europeans, not just Charles de Gaulle. To a very considerable extent, U.S. business has been more internationally minded, quicker than the United States Government to recognize the fact that there is now a single world economy. Today deliveries of U.S. products to foreign markets total about $200 billion, but only a sixth of this comes from factories in the United States: the rest is made and sold abroad by foreign workers employed by American subsidiaries.

As businesses have expanded their product and geographic boundaries, they have been compelled to work in quite novel ways with new groups of constituents and to accommodate themselves to new social, economic, and technological forces. Scientists and science have presented new but unavoidable challenges and near-limitless opportunities. Billions of dollars in Federal research contracts have forged a three-way partnership between government, American industry, and higher education that is completely without parallel in our history. The resulting accelerated pace of technological change broadens business opportunities but presents major risks as well. The management of science and the forecasting of future market trends which will emerge from research efforts now underway have forced corporate managers to place great emphasis on long-term planning. Top-level corporate managers now spend as much time peering into the future, in the manner of lookouts aboard vessels, as they do in running the immediate affairs of their firms. In the "lookout" process a sharp eye must be kept on the future course of the economy—its rate of growth and changes in its composition. The crucial significance of a sufficiently rapid and predictable economic rate of growth—coupled with business's new recognition of the role which the government must play as an expansionary and stabilizing force in regulating the economy—helps further to cement the emerging government-business partnership. An additional bond is being forged by the marked tendency of government to involve business in the resolution of the many complex social problems that are part of urbanized society.

Put all of these elements together and it can be seen that the worlds of business are undergoing fundamental alteration, straining the capacity of corporate executives just as severely as the imagination of the average citizen. Mergers, industrial diversification, internationalization, technological change induced by intensive research commitments, direct involvement in accumulated problems of the society, an expanded constituency: confusing, distracting, complex, dynamic—yet intertwined with all the rest of our unsettled world, affected by it, deeply affecting it. To think of it otherwise is not in the interest of business, the public, or of truth.

The changes that are taking place in the worlds of business are so new in our experience that they outrace our conceptions of the appropriate relationship between business and government. Sixty years ago it was a lot simpler. The barons of capital—John D. Rockefeller, Morgan, Hill, and company—presented sharply etched subjects for political characterization, and Teddy Roosevelt could speak unqualifiedly of the threat the "malefactors of great wealth" posed as "the tyranny of plutocracy." The question, Woodrow Wilson could say in 1913, is "who is going to be master of the government of the United States—the great corporations or the government." In the days of Teddy Roosevelt and Wilson this black-white notion of government's role vis-à-vis business may have been accurate and timely. The issues today are more subtle and less simple. "We must move on from the reassuring repetition of stale phrases," John F. Kennedy said in his 1962 Yale commencement address, "to a new, difficult, but essential confrontation with reality." The debunking of myth and the affirmation of belief in reality are refreshing comments for a President; but their assertion makes it no easier to decide how best to harness business, in its many changing dimensions, to the general welfare and conversely how to insure that government does not unwisely restrict business in its legitimate search for profit.

In considering this central issue of public policy, social critics have offered little of help in dealing with the changing worlds of business, generally taking refuge in the myth and folklore of an earlier day. Whatever the reason, there has been no systematic, continuing attention paid to the business sector and the way it affects all segments of the public. As a result we are burdened with conceptions of the relationship between government and business that are rooted more in myth than fact. We have been marching backward into the future, carrying our heavy burden of myth with us. For many conservatives, business is taken as "good" almost by definition; leave it alone—free it from government regulation—and the public interest will best be served. Most enlightened industrial leaders actually have never accepted this principle, for they know that government offers much of tangible importance and realize that business occupies such a central position in the economy that it cannot expect to live apart.

From the other end of the spectrum, liberals have also taken a simplistic view of business, by and large distrusting it because of its presumed inhuman profit orientation, but conceding its inevitability. Although they regard industry as an amoral force that pursues solely economic goals rather than "other," more desirable social objectives, the liberal critics and their allies in the New Left have not generally paid enough attention to business to enable them to articulate a set of rules that, even from their view, might harness private interests to the public welfare. Rather they have either largely foregone a serious look at the new worlds of business or retreated into the familiar ground of rhetoric, sometimes criticizing business for its lack of a social conscience, yet spasmodically soliciting its involvement in the solution of contemporary social problems.

Within the liberal community there are widely divergent points of view about government's role toward business. Some—a small, earnest group of contemporary antitrust populists who view themselves as the last defenders of competition and the true integrity of the free market—would "break up" big businesses (like General Motors, U.S. Steel, General Electric, Standard Oil of New Jersey, and IBM) through aggressive antitrust action, stop most mergers, put a ceiling on corporate size, and restrict firms to operations in one or two industries. Led for several years by Senator Estes Kefauver, and now by Senator Philip A. Hart, this group has a small band of followers in certain Republican intellectual circles, notably the Economics Department at the University of Chicago. Ideologues like Professor Milton Friedman, an off-and-on economics adviser to Richard Nixon (and previously to Barry Goldwater), believe that greater reliance must be placed on classical market forces if government controls are to be avoided—controls that, in their view, will restrict freedom and lead to other undesirable political consequences. Nixon Cabinet member George Romney, a former president of American Motors and GOP Presidential hopeful, once asserted a similar position, urging that bigness in business must be sternly checked, through antitrust if need be, if the free enterprise system is to work effectively.

For most businessmen—particularly the executives of the nation's largest corporations and financial institutions—and a wide cross section of politicians in both parties, however, any serious talk of vigorous antitrust enforcement aimed at restructuring or dismembering big business firms simply reflects a lack of understanding of economic realities and public needs. This is not to say that antitrust enforcement is not without its uses in certain special situations, such as those that took shape in the last years. Nineteen sixty-nine marked a sudden awakening of interest in the significance of the great contemporary merger movement for the business community. Although corporate mergers soared to a record high of 4,500 in 1968 (they aggregated more than 5,000 in 1969), it was not their number that brought them to the forefront of public attention and produced frantic calls for action by legislators, businessmen, and editorialists to slow down the merger trend. Rather it was their character. What had happened was that the old and well-established corporations were being jeopardized with takeover by the aggressive, new-fangled conglomerates. The fears of the business old guard were well founded. Late in 1968 Jones & Laughlin Steel (one of the top 100 firms, with assets of over a billion dollars) succumbed to Ling-Temco-Vought and Armour was captured by much smaller General Host Corporation. Sinclair Oil escaped conquest by Gulf & Western, one of the most acquisitive conglomerates, only by fleeing into the arms of Atlantic-Richfield. Early in 1969 campaigns were mounted by the Leasco Data Processing Equipment Corporation (whose founder and chairman is twenty-nine-year-old Saul P. Steinberg) to acquire the Chemical Bank of New York, the nation's sixth biggest bank and a full-fledged member of the Wall Street banking club. As the months passed in 1969 additional takeover moves were made known. Pan American Airways was threatened by Resorts International and, in what may have been the straw that broke the business establishment's back, Northwest Industries attempted to seize power at the much bigger and far more staid B. F. Goodrich Company.

This series of challenges for control of several of the country's largest companies produced screams of anguish from highly respected business leaders and pleas for government intervention. It is important to recognize, however, that this pressure came from businessmen who generally have a marked distaste for anything that savors of antitrust and who usually consider mergers as healthy signs, unobjectionable provided they are mutually agreeable to the managements of the companies involved. In taking the unprecedented step in 1969 of urging action by the antitrust enforcers to block, as examples, Northwest Industries' planned takeover of B. F. Goodrich and LTV's purchase of Jones & Laughlin Steel, conservative business executives simply wanted to end, as *Fortune* put it, "the threat to the established way of doing corporate business" posed by conglomerate "upstarts, the outsiders." When it comes to the fact of business bigness itself—the legitimacy of the giant corporations who want to be sheltered by government from the menace of an unwelcome takeover—well, that is an entirely different story.

As the executives of the largest U.S. corporations see it, the bigness of their enterprises simply reflects the way things must be in an industrial economy. This position is shared by many who are commonly thought of as holding radically different points of view—labor leaders, leftish university professors, liberal Democrats, most conservative Republicans, and well-known corporate chieftains. In the view of one, Harvard economist John Kenneth Galbraith, the modern economy requires large-scale industrial planning, carried out by a group of specialists within the mature corporation—the "technostructure," as he terms it. Such planning, Galbraith argues, demands that the firm have effective control over price and the market, the very types of control that are the antithesis of classical economic theory and the *bête noire* of antitrust. His view, interestingly, is shared both by the leaders of the major industrial unions, like United Auto Workers President Walter Reuther, and by the presidents of the country's principal corporations. Bigness in business, they agree, in some cases reluctantly, is inevitable and desirable in that it permits the accumulation of large units of capital, massive continuing research, and long-term product planning. Given this assessment, it is only reasonable to anticipate that government and the corporate community will come to work together, each accepting the other's legitimacy.

Among those who accept bigness in business as unavoidable, there is nonetheless a lack of agreement about its implications. Barry Goldwater, a firm believer in business and hardly an advocate of a "bust-'em-up" antitrust program, criticizes "big businessmen" who "will do almost anything for the dollar" and laments the disappearance of "the old leader of business, the man who would stand up and scrap for what he knew was right for his business and for the country." From the other end of the ideological spectrum, John Kenneth Galbraith, although convinced that huge corporate size and market control are inherent in our kind of economy, also finds the situation distasteful.* Big companies, he feels, even when working in partnership with government, pursue "economic goals," and "if economic goals are the only goals of the society it is natural that the industrial system should dominate the state and the state should serve its ends." In Galbraith's judgment, society's purposes will only be served if "other goals" are given preeminence over "economic goals." But that, too, is more hopeful than realistic for the principal purpose of business *is* the search for profit. To give priority to the "other" goals of which he speaks would require a basic change in our economic-political system, one that would seemingly call for greater state direction and control than most are willing to accept.

Any thought of vesting in government more authority over the economy is, of course, fundamentally unacceptable to businessmen and to most political leaders. They want to work in constructive partnership—in an alliance of equals. But in doing so, both are embarking on a new, untested relationship for which there are no precedents, no accepted rules to govern their association. Here, then, is one of the great challenges to business and government. With big business playing an ever larger role in the economy and becoming more directly involved in problem areas once thought to be "governmental" in character, we are groping for standards by which to judge and influence the effects from the standpoint of the total public interest. Old theories—the decades-old folklore of businessmen and politicians—are no longer adequate. We need a new theory but do not have it, yet, and no theory can be devised without a better factual grasp of the situation in all its complexity.

Never have the leaders of business, or government, been confronted by so many challenges to their established modes of conduct and thought. Business itself is changing radically—in its size,

---

* His views, with customary acidity, are set forth in *The New Industrial State* (Houghton Mifflin, Boston: 1966).

diversification, control—in its trend to globalization—in its pace of technological change—in the constituency with which it must work and serve. At the same time, its relations with government are being altered. A revolution is underway.

PART I

The New Faces of Corporate America

CHAPTER 2

The Corporate Goliaths

If we are to understand what is really going on in the changing worlds of business and identify the problems that lie ahead—problems of no less consequence to businessmen than to the general public—the first thing we must do is get the facts about corporate size, market power, diversification, mergers, and corporate control. That is the purpose of this and the two succeeding chapters.

The starting point must be an examination of the extent to which a few immense corporations dominate American industry. Their incredible absolute size and commanding market position make them the most exceptional man-made creatures of the twentieth century. Indeed, their economic might, political position, and social stature is matched only by a few major nations. In terms of the size of their constituency, volume of receipts and expenditures, effective power, and prestige, they are more akin to nation-states than business enterprises of the classic variety.

General Motors' yearly operating revenues exceed those of all but a dozen or so countries. Its sales receipts are greater than the *combined* general revenues of New York, New Jersey, Pennsylvania, Ohio, Delaware, and the six New England states. Its

19

1,300,000 stockholders are equal to the population of Washington, Baltimore, or Houston. GM employees number well over 700,000 and work in 127 plants in the United States and forty-five in countries spanning Europe, South Africa, North America, and Australasia. Their total cash wages are more than twice the personal income of Ireland. GM's Federal corporate tax payments approach $2 billion, or enough to pay for all Federal grants in fiscal year 1970 in the field of health research. The enormity of General Motors, seen from whatever angle, is stupefying, but it should not be thought of as unique. Some 175 other manufacturing, merchandising, and transportation companies now have annual sales of at least a billion dollars. One, rivaling GM in the grandeur of its operations, is Standard Oil of New Jersey. With more than a hundred thousand employees around the world (it has three times as many people overseas as the U.S. State Department), a six-million-ton tanker fleet (half again bigger than Russia's), and $17 billion in assets (nearly equal to the combined assessed valuation of Chicago and Los Angeles), it can more easily be thought of as a nation-state than a commercial enterprise.

To gain a better impression of the scale of the bigger U.S. companies one has to view them against a larger industrial backdrop. Looked at this way, we find that a mere 100 firms—less than a tenth of 1 percent of a total 300,000 firms—account for fully a third of the value added by manufacturing (sales less the cost of materials and services purchased), employ 25 percent of manufacturing employees (and make a third of all wages payments), make nearly 40 percent of new capital expenditures, and own about half of all assets used in manufacturing. What this means is that the presidents of a hundred companies—a group sufficiently small to be seated comfortably in the reading room of the Union League Club in Philadelphia—represent almost as much wealth and control as large a share of the nation's economic activity as the next largest 300,000 manufacturers—a group that would completely fill four Yankee Stadiums.

Hyperconcentration in business is by no means a new phenomenon, but it has shown a steady tendency to become tighter during the postwar period. At the end of World War II the 100 largest manufacturing companies accounted for 23 percent of the total value added by manufacture. Some thought their position would deteriorate as new companies came on the scene and new products were put on the market. But this did not happen. Steadily the top 100's share rose, so that their present share exceeds 33 percent, nearly half again as large as the sizable position they occupied twenty years ago. In terms of assets the commanding position of the country's biggest enterprises is even more clearly evident. The 200 largest manufacturing corporations now control almost 60 percent of all manufacturing assets, up from less than 50 percent only twenty years ago.

Even this, however, fails to describe sufficiently the proportionate as well as the absolute growth of the top-ranked American corporations. Throughout the postwar years, and especially since the mid-fifties, U.S. firms have invested heavily abroad. In fact, they have expanded their position in other countries more rapidly than they have at home. In barely a decade our direct investments abroad have rocketed from $33 billion to more than $65 billion. The value of U.S. direct investments overseas now increases at the rate of about $10 million a day. The result is that the biggest corporations have substantially increased their share of international production by even more than they have within the United States.

While the industrial titans have continued to increase the size of their position in the economy, it is also true that the subgiants— what might be labeled the second-tier firms—have grown, too, even somewhat more rapidly. This has meant something of an evening-out in comparative firm size—a trend to greater equality. While this has meant somewhat more size uniformity among the biggest industrial companies, it has also marked their growth at the expense of smaller manufacturers—a further step toward even higher levels of corporate concentration in the economy.

Industry: Rule by the Few

While the overall level of concentration is of consequence— primarily because it delineates who has how much of our aggregate economic might—it tells us little about the structure of individual industries. It is conceivable, for example, that a corporation could look very big and powerful in terms of the assets it held (and be of significance for that reason), but be so widely spread across the economic landscape that it would not be a potent factor in any of the markets where it conducts its affairs. A firm that accounted for 5 percent each of the sales of autos and electrical equipment and chemicals and steel and petroleum would be a very big enterprise indeed. It would not, however, be much of a factor in any *one* of these markets.

In closely examining the industrial terrain of the United States, one feature is paramount: the degree to which a very few firms rule most of the principal manufacturing sectors. It is a rare case in which one firm, alone, makes most of the sales for a given product. General Electric continues to make most of the light bulbs, Western Electric produces virtually all of our telephone equipment for its parent, American Telephone & Telegraph, and General Motors sells all but a few of the diesel locomotives put into service by the railroads. The general pattern can be found in the automobile industry where General Motors makes about half of the new autos sold, Ford another 25 percent, and Chrysler approximately 15 percent; in copper (where Anaconda, Phelps Dodge, Kennecott, and American Smelting divide the market); in aluminum, steel, chemicals, heavy electrical equipment, cigarettes, rubber tires, flat glass, cereal foods, farm equipment, and a long list of other industries. The key fact is that in each, no one firm is dominant (there is no monopolist in the classical sense that one seller makes just about all the sales of the product in question), but rather power is shared by a handful of large companies. Result: what the economists call an oligopoly (Greek for a "few sellers").

An industry-by-industry survey of the U.S. economy reveals that oligopolistic patterns characterize most of the bigger industries, particularly those engaged in the manufacture of consumer durables and goods used by producers of other products. In all, about two thirds of our manufacturing industries can be regarded as highly concentrated. Given the crucial position of manufacturing

CHART 1
Industries Dominated by a Few Big Firms

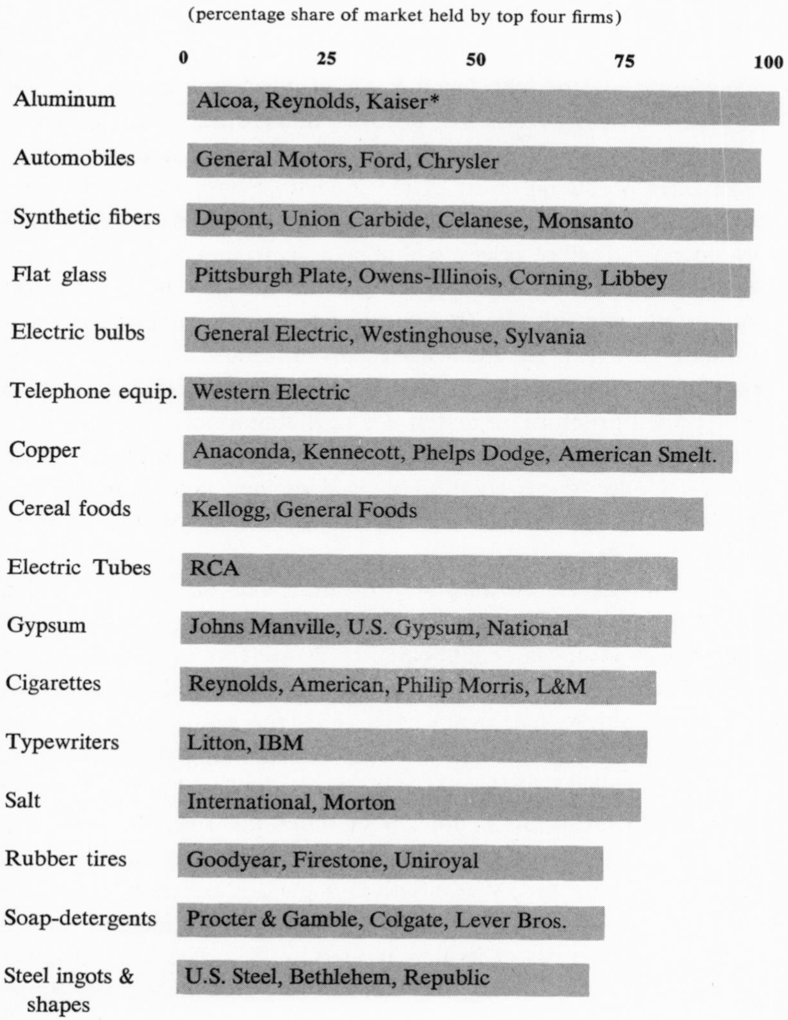

(percentage share of market held by top four firms)

	0	25	50	75	100
Aluminum	Alcoa, Reynolds, Kaiser*				
Automobiles	General Motors, Ford, Chrysler				
Synthetic fibers	Dupont, Union Carbide, Celanese, Monsanto				
Flat glass	Pittsburgh Plate, Owens-Illinois, Corning, Libbey				
Electric bulbs	General Electric, Westinghouse, Sylvania				
Telephone equip.	Western Electric				
Copper	Anaconda, Kennecott, Phelps Dodge, American Smelt.				
Cereal foods	Kellogg, General Foods				
Electric Tubes	RCA				
Gypsum	Johns Manville, U.S. Gypsum, National				
Cigarettes	Reynolds, American, Philip Morris, L&M				
Typewriters	Litton, IBM				
Salt	International, Morton				
Rubber tires	Goodyear, Firestone, Uniroyal				
Soap-detergents	Procter & Gamble, Colgate, Lever Bros.				
Steel ingots & shapes	U.S. Steel, Bethlehem, Republic				

* Only the names of leading firms in each industry are identified. In some cases there is only a single dominant company, in others there may be two, three, or four.

in the economy, its marked oligopolistic characteristics have great consequence for the way industries behave in their dealings with the public.

In an oligopolistic market, prices and profits typically are higher than they would be with lower levels of concentration. Price competition is severely restricted, if not eliminated outright. No formal price-fixing conspiracy is necessary. Where there are, say, three companies producing most of the industry's output (automobiles, for example), the condition, once nicely described as "spontaneous coordination" of prices, will almost invariably be present: each seller knows that it both affects and is affected by the market choices of its rivals. If, therefore, company A establishes a significantly lower price than what has prevailed, its share of the market will increase considerably; its rivals, B and C, can thus be expected promptly to match A's newly announced price. Whatever gain A might originally have anticipated by cutting its price is lost. Under these conditions, it does not take long for the parties, independently, to price in a uniform noncompetitive fashion.

General Motors, the auto industry titan, sets the prices at which it will sell its cars in such a way as to yield a rate of return that will provide after-tax profits equal to 20 percent on its net investment. Such a profit rate is nearly twice that of the average corporation and almost half again as large as the profits of most large manufacturing firms. Because of its commanding position in the auto industry GM tends to set the lead and Ford, Chrysler, and American Motors fall in line. Sometimes the smaller auto companies gleefully boost the prices they have already established in order to conform to GM's initiative. A good illustration took place just a few years ago. Ford announced an average increase of 2.9 percent in the prices of its new models. A few days later GM announced it was increasing its prices on comparable models by an average of 6.1 percent. Some might be so unrealistic to think that Ford would have let its lower prices remain in effect, hoping thereby to steal sales away from its bigger rival. Ford (and, later, Chrysler) promptly hiked its prices to match the GM prices almost dollar for dollar. More commonly, as with the 1970 model cars, the others wait for GM to post its prices, then follow along in lockstep fashion.

This kind of pricing interdependence is a continuing feature of the many oligopolistic industries in which a small group of "competing" firms account for most of the sales. By the very nature of such industries there can be no meaningful price competition. Prices are substantially identical at almost any given moment in time. Such rivalry as takes place (and this is limited to products, like autos or gasoline or cigarettes, which can be merchandised in such a way as to create in the prospective consumer's mind the impression of distinctiveness) is confined to product differentiation, advertising, and assorted psychosocial selling techniques.

In most markets a small group of manufacturers long ago established a tight hold and their grip is not being weakened by competition or the entry of new firms. Data for the 1960s show that in industries where concentration was already high (where the top four firms accounted for at least half the industry's sales) there was no significant net change at all. In about half of this group of fifty-three industries, there was very little movement, up or down. In fourteen cases concentration declined a little, but in twelve it rose by at least an equal amount. What has happened is that over the years large companies have succeeded in achieving a high-level oligopolistic plateau in most key industries. And that redoubt appears substantially impregnable to change through the operation of normal economic forces.

It is equally important to put aside the views of those who assert that industry is in such a constant flux that no firm, however mighty, can be certain of preserving its position, preeminent though it may be. One way to gauge this issue is to consider the facts pertaining to turnover within the ranks of the largest industrial corporations. Take the fifty biggest companies in 1947. By 1963, twenty of these firms had fallen outside the ranks of the biggest fifty; but they had not slipped very much. Sixteen were ranked among the next fifty. If the situation is turned around, the record shows that of the fifty top firms in 1963, thirty were in the top fifty in 1947 and another ten were in the next fifty in that earlier year. Consider a more recent period. Of the twenty biggest industrial firms in 1955, sixteen were counted among the top twenty in 1967 and all twenty were ranked in the biggest thirty-five. Conversely, of the four firms which had soared into the upper-twenty category in 1967, three were ranked in the biggest thirty-five, twelve years earlier. The giants change positions but not radically so, even over a span of years that is distinguished by rapid economic growth and the introduction of many technological innovations.

Merger Mania

The United States has for some time been in the midst of the greatest merger movement in the nation's history—greater in magnitude than even the floodtide of the early 1900s and 1920s. In 1968 the number of mergers between corporations rose to the record level of 4,462 * and there is no sign that they will lessen in number or economic consequence in the foreseeable future. In 1969 there were an estimated 5,400 mergers.

Corporations have always been in the marriage business (there is virtually no large corporation that you can think of that at some point has not acquired, merged, or consolidated with some other corporation), but what is different now is the vast number of mergers and especially the size of the participants. Once it was common—probably typical—for competing or related enterprises to join together, often for the principal objective of gaining sufficient size to match the strength of a rival or simply to gain dominance over a market. Such mergers still occur, but we are finding that the acquirer and often both partners are already large firms. Moreover, they are frequently in completely unrelated industries (the diversification or "conglomerate" aspect of the merger movement will be taken up in the next chapter). From 1948 through 1968, 1,275 firms with assets of $10 million or more were acquired—in more than half the cases by a company with assets of

* The number 4,462 refers to all mergers in the United States, including those in trade and in other industries where mergers often take place with little publicity. The official data, reported in Table 1, deal only with mergers in manufacturing and mining.

TABLE 1

Manufacturing and Mining Firms Acquired, 1948–1968,
by Number and Size

Year	Number	Total Large Acquisitions [a]		Total Firms Acquired by 200 Largest Firms [b]	
		NUMBER	ASSETS (millions $)	NUMBER	ASSETS (millions $)
1948	223	4	$ 66	4	$ 66
1949	126	5	67	5	67
1950	219	4	173	2	107
1951	235	9	201	5	125
1952	288	13	327	6	187
1953	295	23	679	17	561
1954	387	35	1,425	17	906
1955	683	68	2,129	33	1,412
1956	673	58	2,037	37	1,527
1957	585	50	1,472	29	1,104
1958	589	38	1,107	24	707
1959	835	64	1,960	36	1,425
1960	844	62	1,710	33	978
1961	954	59	2,129	25	1,240
1962	853	72	2,194	31	1,095
1963	861	68	2,917	34	1,843
1964	854	91	2,798	37	1,221
1965	1,008	93	3,900	29	2,061
1966	995	101	4,100	31	2,215
1967	1,496	170	8,246	66	5,392
1968	2,300	188	12,366	70	6,755

[a] Acquired firms with assets of $10 million or more.

[b] For years 1948–1965, the 200 largest firms are ranked by 1965 assets; for years 1966–1968, acquirers are 200 largest firms ranked by 1966 assets.

Source: Federal Trade Commission.

more than $100 million. Of the 500 largest U.S. industrial corporations listed by *Fortune* in 1962, eighty have since disappeared through mergers. As many as thirty of the companies which appeared on *Fortune*'s top-500 list in 1968 did not appear in 1969 because of merger. Actual cases tell much of the story. Consider this list of mergers in Table 2 and note especially the size of the well-known corporations that have been absorbed:

TABLE 2

Large Mergers Occurring in 1967, 1968, and 1969

Year	ACQUIRING COMPANY Name	Assets*	ACQUIRED COMPANY Name	Assets*
1967	Signal Oil & Gas	678	Mack Trucks	303
1967	Hunt Foods	461	McCall Corp.	149
1967	Ethyl Corp.	382	Oxford Paper	119
1967	North American Aviation	574	Rockwell Standard	391
1967	Ling-Temco-Vought	298	Wilson & Co.	196
1968	E. R. Squibb & Sons, Inc.	253	Beech-Nut Life Savers, Inc.	172
1968	Gulf & Western Industries	749	Consolidated Cigar	127
1968	Occidental Petroleum Corp.	779	Island Creek Coal Co.	115
1968	Kennecott Copper Corp.	1,075	Peabody Coal Co.	316
1968	Ling-Temco-Vought, Inc.	845	Jones & Laughlin Steel Corp.	1,093
1968	American Standard, Inc.	539	Westinghouse Air Brake Co.	303
1968	International Telephone & Telegraph	2,961	Continental Baking Co.	187
1968	Singer Co.	1,049	General Precision Equipment Corp.	323
1968	Occidental Petroleum Corp.	779	Hooker Chemical Corp.	367
1968	Tenneco, Inc.	3,589	Newport News Shipbuilding & Dry Dock Co.	139
1968	Glen Alden Corp.	470	Schenley Industries, Inc.	571
1968	Montgomery Ward (now MARCOR, Inc.)	1,709	Container Corp. of America	397
1969	Atlantic Richfield Co.	2,451	Sinclair Oil Corp.	1,451
1969	Lykes Corp.	377	Youngstown Sheet & Tube Co.	1,027
1969	International Telephone & Telegraph	4,022	Hartford Fire Insurance Co.	976
1969	R. J. Reynolds Co.	1,197	McLean Industries, Inc.	281
1969	Walter Kidde & Co.	375	United States Lines	233

* Dollars in millions.

Such a list of recent mergers could be extended for several pages, but a close look at the pattern of corporate consolidations shows that it has had much greater impact on some industries than others. In textiles, for example, a few aggressive firms have acquired dozens of previously independent companies, pulling them together into large, completely integrated corporations that can make and sell virtually any type of fabric. Partly reflecting the shift from natural to synthetic fibers, and an accompanying emphasis on chemical processes, this wave of mergers has affected every segment of what had previously been an industry composed of hundreds of firms performing distinct tasks. Since the end of the war, approximately a quarter of all the production facilities in the textile industry have changed hands. In this surge of consolidation Burlington Industries was a leader, growing from a relatively small domestic company to a world corporation with sales in excess of a billion dollars. It acquired companies in dyeing and bleaching, converting, hoisery manufacture, and producers of woolens, blankets, cotton, rayon, and fiberglass fabrics, velvets, and carpets and rugs. Other companies, like J. P. Stevens, Dan River Mills, and Kayser-Roth have engaged in a similar process of growth and consolidation through the merger and acquisition of dozens of smaller, once-independent firms. From an industry once distinguished by the competition of a very large number of sellers, textiles is well on its way to a pattern as concentrated as autos, copper, or aluminum. By 1975, one industry official predicts, there will be not more than four diversified textile companies, with annual sales each of at least $1 billion.

In petroleum the principal companies have been buying up dozens of independent producers of crude oil and natural gas (since 1950 the twenty biggest integrated companies have bought more than $2 billion worth of production properties). Simultaneously they were acquiring control of refiners—the firms, usually operating in a limited geographical area, that turn crude oil into gasoline and other products for use by consumers. In the dairy industry the leading national companies, National Dairy Products (Sealtest), Borden, Beatrice Foods, and Foremost, have marched from border to border, north to south and east to west, purchasing hundreds of local and regional dairies. An industry that had once been distinguished by local ownership, the dairy trade has been recast into a market ruled by nationally owned and operated corporations. The local dairy had become little more than a branch for a corporation with national, and often global, interests.

The forces at work in textiles, petroleum, and dairy products have left no market unaffected. Even in farming, the supposed last bastion of the rugged individualist, there is a powerful movement to bigger units and corporate ownership. More than half the value of farm real estate is owned by absentee interests, like CBK Industries, Inc., once a garment maker but now the owner of a string of 10,000-acre "farms" located from Texas to the Canadian border. Mergers have markedly changed the character of industrial chemicals, paper products, transportation, and electrical equipment industries. Closely held, narrowly specialized, and local-regional firms have disappeared in great numbers in recent years, leaving more and more industries dominated by big, broadly diffused, and nationally—often internationally—based companies. They represent a major new element in the economy.

The Anonymous Managers

In the trend to bigness there has been an accompanying shift away from personalization in business affairs. The tycoons who founded and shaped most of the corporations that still hold sway have disappeared, replaced by professional managers—figures whose names and faces are unknown to the public. John D. Rockefeller created Standard Oil in a quest for monopoly in petroleum. But who is president of Standard Oil of New Jersey? or General Motors? or General Electric? J. Pierpont Morgan put together the U.S. Steel Corporation with the goal of controlling the entire steel industry. He did not quite succeed (Rockefeller came closer to *his* objective), but he still served as the focus of attention in discussions of government-business relations. For Andrew Carnegie, Henry Ford, James Hill, and Edward H. Harriman, there too was prominence. All were in the public domain—the subjects variously of vituperation, deification, and caricature. They were nationally known figures and personally embodied their enterprises, exercising near-absolute control and serving as a link with the public. Today that link has been severed. In all but a very few corporations control has been broadly distributed and effective power over company affairs has been assumed by groups of executives typically unknown to laymen.

Sears, Roebuck acutely illustrates the trend to size, executive anonymity, and diversification that is becoming so characteristic of contemporary business. With annual sales of more than $8 billion and assets in excess of $6 billion, Sears is the biggest merchandiser in the world. It literally operates around the world, selling, not just goods for the home, but almost everything that the consumer could possibly want in the way of products and services. Through acquisitions and internal growth, it has gained a position and developed a raison d'être that has pioneered the way for many other businesses. Sears is oriented to a function, namely meeting the needs of the household. To satisfy that demand the company has diversified wildly, not only selling through nearly a thousand retail stores (located in the U.S., Canada, South America, and Europe) but making many of those goods in wholly or partly owned subsidiaries.

Sears manufactures and sells a full line of appliances, electronic goods (ranging from TV sets and radios to tape recorders and organs), lawn mowers and garden tractors, venetian blinds, wallpaper, paints and chemicals, outdoor cooking equipment, plumbing fixtures, sporting goods, and family apparel. It also services most of what it sells through wholly owned service affiliates and will install anything from a swimming pool to a heating-air conditioning unit. It offers comprehensive insurance, operates a savings and loan association, and provides the credit for its billions in installment sales. Sears also franchises and operates restaurants in some twenty-eight states and supplies vending services for industrial plants and office buildings. In the breadth of its operations, in its aggressive search for new markets here and abroad, and in the degree of its self-sufficiency, Sears probably has no equal. It is exemplary in another way, too. It actually owns itself. The Sears employee pension and profit-sharing funds, managed by men directly or indirectly appointed by the company's management, own more than 25 percent of all Sears outstanding common stock, quite adequate for effective control. It is a world of its own.

Globalization of Business

There is one other significant dimension to the prevailing trend to depersonalized corporate bigness: its internationalism. Fifty, even twenty, years ago, most companies, even the biggest, operated pretty much within the borders of a single country. They sold their goods to foreigners, but in finished form; the goods themselves were manufactured in "home-country" factories. Transactions between countries thus took the form simply of trade: American firms made goods in American factories and shipped them to foreigners. Now, world commerce takes the form of world production. Today a typical American firm makes goods in a score of countries and transports them to buyers from foreign-based factories and distribution centers. In all, U.S. companies now sell about $200 billion abroad, but five sixths of this comes from goods produced *outside* the United States!

With facilities in twenty-five or more countries, with employees of several nationalities, with stockholders in significant numbers in a dozen or more countries, and with a score of subsidiaries incorporated in as many nations, it is impossible to associate a major company with any particular country. One result is that the principal manufacturing industries of the world—steel, oil, autos, aluminum, chemicals—are beginning to show the same trend to concentration that has already taken place in the United States. To this theme we will return in Chapter 17.

The Uses of Corporate Power

No corporation, anymore than a political person or entity (President, Congress, Cabinet Secretary), has absolute power to do as might be wished. That is no less true today than in the past. What must be acknowledged, though, is the range of discretion within which the contemporary enterprise has to function. In this sense, the large modern corporation has considerable effective power. It has significant control over the price at which it will sell and can establish what it regards as an acceptable level of profits; it has sufficient influence over the market so that it can plan and make buyers respond to its initiatives instead of the other way around, and it can mold consumer preferences through its own advertising and promotional activities. In no one of these respects, of course, is its power unrestricted. It cannot establish any level of prices, or seek any rate of return, or behave as if consumers were nothing more than dolls on the end of a string. And it can be outflanked, as steelmakers found out when they maintained high prices and lost sizable markets to foreign steel firms and aluminum, cement, and glass materials producers. In admitting these limitations one should not be so impractical or unwise as to overlook the substantial area of discretion—to price, plan, and market—that is within the control of the typical large corporation.

The power of the big, contemporary corporations to pursue pricing policies independent of the constraint theoretically exercised by the marketplace poses serious problems both to the economy and to the corporation itself. "Discretion" means freedom and that carries with it all the conflicting demands and frustrations that beset anyone with power. To what extent, for instance, should a company refrain from raising its prices because this might contribute to inflation? Should a union's wage demand well in excess of productivity be resisted because of its inflationary potential even though the company knows it can pass it along through a prompt price increase? Should a corporate president adhere to the wishes of the White House not to raise prices even if this will mean less profits? How does the board of directors exercise its trusteeship when, given its power, it is confronted by conflicting demands on the company treasury? Should a company voluntarily refrain from investing abroad in order to protect the nation's balance of payments even if it could earn significantly more for its shareholders than if it invested an equivalent amount at home?

For the officers of the modern corporation these are precisely the kinds of question that must be confronted almost daily, for they reflect the fact that the company does have discretion—it can make choices—it is not the helpless pawn of a market system and can either exercise its considerable power responsibly or irresponsibly. Surely one of the toughest problems facing the contemporary business firm is the way it uses its power. There are no guidelines, no accepted bounds, and yet the manner of its exercise affects the entire society. This is why the power of the corporation—reflected in industrial concentration, accentuated by mergers, extended by product and geographic diversification—is of such immense concern both to businessmen and to citizens.

CHAPTER 3

The Industrial Octopi

"One can't help thinking that . . . the whole country will soon be merged into one company."

—*Art Buchwald*

The face of American industry, and U.S. corporations, is being remade by the greatest wave of mergers in the country's history. More than twenty-five hundred companies are disappearing annually through amalgamation with other businesses. This is significant in itself, but even more important is the nature of the current merger movement.

Not many years ago most mergers between companies consolidated firms engaged in the same or closely related lines of activity. Today that type of consolidation (sometimes called "horizontal") is passé. The modern form of merger brings together firms in unrelated markets, coalescing them into vast holding companies, often operating internationally. In current parlance these amorphous, smorgasbord-like corporations are termed "conglomerates."

The Ogden Corporation, a strikingly diverse company well on its way to a billion dollars in annual sales, wrecks autos, serves hotdogs at Dodger Stadium, raises cattle in Paraguay, processes fruits and vegetables, provides architectural and engineering services, runs a savings and loan association, and engages in worldwide transportation. The only thread that binds together its disparate pieces is a management core, operating under the direction of President Ralph Ablon, an articulate proponent of agglomeration who sees it as the natural evolution of business, the outgrowth of basic changes in technology, communications, and management science.

Whatever the reason for their spread (and that's a point to which we will turn later), the unmistakable and unavoidable fact is that the conglomerate firm was the most vivid industrial feature of the 1960s. What's more it gives every promise of becoming the dominant form of American business in the last third of the century. Hundreds of major corporations have taken the route to diversification, typically by acquiring a string of established firms. The result is that well-known companies have departed so sharply from the markets which identified them to the public that they have even felt obliged to change their names. Remember U.S. Rubber? It's now Uniroyal, and behind that name change stand two features common to much of recent industrial activity: the corporation no longer is a maker of rubber products nor is it a U.S.-based firm. Fewer than half the things it makes have anything to do with rubber. With twenty-eight research and manufacturing centers in twenty-three countries, it has also lost its exclusive or principal ties with the United States.

R. J. Reynolds, once nothing but a maker of cigarettes (Chesterfields, among other brands), now sells poultry, canned soups, egg noodles, pie mixes, and soft drinks, and operates a large freight shipping company. (The company took "tobacco" out of its corporate name in 1969; it's now R. J. Reynolds Industries.) Liggett & Myers has added dog food to its array of cigarettes. Borden sells coffee, coated fabrics, pressure-sensitive tape, and a long line of chemicals ranging from cosmetics to fertilizers. Campbell Soup vends a complete range of frozen foods (under the Swanson label) and baked goods. Coca-Cola still sells around the globe "the pause that refreshes," but it also makes instant coffee, cattle feed, and Minute Maid concentrated orange juice. Firestone "Tire & Rubber" manufactures recoilless rifles and jet engine parts. Pepsi Cola is another organization that found it expedient to change its name, a symbol of the new quest for superdiversification. Pepsico, as it is now called, offers a wide assortment of snacks to go with your soft drink; it will also move your goods across the country, or around the world, in its North American vans. U.S. Steel has a stake in plastics, fertilizers, real estate, and has joined with Burlington Industries in a jet aircraft leasing enterprise. When the New York Central merged with the Pennsylvania Railroad, the happy couple promptly changed their name to Penn Central, struck from the corporate name or press releases any mention of railroading or transportation, and announced it would henceforth invest widely in things like Florida and New York real estate development and textiles.

Most of the conglomerates have been the product of mergers— hundreds of mergers. In the process, many well-known firms have been swallowed into bigger diversified enterprises. You can test your familiarity with what's been going on by comparing the product of the firm on the left with the company in the right column that controls it (answer key in footnote) : *

(1) Squibb	(a) R. J. Reynolds
(2) Avis Rent a Car	(b) LTV
(3) Random House	(c) Ford
(4) N.Y. Yankees	(d) Olin
(5) Miller High Life Beer	(e) Signal-Occidental
(6) Chun-king foods	(f) Philip Morris
(7) Hertz Rent a Car	(g) Laird Industries
(8) Consolidation Coal	(h) RCA
(9) Fanny Farmer candies	(i) W. R. Grace
(10) Philco	(j) CBS
(11) S. S. Pierce	(k) ITT
(12) Mack Truck	(l) Continental Oil
(13) Wilson "tendermade" ham	
(14) Teaberry gum	

Regardless of how well you scored, the game helps demonstrate the scale, significance, and character of the present merger movement. It has already fundamentally changed established business relationships, and it promises to go right on doing so, with the

---

* (1)-(d); (2)-(k); (3)-(h); (4)-(j); (5)-(i); (6)-(a); (7)-(h); (8)-(l); (9)-(i); (10)-(c); (11)-(g); (12)-(e); (13)-(b); (14)-(f).

effects as much social and political as they are economic. A closer look is in order.

Diversification by Acquisition

Currently about five thousand mergers are taking place each year in the United States, four times as many as in a typical pre-World War II year and seven times the number reported in the late 1940s and early 1950s. Beginning with the decade of the sixties the number of mergers jumped sharply and it has continued to rise steeply. Although the figures are impressive however viewed, the number of *large* mergers is even more striking—and of greater economic consequence.* From 1948 through 1968, nearly thirteen hundred manufacturing and mining firms with assets of $10 million or more were acquired by other companies. All told, their assets exceeded $50 billion. Their purchasers were the largest industrial concerns in the country, giant firms in search of even greater size and diversity. In the 1948–1968 period the 200 *largest* manufacturers acquired nearly six hundred companies, with assets of over $30 billion. Fully half of these assets were absorbed in just five years, 1963 through 1968. Particularly in a few industries—petroleum, chemicals, paper and allied products, and machinery—many substantial independent firms have been eliminated. These industries, as with dairy products and textiles, have been thoroughly transformed in the last decade.

While there have been a large number of sizable mergers in recent years, what is more important for purposes of long-term economic policy is the changing character of corporate consolidation. In the past, firms typically merged with their competitors or with their suppliers or customers. For illustration, the U.S. Steel Corporation was forged in 1901 out of the stuff of the competing Carnegie and Moore interests, consolidating in one move more than two thirds of the nation's steel capacity. In much the same fashion, John D. Rockefeller assembled his Standard Oil trust out

---

* Pertinent data, including figures on the significance of large mergers, are in Table 1 (page 27).

of the assets of dozens of refineries, pipelines, and sales companies he purchased in the late nineteenth century. The merger movement that took place in this way at the turn of the century, like the merger wave of the 1920s, brought together competing interests in a quest for control of the market, in an oft-admitted grab for monopoly. In this manner were formed many of the billion-dollar companies that today continue to dominate many of our key industries. The roster is long and impressive: American Tobacco (American Brands, as of 1969), U.S. Rubber (Uniroyal), National Biscuit, International Paper, American Can, Eastman Kodak, International Harvester, du Pont, and International Nickel; and dating from the 1920s, Bethlehem Steel, Allied Chemical, and General Foods. All had one ingredient in common: they were the product of mergers between competitors, with a few customers or suppliers thrown in to round out the picture.

Now mergers between rivals are rapidly approaching the status of historical anomalies. More than 80 percent of all mergers in manufacturing and mining are now of the conglomerate type, and the trend is definitely upward, as Chart 2 shows. Some conglomerates involve firms in related but noncompetitive markets (a dairy in New York joining with a dairy in Los Angeles), but, significantly, the proportion of mergers that link up companies that are in *completely* unrelated lines of activity (the "other" category in the chart) has skyrocketed since 1965. Almost half of all merger activity is purely conglomerate in form, up from only 15 percent in 1963.

There is clear evidence that the biggest corporations are broadening their conglomerate areas of industrial interest, primarily through merger. Of the 1,000 largest industrial firms, 560 were engaged in the manufacture of six or more distinct products in 1950. By 1962 their number rose by about 30 percent, to more than 700. Today the 200 biggest companies operate in more than 2,200 separate industrial categories. Further, the bigger the company, generally the greater the scope of its operations and the more rapid its rate of diversification. This latter point suggests, quite correctly, that the largest manufactuing firms were uncommonly active participants in the conglomerate merger derby. Of

CHART 2
Distribution of Large Mergers,* by Type
1948–1968
(percentage of total acquired assets)

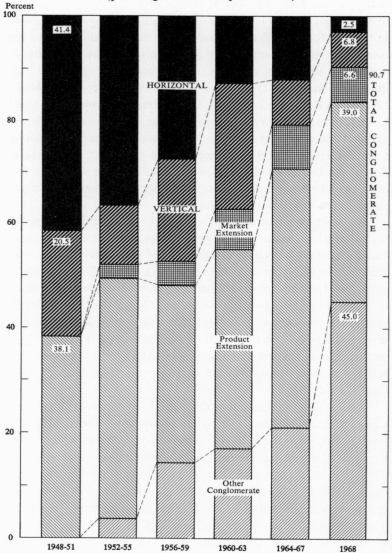

* Firms with assets of $10 million or more.
  Source: Federal Trade Commission.

acquisitions made by the 100 most active merging firms, four out of five recently have represented moves into industries different from those in which they are dominant.

To dramatize the kind of diversification, or conglomerate, acquisitions made by the country's largest firms in recent years, take Borden as an example. Once a producer of dairy goods, it has acquired firms that process fruits and vegetables, make confectionery products, glue, coated fabrics, plastics, toilet preparations, and surgical appliances. Comparable diversification moves were being made by virtually every other large corporation. The consequence: about half of the 500 biggest industrial firms currently operate in four or more broad industrial categories. The days have ended when a company stuck to a single industry.

Many companies are entering a new era, erasing their old image, and putting on the face of diversification. Their own words tell the story. The Transamerica Corporation, with yearly sales over a billion dollars, says it is "hip deep in a dozen different services"— life insurance, real estate, personal finance, consumer investment and revolving credit, and air charter transportation. The Hershey Corporation substituted "Foods" for "Chocolate" in its title and added macaroni, spaghetti sauce, cookies and biscuits to its list of products. When it acquired Cory, a maker of electric appliances, it rightly said that "today Hershey means a lot more than chocolate." And remember the Hercules Powder Company, whose name for decades was almost synonymous with munitions? It is now simply the Hercules Corporation. In making the change the company pointed out that "the types of products for which the company was named in 1912 now constitute less than ten percent of Hercules sales."

The Union Bag-Camp Paper Corporation (the hyphen in corporate names is a standard symptom of mergers, particularly in the newspaper field) once made bags and paper, but then it spread out and adopted a shorter title. If it had not done so, confessed the company, "we would have had to change our name to Union Bag-Corrugated Box-Chemicals-Lumber-Packaging Machinery-Folding Carton-Honeycomb-Camp Paper Corporation." It wisely avoided that fate and switched to the Union-Camp Corporation, a simple name—and one, significantly, that suggests, quite wisely, no association with any particular industry. Tennessee Gas found itself in a similar plight, burdened with a name that was inconsistent with its diversification aims. It plunged into chemicals, oil production and marketing, paperboard and packaging (with the purchase of the Packaging Corporation of America), shipbuilding (with its $123 million acquisition in 1968 of the Newport News Shipbuilding & Dry Dock Company), real estate development (Kern County Land Company), farm and construction equipment manufacture, and insurance and banking. It put up a new sign: Tenneco, explaining that it is now "a highly diversified corporation" with six divisions, any one of which alone would rank among the country's top 500 industrial corporations. For MMM (remember when it was Minnesota Mining & Manufacturing?), Olin ("Olin is chemicals, metals, Squibb pharmaceuticals, paper and packing, Winchester arms and ammunition"), FMC, and a list of other taffy-like enterprises the same manifestations of growth through diversification have been vividly on display. Sometimes the game moves so fast that it is difficult to keep up with the players. Signal Oil & Gas Company, for example, decided in 1966 to diversify its interests. It acquired Mack Truck, Arizona Bancorporation, and Allis-Chalmers (paying $475 million for the latter, a company with a varied product line stretching from farm implements to fuel cells). But just as it began to digest these large bites it was itself swallowed into an even more diversified enterprise through merger with Occidental Petroleum Corporation. Occidental's own name is misleading, by the way, because it has been actively broadening its own interests—in home building, chemicals, and coal. Together Occidental and Signal have sales well over $3 billion a year, an adequate dowry but not atypical for a major corporate marriage.

The conglomerate octopi spread out across national boundaries as commonly as they do across industries. International Telephone & Telegraph (it prefers to be called ITT, for reasons that will shortly be obvious) is a splendid illustration. Founded in 1920, it was principally engaged in the communications business for its first forty years. Then Harold Geneen took over as president and launched the company in a feverish search for diversification acquisitions. About fifty companies have been purchased in the last ten years, most of them outside the communications-electronics industries. ITT acquired Avis Rent a Car (it rents a lot of other things too), Hamilton Management (a half-billion-dollar mutual fund), Aetna Finance (consumer finance and life insurance), the Sheraton Corporation (the world's largest hotel chain), Levitt & Sons (the big tract homebuilders), the Rayonier Corporation ($300 million in assets at the time it was acquired), and Continental Baking (the country's biggest bread producer). Yet to be consummated is ITT's acquisition of the Hartford Fire Insurance Company, with assets of a billion dollars. In five years, then, ITT doubled its sales and assets, soaring into the $4 billion league on a broad base of mergers.

This may imply that the company is principally oriented to the United States, but in fact ITT does the majority of its business outside of its borders. In its global sweep, it embraces over 150 companies, employs 300,000 people (over half of them non-U.S. citizens), carries on research and manufacturing operations in fifty-seven countries, and has sales outlets in more than a hundred. The boards of its foreign-owned subsidiaries are liberally dotted with officials and ex-members of other governments and its stockholders include thousands of investors from other nations. ITT is a prime but not unique illustration of the modern corporation— big, actively expansionist, diversified widely, both industrially and geographically. It typifies the kind of business enterprise to which governments, and the public, must become accustomed in the years immediately ahead. "In ten years," predicts the head of one conglomerate in a characteristically ebullient remark, "there will be only 200 major industrial companies in the United States, all conglomerate."

The Philosophy of Conglomerateness

The forces that underlie the growth of conglomerates are many, but chief among them is a new managerial attitude that envisions the conglomerate enterprise as the next evolutionary step in business development. The advocates of conglomerateness speak in neo-religious terms, espousing a gospel of growth through diversification that sometimes borders on the messianic. It has two basic themes: growth and synergism.

For the conglomerate firm growth is a goal in and of itself, even more important than the quest for profit. Charles B. "Tex" Thornton, founder of Litton Industries (perhaps the archetype of the conglomerates), explains his philosophy this way: "We grow not just to stay in business but to have a virile, stimulating atmosphere. Growth is associated with progress, the means to accomplish more things. Profit is only one of the motives. A stronger motive is a deep, pioneering spirit." This same attitude, with its emphasis on growth, growth, and still more growth, has permeated all of the conglomerates and has even infected many older firms. Former Ford Motor President Arjay Miller stressed his company's search for greater sales revenue as an energizer of paramount significance —a force that transcends other considerations and is the firm's principal economic objective. With growth as the touchstone the wave of mergers and acquisitions becomes more understandable, for they typically afford the fastest, surest way to increase sales.

Synergism (the whole is greater than the sum of its parts) is the other key element that explains the trend to conglomerateness. As the Sperry Rand Corporation puts it: "We do a lot of different things, and we do each one better because we do all the rest." In a conglomerate, synergism takes the form of meshing independent firms in a way that provides greater strength and growth than if they had retained their individual sovereignty. Litton Industries, for example, envisioned the formation of a transportation system group. To implement its plan, it acquired Hewitt Robbins, a material handling equipment company; Ingalls Shipbuilding Company; and Alvey-Ferguson, a maker of computer-controlled warehouse handling systems. Each piece had value in itself, but united— under central direction and oriented toward a broad functional objective—the theory was that their potential could be more fully realized.

This notion of synergism is closely related to the concept of decentralized operations under centralized managerial control. For the conglomerate proponent this blend is the key to success and to accelerated growth. Given the advantages of modern communications and computerized information systems, conglomerate managers are supremely confident that they can run a widely diversified organization by continually monitoring certain performance variables and pulling on a few control strings as conditions warrant. One conglomerate executive boasts that his central staff of ninety experts can "run any company in the world, any company."

Conglomerate managerial self-confidence—the belief that a widely diversified industrial empire can be run successfully by a small core headquarters staff—has been expanded into a new philosophy of corporate management. Using his conglomerate as an example, Consolidated Foods President William Howlett explains: "What we have here is an autonoplex—a complex of autonomous companies—each run as a separate business. This is the fundamental concept. Within a prescribed range of know-how, the way to build a business is to develop a multiplicity of small businesses tied to a central headquarters through financing." What Howlett, Tex Thornton, and others passionately believe is that the conglomerate is really a fundamentally new form of business organization, not just bigger or more diverse, but different in kind. It combines the strengths of experienced central staff experts with the operational advantages of decentralization. It affords the benefits of size, particularly in management, without losing the benefits which accrue when an executive can have close continuing contact with production, sales, or research. This new breed of executives feels that the conglomerate represents the best of all possible business worlds and clearly represents the way of the future.

It would be a mistake to think, however, that conglomerate empires have resulted simply from the immutable forces of an inexorable technocracy. There are empire builders today just as there were sixty years ago. As good an example as any of the contemporary conglomerate merger barons is James Ling, impresario of Ling-Temco-Vought (LTV). In barely a decade he managed, primarily through merger, to parlay a $2 million a year electronics business into a $2 billion diversified enterprise with interests in a dozen major industries. Ling's first major acquisition came in 1960 with the purchase of the Temco Aircraft Corporation (sales: $100 million). In 1961 the Chance Vought Corporation (sales of $200 million) was added, followed later by the purchase of Okonite, a wire and cable producer ($68 million). Then, in 1967, LTV merged with an even bigger firm, Wilson & Company, a billion-dollar producer of meat and food products, sporting goods, and chemicals. Hard on the heels of this giant acquisition LTV added to its holdings a controlling interest in Greatamerica Corporation, which, among other things, owned most of the stock in Braniff Airways. In 1968, LTV chased and caught Jones & Laughlin Steel. Ling explains this succession of moves as carefully measured steps in an effort to reduce dependence on any one product or technology or business through "optimum decentralization."

Two other considerations help explain the accelerating merger trend in the United States. One is our Federal income tax laws. They can have great significance for a company that is familyheld, making it highly desirable and economically advantageous to sell out to a bigger and especially a publicly held corporation. Not only can this minimize taxes and eliminate uncertainty about future estate tax liability but it enables a family to diversify its investments. The tax laws can also help promote mergers between larger companies. A shareholder in one company owning stock worth, say, $5,000 may be offered stock (or perhaps convertible debentures) in a merged corporation that might be worth $7,500. He pays no tax on this profitable exchange of securities. Further, if he is given convertible debentures, the interest he receives is treated as a tax deduction by the company. These tax attributes have been shrewdly exploited by the conglomerates and in 1969 Representative Wilbur Mills, chairman of the House Ways & Means Committee, introduced legislation designed to modify some provisions of the Federal tax laws that have helped encourage corporate mergers. These changes are relatively modest in scope, however, and they are unlikely to have more than a temporary impact on the merger movement. Its causes are far greater in number and more basic than taxes.

There is another impetus, related to the oft-inexplicable propensity of the stock market to put a higher value on the earnings of conglomerate companies than on less aggressive enterprises. A dollar of earnings on the books of a conglomerate may produce a stock market price of, say, $45 whereas another company with earnings of a dollar a share might find its shares selling for only $15. The result is that a conglomerate can often offer stock for another corporation's shares that makes a merger well nigh irresistible. If, for example, the hypothetical conglomerate whose stock is selling at $45 a share were to offer to exchange one of its shares for two of the company whose stock is selling at $15, the latter's stockholders would receive a sizable 50 percent premium since they would be giving up stock worth $30 for stock worth $45. It is precisely this technique that triggered off a number of takeover bids in 1968 and 1969, as conglomerates sought to gain control of other companies, despite the opposition of their managements, by making highly attractive exchange offers direct to the shareholders. Takeover bids were used by LTV to acquire Jones & Laughlin Steel, by the Lykes Corporation to buy Youngstown Steel, and by the General Host Corporation to purchase a sizable stock interest in Armour. Of course, the takeover tactic can provoke open warfare if the management of the target company fights back.

Generally, though, the conglomerates have had little difficulty in purchasing the companies they wanted to because of the attractiveness of the terms they have been able to offer. But, one asks, how can they work what almost seems like magic? The answer, in part, is that so long as the stock market values the earning of a conglomerate more highly than those of a nonconglomerate there is no magic involved; the conglomerate's management is simply taking advantage of the psychological vagaries of the market. It is absolutely essential, however, that the conglomerate keep growing, and growing rapidly. There are certain resemblances to a treadmill, however, for without continued growth in earnings the firm loses the momentum that is necessary to permit it to carry the burden of the acquisitions it has already made. This is just one of the potential problems that conglomerates encounter in their excited search for expansion. Their reach may prove to exceed their grasp —their managerial capacity may not match their claims or their theory—but it would be foolish not to recognize the broad significance of the principle they carry to its extreme, namely diversification.

Molding New Industries

Under pressure of diversification mergers the industrial road map of the United States—and, for that matter, of the entire developed world—is being redrawn. Previously distinct industries are being coalesced and new ones are being formed to take their place. One that is emerging might be called the information-entertainment industry, which will draw together large portions of the publishing, electronic, and existing entertainment industries. Its general contours can already be discerned. Major electronic companies, anxious to tap the growing education and leisure market, have moved aggressively into publishing, acquiring a number of long-established book and magazine organizations. RCA merged with Random House (which previously had bought Knopf and Pantheon); Xerox bought American Education Publications, University Microfilms, and the Heritage Library; Raytheon acquired D. C. Heath; IBM took control of Science Research Associates; and Litton, the ubiquitous conglomerate, added the American Book Company to its corporate family. Almost simultaneously, General Electric was joining with Time, Inc., in a $40 million venture to explore new approaches to education; Sylvania was affiliating with *Reader's Digest* on a similar endeavor; and MMM, also a major factor in electronics, was developing an arrangement with *Newsweek* to publish and distribute current-events materials.

Not only electronics manufacturers are spilling over into publishing. Other media are beginning to sense that books and magazines are no more than a form of communication and can occupy a logical place in an information enterprise. In the last few years, the *Los Angeles Times* acquired World Publishing, the Cowles newspapers bought control of *Harper's Magazine,* and Time, Inc. (already the owner of five TV-radio stations), acquired Little, Brown. Meredith Publishing, which puts out *Better Homes & Gar-*

dens, merged with two book publishers, Duell Sloan & Pearce and Appleton-Century-Crofts. *Esquire,* once a synonym for naughtiness, purchased Globe Book Company, a publisher of school books. Crowell Collier and Macmillan moved into the music field, buying the century-old Schirmer organization.

Just as books, electronics, newspapers, and magazines have become thoroughly intermeshed, so too have the other media begun to coalesce. National General, a producer and distributor of motion pictures and television programs, purchased Grosset & Dunlap and its paperback subsidiary, Bantam Books. Earlier, CBS, an electronics firm as well as a television network (so too is RCA, of course, with its ownership of NBC) bought the New York Yankees, just as a few years before it had taken a financial interest in *My Fair Lady* among other Broadway musicals. In 1967, CBS had acquired Holt, Rinehart & Winston, a well-known book publisher with sales of $60 million. Earlier, United Artists and Paramount had been swallowed up by other conglomerates and MCA, an entertainment colossus, had taken control of Universal Pictures and Decca Records.

Of special interest is the ownership of television stations in major cities. While newspapers are still the single biggest factor (of seventy-four television stations in the top twenty-five cities, thirty-four are owned by newspapers), a substantial percentage is owned by diversified industrial companies for whom broadcasting is little more than a profitable sideline. Westinghouse, Avco, Chris-Craft, Storer (which also controls Northeast Airlines), General Tire, and the Rust Craft Greeting Card Company have substantial investments in local broadcast outlets. When it is recalled that NBC and CBS are essentially broad-based electronics concerns, the spillover between industries is once again vividly in evidence.

What this summary account makes clear is that the old lines between the publishing, mass media, entertainment, and electronics industries have been almost completely erased by diversification mergers. A new industry—call it "information" or "entertainment" —is evolving, although its exact character cannot yet be delineated.

The central point to note is that mergers are not merely forming bigger firms, but are fundamentally changing the nature of several industries whose public significance is immense.

What is taking place in the field of publishing-information-entertainment is being duplicated in many other sectors of the economy. In energy, for example, we have become accustomed to thinking of coal, gas, oil, and nuclear power as constituting distinct industries. That was once true, but it no longer is. The major oil companies, no doubt anticipating the day when coal may be converted into gasoline at low cost, have moved aggressively into coal, buying up the country's biggest producers. Continental Oil started the parade in 1966 with its acquisition of the number one firm, Consolidated Coal. Then Occidental Petroleum bought Island Creek Coal, the third-ranked firm. Gulf Oil and other petroleum companies were making similar moves.

In another related area, nuclear energy, oil companies have also staked out a dominant position. Kerr-McGee has gained a key spot in the production and refining of uranium. Other oil and several major chemical companies are seizing sensitive points in the nuclear fuel industry, something that will take on increasing importance as the proportion of electricity generated by nuclear power increases, as it is certain to in the near future. By 1980 costs of producing electricity with nuclear power will be as low as any source. But whatever the means used to generate electricity, nuclear power or steam generation, the oil companies of today will control the fuel. Humble Oil Company, Standard Oil of New Jersey's principal domestic subsidiary, has changed its marketing name from Esso to Enco, signifying its new status as an "energy company." It is symbolic of what is happening throughout the economy as companies break out of their old confines and diversify into other industries.

Great changes are also taking place throughout transportation, one of the stuffiest and most tradition-bound sectors of the American economy. For years and years each of the principal forms of transportation, rail, truck, air, pipeline, water, operated in its own little world, seemingly uninterested and unaware of what was going on elsewhere. Gradually this has changed, as much because of new technological forces as any modernization in managerial attitude. The first major force for unification came with the piggyback movement of truck trailers on railroad flat cars (at first most railroads fought the idea bitterly, but now it is a highly profitable source of railroad business). Recently the freight container has come on the scene: a metal box, usually about eight feet square and from twenty to forty feet in length, it can be loaded with freight and moved intact directly from shipper to destination by truck, rail, sea, or air. Simple though the container is, it constitutes a powerful force for change—for unification—between and among the fragmented transportation industries. The biggest freight forwarder, U.S. Freight, not only has invested heavily in containers, but has set up comprehensive trucking and intercontinental container services. With the container as a common denominator, nontransportation interests now envision the possibility of creating an international transportation system. In 1968 Walter Kidde & Co., an emerging conglomerate which has increased its sales ten times in four years, bought U.S. Lines, a leading American ship line with substantial existing and planned commitments in container operations. U.S. Lines operates extensively in Europe-United States routes and a subsidiary, Waterman Steamship (acquired in 1967), transits the Pacific. Kidde, through these moves, has now established a highly integrated containerized transportation service between America, Europe, and the Far East.

While direct ties between many different forms of transportation are still forbidden by anachronistic, decades-old Federal legislation (a railroad, for instance, can buy a pipeline but not a truck or water carrier), transportation companies are diversifying outward into other industries and some outside enterprises are buying their way in on a highly selective basis. Tennessee Gas Transmission (Tenneco, if you will recall) bought American Commercial Barge Lines in 1967 and Chromalloy, a metals firm, owns a truck company, American Transit. More typical, though, have been the moves of railroads to withdraw their earnings and invest elsewhere. The Illinois Central Railroad, through a parent holding company, has acquired chemicals producers and other manufacturers. Big Western railroads have expanded beyond their commitments in oil and timber extraction (over a third of the Santa Fe Railway's earnings come from its nonrailroad subsidiaries) and the Penn Central has made clear that it will be more interested in nonrail investments, like real estate, than in transportation. The fresh winds of merger and diversification are blowing across the once-quiescent fields of transportation. Most people welcome them, but their impact on an industrial complex that represents nearly a sixth of the nation's annual output and permeates every product and service market is revolutionary.

The Challenge of Conglomerateness

The highly diversified conglomerate enterprise, operating in many industries and many countries, is essentially a new creature and, not surprisingly, it is looked upon with suspicion and treated by some as if it were a momentary aberration. For more traditional business, a number of politicians, and even some financial analysts, the diversified firm simply doesn't conform to the established mold and thus will fade away as the old values reassert themselves. But the theory of business, premised on the view that firms should operate and compete within a single industry, has lost its relevance. The reality is that broad industrial and geographic diversification is now being accepted as a way of life by firms, new and old, and is outmoding customary ways of thinking about business. The modern corporation is increasingly likely to be, and in many instances has already become, a large, widely diversified international holding company without unequivocal ties to any single industry or country. It must be analyzed and dealt with on those terms.

CHAPTER 4

Who Controls Corporate America?

"Illusions are a danger, truth is wholesome."

—*Gunnar Myrdal*

"Who's in charge here?" It's an old, often-asked question but it is now as applicable to corporate America as it could be to any conceivable situation. Just as business firms have increased their bulk and diversified industrially and geographically, their "control" has been altered to such a degree that it is now impossible to tell who really "owns" a big modern corporation. Indeed, the very question of ownership is no longer meaningful and posing it in the same way one would inquire who "owns" a house or a local hardware store is nearly a sign of mental obsolescence.

Our customary mode of thought regards individuals as sharing ownership of a corporation, determining its destiny at the corporate ballot box. For at least forty years, however, most people have conceded that corporations are so large and their stockholders so many and so widely diffused that a shareowner is rarely more than a passive beneficiary of what management decides to dish out in the way of dividends. Realistically the modern stockholder is no more than an owner of a piece of impressively inscribed paper that gives him about the same rights as the owner of a corporate debenture. He takes what is conferred upon him and management is in the corporate driver's seat.

In 1929, when Adolph Berle and Gardiner Means took a careful look at the situation, in their book, *The Modern Corporation and Private Property,* fewer than half of the 200 largest nonfinancial corporations were under management control. Individuals, families, or other identifiable groups dominated many companies through their majority or sole stock ownership. Today there are few comparable situations in the United States. A few, a very few, families and individuals still reign unchallenged over some of the country's biggest corporations (the Pews in Sun Oil and Howard Hughes's Tool Company); normally, where families are significant at all, they hold no more than a minority stock position. Du Pont remains under the wing of the du Pont family and their personal holding company, Christiana Securities, but still they own only a third of the company's stock (that stock is worth about $2.5 billion at current market prices). Ford Motor is run by the family through their ownership of its class B stock, which is entitled to 40 percent of the votes (the Ford Foundation holds most of the nonvoting class A stock). The Mellons, directly and indirectly (through the Mellon National Bank), dominate Alcoa and the Firestone family and their trusts hold about a quarter of the tire firm's stock. Olin, Kaiser Aluminum, Pittsburgh Plate Glass, W. R. Grace, General Tire, Seagrams, and Schenley Industries are similarly controlled by families or individuals who own a big chunk but still a minority of their stock. These are significant cases, but they are still rare exceptions. Incontrovertibly, most U.S. corporate wealth is controlled—not by individuals, or families, but by an alliance of management and financial institutions.

Growing Influence of the Institutions

Managerial control of the world's largest public enterprises is a crucial distinguishing characteristic of twentieth century capitalism, but that is hardly a recent discovery. What is new, a contribution of the postwar years, and particularly the last decade, is the shift from individual to institutional corporate shareownership. This is the era of the financial institution, not the personal investor. Increasingly, individuals are investing in U.S. industry indirectly, via mutual funds, pension funds, and bank-managed trusts. One in six adults now owns stock in a corporation listed on the New York Stock Exchange compared with only one in sixteen in 1952. That proportion, though, has not increased since 1962 for a very simple reason: currently individuals are selling more stock than they buy. In the years 1962 through 1969 their individual corporate stock declined in value by over $10 billion. While people have added greatly to their personal savings (up from an annual rate of $22 billion in 1962 to near $60 billion in 1969), it has not been through the *direct* purchase of corporate stock. Instead, in the last decade individuals have been indirectly enlarging their stake in American industry through institutional investments.

These institutions take many forms, but primarily they are the mutual funds, pension funds, and insurance companies—all with varying degrees of bank involvement. Collectively, these institutions own securities representing more than a third of the value of all listed stocks on the New York Stock Exchange. Their role makes them the major new force in the trading of stocks and bonds and establishes their preeminent position in the control of corporate America.

Among the major institutions holding New York Stock Exchange-listed stock, the pension funds are the fastest growing. Presently they hold over $40 billion in stock, but, fed largely by the contributions of employers, they are increasing their holdings at the rate of more than $5 billion a year. In 1949, to show just how rapid has been their expansion, they held less than a billion dollars in stock. Now their annual increment is five times the value of their holdings barely two decades ago. Running a close second are the mutual funds. Their stockholdings now amount to about $53 billion, up from $1.4 billion in 1949 and $7 billion in 1956. In terms of total assets, however, the nation's commercial banks—primarily through their administration and effective control of personal and common trusts—must be accorded the biggest position of all, with assets estimated at over $600 billion. Actually, the banks whose role is appraised later, exert even greater influence than this would suggest for they decide upon many and execute most of the transactions for the pension funds.

Mutual Funds, Pension Funds: $$$

The growth of mutual funds in the last two decades has been astonishing. In 1948 only seven hundred thousand people had accounts with the fewer than 100 mutual funds then in operation. Their net assets totaled $1.5 billion and annual sales amounted to $274 million. Most Americans then still saved in the traditional ways—life insurance, bank deposits, and personally owned corporate securities. But about 1950 things began to change and the mutual funds skyrocketed in financial significance. By the mid-fifties mutual fund investors exceeded two million and annual fund sales soared above a billion dollars. Currently some 10 million people purchase $5 billion a year in shares in 200 mutual funds. In 1967, the funds themselves reported assets of over $50 billion, fifty times their 1948 holdings. Bear in mind that since 1948 the population has increased by only a third and the Gross National Product (in real terms, taking out the element of inflation) has just slightly more than doubled. The relative growth of the mutual funds, when set against these indicia, is indeed remarkable and strikingly shows the extent to which the mutual funds have quickly become a major force in the economy.

Of even greater financial consequence than the mutual funds are the pension funds. Set up under a variety of arrangements and encouraged by favorable tax treatment (payments into the funds are a deductible expense for the employer, but not taxable to the worker until paid out), the pension funds have swollen fantastically since the middle of World War II. In 1940 only some four million jobholders were covered by a pension plan (Social Security excepted, of course) and plan reserves totaled less than $2.5 billion. Today the nation's pension funds take in that much every six months in the form of employer-employee contributions! Presently more than twenty-eight millon people in industry are covered by a pension fund and employers contribute about $8 billion a year to finance prospective retirement benefits (employees add about $1 billion in their own right). This huge, steadily swelling influx of revenue has increased the assets of private pension funds to

more than $80 billion. If the various government employee funds
are taken into account, they add another $100 billion (about half
of this is in state and local funds, with the Federal Civil Service
and Social Security funds just about evenly splitting the remainder).
There are now ten individual state and city retirement systems
each with more than a billion dollars in assets (California, New
York, New Jersey, among others); the du Pont and Western Electric funds are almost this big. All told, public and private unin-
sured pension funds currently have assets of approximately $180
billion—equal to those of the entire life insurance industry.

In terms of book value, just about half of the pension funds'
assets—$40 billion out of $80 billion—are held in the form of
common stock (in terms of market value common stock accounts
for more than half the total). An additional third is invested in
corporate bonds.

If one looks ahead, the pension funds take on even more awesome proportions. It is estimated that by 1976 workers included
in private and state-local government plans will number forty-eight
million, compared with thirty-five million in 1966. By 1981 more
than fifty-five million employees will be covered. As contributions
continue to mount, total pension fund assets will rise from their
present level of $150 billion to more than $400 billion. Then the
funds will be taking in nearly $20 billion in new funds each year.
That is about equal to the proceeds of all the new securities currently sold annually by corporations. What this suggests is that
in a few years the pension funds alone could finance most new
corporate cash requirements. This point underscores the fact
that in barely two decades, we have created in the United States
two enormous new financial empires—the mutual funds and the
pension funds. Their position in the economy and the pattern of
their investments—heavily centered in corporate securities—have
sharply diffused, and altered in many other significant ways, ownership in public enterprises. Indeed, in assessing the role of institutions, reports of their assets seriously understate their actual significance in securities trading. One reason is that institutional
securities holdings are heavily concentrated in a few stocks. Out
of more than twelve hundred companies whose stock is sold on the

New York Stock Exchange, twenty-five account for a third of all stock purchases by institutions and a mere sixty account for two thirds. Mutual funds held more than a quarter of such high-flying stocks as Burroughs, Control Data, Raytheon, and Ling-Temco-Vought. A second factor lies in the propensity of institutions, especially the so-called performance or growth mutual funds, to "turnover" their holdings often, sometimes buying and selling a given company's stock several times in a single year in large, 10,000-share transactions. Institutions on the average will trade a fifth of their stock annually, but the fast-paced mutuals will sell anywhere from 50 to over 100 percent in a year. The volatility of their trading emphasizes the power of the institutions in the nation's stock markets and potentially in the affairs of all large publicly held corporations.

In assessing their increasingly important role in the economy, what is worth even greater stress is the very recent trend for the institutions to coalesce. There have long been intimate financial ties between the various institutions (a fact to be considered later in this chapter), but a merger trend is developing that will bring many more under common ownership. Most notable are the moves by life insurers to enter the mutual fund business, often by acquiring one or more established fund managers. The most dramatic move came in 1968 when the CNA Financial Group (formed in 1967 as a holding company to control Continental Casualty and Continental Assurance) paid $22 million for the Tsai Management & Research Corporation, which runs the highly publicized Manhattan Fund. New England Mutual, American General, and Fund American also acquired mutual funds. By the beginning of 1969 insurance companies had bought mutual funds with assets approximating $3 billion. Meanwhile other prominent insurers like John Hancock and Omaha Mutual started mutual funds of their own. These developments, striking as they are, are perfectly understandable for the life insurance companies have been getting a smaller and smaller piece of the family investment dollar. The nation's insurance companies have $190 billion in assets, twice what they were in 1956. But mutual fund assets now amount to over $50 billion, up five times since 1956.

Just as the insurance companies have begun to diversify, so too have the banks. For years the nation's banks pretty much stuck to their banking chores, largely because Federal law prohibits commercial banks from directly engaging in general business. A bank, for example, cannot, in the United States, buy stock in its own right in, say, General Motors or IBM (banks, of course, hold stock as security for loans and they manage billions of dollars in investments as trustees). Beginning about 1965, however, the banks started to take advantage of a loophole in the Federal law that had generally gone unnoticed in financial circles for more than thirty years. It permitted banks to set up so-called one-bank holding companies that could engage in diversified business activities. What a bank could not do directly, therefore, it could do indirectly, through a holding company it created and controlled. Such holding companies can sell insurance, lease equipment, operate mutual funds, act as stockbrokers, serve as travel agents, or perform any of a number of services, whether or not related to traditional banking operations. The temptation to diversify in this fashion was uncontrollable. Between 1965 and 1968 more than twenty large one-bank holding companies were established by banks with assets of more than $15 billion. While legislation before the Congress in 1969 would curtail the further expansion of one-bank holding companies, the banks, using the holding companies which they previously created, have become an important new commercial participant in the trend to diversification.

Internationalization of Finance

The shift away from personal investment in corporate securities and the marked trend for individuals to invest via institutions, especially pension and mutual funds, has introduced a vital new force in the U.S. economy. It is removing individuals still further from direct participation in corporate affairs, which is hardly a new phenomenon, and it is concentrating vast financial power in the hands of a relatively small number of institutions. There is another fact, however, that warrants attention, namely the internationalization of investment. The contemporary business firm is increasing in size, diversifying through merger, and expanding greatly, industrially and geographically, in the number of markets it serves. Corporations are going international in a big way, and investment services are following right along. This in itself poses new challenges for the United States and other countries that remain nationalistic in their approach to international corporate activities.

The internationalization of finance is only another facet of the new economic environment. The securities of foreign companies, of course, have long been traded on American exchanges, just as U.S. stocks and bonds are traded in London, Paris, Amsterdam, Frankfurt, Zurich, and other world financial centers. The common stock of some twenty-six foreign companies is regularly traded on the New York Stock Exchange, including such well-known firms as Unilever (parent of Lever Brothers—the maker of Pepsodent toothpaste, Lux and Rinso soaps, and Spry shortening), Shell, International Nickel, Aluminium of Canada, and Seagrams. Foreigners deal extensively in the United States in corporate securities: in 1969 their net purchases of stocks of American companies totaled around $5 billion. Meanwhile, Americans bought and sold almost $2 billion in foreign stocks traded on U.S. markets. Result: at the end of 1967 foreigners held nearly $15 billion in U.S. corporate stocks while U.S. citizens held approximately $5 billion in foreign corporate stocks. There are other important dimensions of international investments, notably direct ownership of property in other countries, but it warrants the closer attention provided in Chapter 18.

Careful note should be taken here, though, of the growing significance of mutual funds and other institutions in international investment by individuals. Just as people have tended domestically to funnel their investments in corporate securities through intermediaries, much the same has been occurring around the world. Foreigners now invest more than $200 million a year in U.S. mutual funds. Moreover, foreign-based funds, often owned or managed by Americans (the Chase Manhattan Bank, for instance, manages the Neckermann Fund, a subsidiary of the big German mail order firm, Neckermann Versand), have become extremely attractive investment outlets for citizens of other countries who are anxious to participate in the booming American economy.

The biggest of the global mutual funds is Fund of Funds, a billion-dollar subsidiary of Panama-based Investors Overseas Services—a firm controlled by Bernard Cornfeld, an expatriate Brooklynite. With some fifty subsidiaries scattered around the world (in part to minimize income taxes, which now take only about 7 percent of its profits), IOS ingests approximately $2.5 million a day. Before 1967 it invested most of this money in U.S. mutual funds (thus the name of its key affiliate, Fund of Funds). Although that approach is now banned by an order issued by the U.S. Securities & Exchange Commission, IOS nonetheless continues to invest heavily in American stocks through a London dealer. On some days its transactions equal 4 percent of all the trading on the New York Stock Exchange. With operations in fifty countries and a quarter of a million shareholders, IOS is a prototype of tomorrow's international financial enterprises which will operate transnationally, investing billions of dollars drawn from many countries in a vast number of companies with equivalent global breadth.

Not only do mutual funds operate easily across national boundaries, but they conceal the identities of their stockholders. Clandestine international investment is one of the more puzzling developments in recent corporate financial history. Quite literally we often do not know who owns what. Through numbered Swiss or Panamanian bank accounts (and sometimes both, providing a double layer of "paper" insulation) and Lichtensteinian "establishments," or holding companies, funds are moved about the world in a completely secret manner and invested surreptitiously in legitimate enterprises. No one knows the identity of the actual owner and yet that fact may be of great importance to any of a number of governments if, for example, the purchaser of a firm's stock is a competitor or an illicit gambler or a foreign investor.

To show what can take place, even in the case of a major American corporation, take note of the facts relating to ownership of the Pennsylvania Railroad just prior to its merger with the New York Central. The ten biggest stockholders included two Swiss banks, Crédit Suisse and Société de Banque Suisse, who between them owned 550,000 shares. These banks, of course, merely held legal title on behalf of their depositors—and who were their depositors? American interests, Middle East oil sheikhs, the Vatican, the English Government, or who? No one can say, and not even the Swiss banks may know because they normally buy shares for and at the direction of the "representatives" of numbered accounts. Of the other eight biggest Pennsylvania Railroad stockholders, five were well-known U.S. brokerage houses, led by Merrill Lynch. In total they controlled 1.7 million shares, worth more than $100 million at current market prices. Their stock was held in street name, meaning that the actual owners had asked their brokers to keep title in the broker's name rather than in their own. One is forced to speculate—in this instance, as in many others—about the actual ownership of one of the country's principal corporations operating in a supposedly regulated industry.

Large secretive holdings in big international enterprises are of major policy consequence. While they have the mysterious aura about them that always surrounds clandestine dealings, in fact they are only suggestive of a much wider range of financial relationships that draw seriously into issue all of our traditional conceptions of "ownership" and "control" in the context of the modern corporation. Earlier we noted that most individuals are tending to withdraw from direct stock ownership in companies and to funnel their investments through institutions, especially pension funds and mutual funds. This latter development has substantially increased the power of institutions—pension funds, banks, insurance companies, and mutual funds—in the affairs of even the largest corporations. What's more, these institutions—big though they are even in their own right—do not operate independently, but rather are intricately interwoven in a web of de facto economic alliances.

Financial Interconnections: Money Is the Glue That Binds

An examination of the affairs of almost any large corporation shows the interconnections between the various financial institutions. The major airlines, like American, TWA, and Eastern, have borrowed hundreds of millions of dollars from closely allied groups of banks, pension funds, and insurance companies. In the process they have not only agreed to terms that give the lenders a big voice in their continuing business affairs, but they also accept representatives of these creditors on their boards of directors. Natural enough, of course, but it gives the key credit interests considerable effective power over the entire airline industry. The same family of banks, insurers, and pension funds has directors on the boards of directors of just about every air carrier. Making the web even tighter, executives of the airlines serve as directors of New York banks, often sitting alongside their aviation competitors.

An investigation completed in 1968 by a House of Representatives subcommittee showed that a small group of large banks and insurance companies, knitted together in a web of interlocking directorships, typically supplies most of the capital needed by the airlines to buy their new jet aircraft. At one recent point, for instance, a syndicate composed of Prudential Insurance, Metropolitan Life, Equitable Life Assurance, the Chase Manhattan Bank, the First National City Bank, and Morgan Guaranty effectively controlled the affairs of TWA, the big international airline. The group held more than 16 percent of the airline's stock, had loans outstanding to it amounting to nearly $200 million, and owned the overwhelming interest in a substantial portion of TWA's jet fleet. Most members of the syndicate held comparable positions of power with respect to the other major air carriers.

Similar intricate relationships exist for every big industry, with banks serving as the glue that binds together an industry's top-ranked firms. General Motors, Ford, and Chrysler do not have representatives on each other's boards of directors (to do so would be a violation of Federal law), but one of the biggest Wall Street banks, Morgan Guaranty, has an officer on each of these three auto company boards. Not only does this give immense practical power to Morgan Guaranty, but it also provides a bridge between these erstwhile auto rivals. Looking at the situation more generally, a Congressional study showed that of the 373 members of the boards of the nation's fifteen biggest commercial banks, 324 held more than fifteen hundred management positions (primarily directorships) in other financial institutions, insurance companies, and industrial concerns. Big banking influence in the American economy clearly extends far—very far indeed.

Commercial Banks: The Kingpins of Finance

Despite their large, growing significance in the economy, the mutual funds and pension funds look very small when placed alongside the nation's commercial banks. Presently the assets of all institutional investors total about a trillion dollars, and of this the banks, either in terms of the assets they own in their own right or those which they administer as trustees, control about 60 percent. Big though it is, even this sum, in all its $600 billion magnificence, understates the powerful role the banks play in the U.S. economy, for banks, as the principal lenders of capital, add even more to their strength. In their capacity as trustees the banks manage most of the nation's pension funds and control more than $125 billion in private trust accounts. As lenders they have loans outstanding to business that exceed $70 billion.

Accentuating their power still more, bank wealth is highly concentrated in a few huge institutions which exert their power to acquire key positions of influence in major corporations. Just forty-nine banks, of the size and notoriety of Morgan Guaranty, Chase Manhattan, Bank of America, and First National City, hold more than half of the country's total bank trust assets. With this immense sum at their disposal, backed up by their position as primary lenders of capital, these bank colossi have acquired trustee ownership of enough common stock, in the judgment of most realistic observers of the corporate scene, to provide effective control of almost 150 of the 500 largest U.S. industrial corporations. To ensconce this massive position further these forty-nine banks have placed their representatives on the boards of directors of 300 of the nation's 500 biggest companies.

What this can mean is vividly illustrated by a brief examination of the complex affairs of Morgan Guaranty, the big New York bank whose trust department is the largest in the United States, with assets of over $17 billion. In its trust accounts it holds 5 percent or more of the common stock in seventy-two corporations. Its officers sit on the boards of more than a hundred companies, rubbing elbows with their brethren from other billion-dollar manufacturing, transportation, and insurance corporations. The full array of its incredible position is dramatically shown in the accompanying chart (Chart 3), which shows the extent of its stockholdings and representation on the boards of the largest U.S. corporations. Repeat this same picture several times, substituting for the name of Morgan Guaranty that of any of a number of other banks, and you begin to realize why Congressman Wright Patman has declared that the banks are "the single most important force in the economy." What makes them particularly potent is that they so often work in close alliance with one another, backstopping, as it were, their own already powerful individual positions.

One final twist: the banks often own themselves! By investing the trust funds over which they have control in their own stock, and then voting this stock to elect the incumbent officers as members of the board of directors they become self-perpetuating institutions, like the Catholic Church or a university board of trustees. Given the enormity of their wealth, the banks' insulation from even the customary formalities of ownership control makes it almost essential that ways be devised to check their power.

The effective authority of the officers who run the affairs of the typical big public corporation is not to be discounted, however, despite the growing presence of institutional investors. Many pension and mutual fund managers make only limited overt use of the power they possess. If, for one reason or another, they become disenchanted with a company, their usual inclination is simply to dispose of their interests and shift their funds into another situation. This leaves corporate management with considerable discretion. Nonetheless, the fact that institutions hold a large block of shares in a corporation constitutes a special factor that the firm's management inevitably must take into account. The whisper of a giant, after all, is much more likely to be heeded than the shout of a midget. Moreover, there is evidence that institutional man-

CHART 3
The Sweep of Morgan Guaranty Trust Company

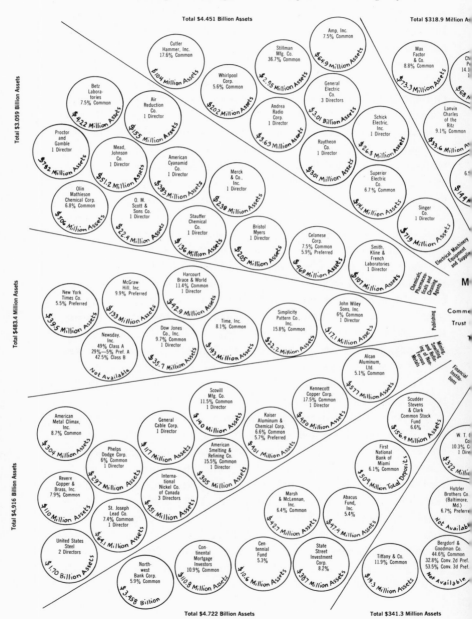

Total $4.451 Billion Assets

Total $318.9 Million A...

Total $3.059 Billion Assets

Cutler Hammer, Inc.
17.6% Common
$104 Million Assets

Amp. Inc.
7.5% Common
$64.9 Million Assets

Stillman Mfg. Co.
36.7% Common
$2.95 Million Assets

Max Factor & Co.
8.8% Common
$73.3 Million Assets

Chi...
Pe...
14.1...
$68 N...

Betz Laboratories
7.5% Common
$422 Million Assets

Whirlpool Corp.
5.6% Common
$202 Million Assets

General Electric Co.
3 Directors
$3.01 Billion Assets

Air Reduction Co.
1 Director
$155 Million Assets

Andrea Radio Corp.
1 Director
$3.63 Million Assets

Schick Electric, Inc.
1 Director
$26.8 Million Assets

Lanvin Charles of the Ritz
9.1% Common
$33.6 Million A...

Proctor and Gamble
1 Director
$782 Million Assets

Mead, Johnson Co.
1 Director
$51.2 Million Assets

American Cyanamid Co.
1 Director
$393 Million Assets

Raytheon Co.
1 Director
$301 Million Assets

6.9...
$141 M...

Olin Mathieson Chemical Corp.
6.8% Common
$1.06 Million Assets

O. M. Scott & Sons Co.
1 Director
$22.4 Million Assets

Merck & Co., Inc.
1 Director
$238 Million Assets

Superior Electric Co.
6.7% Common
$14.1 Million Assets

Singer Co.
1 Director
$719 Million Assets

Stauffer Chemical Co.
1 Director
$136 Million Assets

Bristol Myers Corp.
1 Director
$205 Million Assets

Celanese Corp.
7.5% Common
5.9% Preferred
$169 Million Assets

Smith, Kline & French Laboratories
1 Director
$107 Million Assets

Electrical Machinery Equipment and Supplies

Chemicals Pharmaceuticals and Cleaning Agents

M...

Total $483.4 Million Assets

New York Times Co.
5.5% Preferred
$39.5 Million Assets

McGraw-Hill, Inc.
9.9% Preferred
$133 Million Assets

Harcourt Brace & World
11.4% Common
1 Director
$42.9 Million Assets

John Wiley Sons, Inc.
6% Common
1 Director
$17.1 Million Assets

Newsday, Inc.
49% Class A
29%—5% Pref. A
42.5% Class B
Not Available

Dow Jones Co., Inc.
9.7% Common
1 Director
$35.7 Million Assets

Time, Inc.
8.1% Common
$193 Million Assets

Simplicity Pattern Co.,
Inc.
15.8% Common
$22.2 Million Assets

Publishing

Comme...

Trust

Mining Smelting and Refining of Non-Ferrous Metals

Financial Institutions

Total $4,916 Billion Assets

Scovill Mfg. Co.
11.5% Common
1 Director
$140 Million Assets

Kennecott Copper Corp.
17.5% Common
1 Director
$150 Million Assets

Alcan Aluminum, Ltd.
5.1% Common
$577 Million Assets

American Metal Climax, Inc.
8.7% Common
$304 Million Assets

General Cable Corp.
1 Director
$117 Million Assets

Kaiser Aluminum & Chemical Corp.
6.6% Common
5.7% Preferred
$101 Million Assets

Scudder Stevens & Clark Common Stock Fund
6.6%
$156.9 Million Assets

W. T. C...
Co...
10.3% C...
1 Dire...
$322 Millio...

Phelps Dodge Corp.
6% Common
1 Director
$297 Million Assets

American Smelting & Refining Co.
15.5% Common
1 Director
$305 Million Assets

First National Bank of Miami
6.1% Common
$509 Million Total Deposits

Revere Copper & Brass, Inc.
7.9% Common
$110 Million Assets

International Nickel Co. of Canada
3 Directors
$451 Million Assets

Marsh & McLennan, Inc.
6.4% Common
$427 Million Assets

Abacus Fund, Inc.
5.4%
$47.4 Million Assets

Hutzler Brothers Co. (Baltimore, Md.)
6.7% Preferred
Not Available

St. Joseph Lead Co.
7.4% Common
1 Director
$641 Million Assets

United States Steel
2 Directors
$1.70 Billion Assets

Northwest Bank Corp.
5.9% Common
$3,458 Billion

Continental Mortgage Investors
10.9% Common
$10.8 Million Assets

Centennial Fund
5.3%
$10.6 Million Assets

State Street Investment Corp.
8.2%
$387 Million Assets

Tiffany & Co.
11.9% Common
$19.3 Million Assets

Bergdorf & Goodman Inc.
44.6% Common
32.8% Conv. 2d Pref.
53.5% Conv. 3d Pref.
Not Available

Total $4.722 Billion Assets

Total $341.3 Million Assets

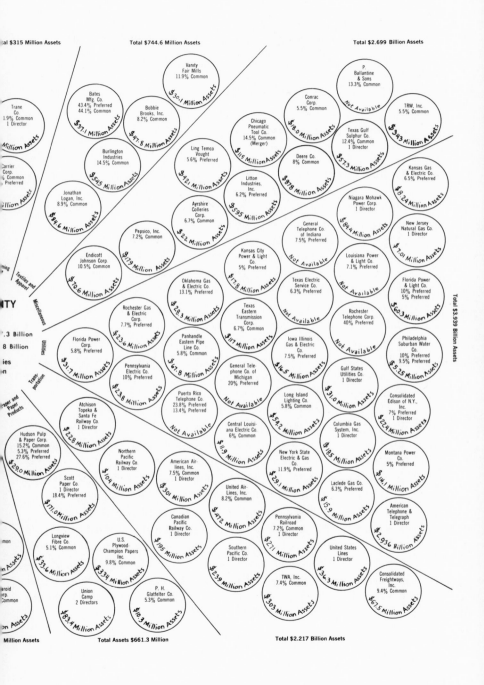

Total $315 Million Assets

Total $744.6 Million Assets

Total $2.699 Billion Assets

Vanity Fair Mills
11.9% Common
$30.1 Million Assets

P. Ballantine & Sons
13.3% Common
Not Available

Trane Co.
1.9% Common
1 Director
Million Assets

Bates Mfg. Co.
43.4% Preferred
44.1% Common
$37.1 Million Assets

Bobbie Brooks, Inc.
8.2% Common
$47.8 Million Assets

Conrac Corp.
5.5% Common
$8.0 Million Assets

TRW, Inc.
5.5% Common
$343 Million Assets

Carrier Corp.
% Common
% Preferred
illion Assets

Burlington Industries
14.5% Common
$545 Million Assets

Chicago Pneumatic Tool Co.
14.5% Common
(Merger)
$115 Million Assets

Texas Gulf Sulphur Co.
12.4% Common
1 Director
$573 Million Assets

Ling Temco Vought
5.6% Preferred
$421 Million Assets

Deere & Co.
8% Common
$878 Million Assets

Kansas Gas & Electric Co.
6.5% Preferred
$824 Million Assets

Jonathan Logan, Inc.
8.9% Common
$84.6 Million Assets

Litton Industries, Inc.
6.2% Preferred
$595 Million Assets

Niagara Mohawk Power Corp.
1 Director
$894 Million Assets

New Jersey Natural Gas Co.
1 Director
$7.01 Million Assets

Pepsico, Inc.
7.2% Common
$179 Million Assets

Ayrshire Collieries Corp.
6.7% Common
$22 Million Assets

General Telephone Co. of Indiana
7.5% Preferred
Not Available

Louisiana Power & Light Co.
7.1% Preferred
Not Available

Florida Power & Light Co.
10% Common
5% Preferred
$60.3 Million Assets

Endicott Johnson Corp.
10.5% Common
$70.6 Million Assets

Kansas City Power & Light Co.
5% Preferred
$17.8 Million Assets

Texas Electric Service Co.
6.3% Preferred
Not Available

ning

Textiles and Apparel

TY

Miscellaneous

.3 Billion
8 Billion

ies
on

Utilities

Trans-
portation

Oklahoma Gas & Electric Co.
13.1% Preferred
$28.3 Million Assets

Rochester Gas & Electric Corp.
7.7% Preferred
$23.6 Million Assets

Texas Eastern Transmission Corp.
6.7% Common
$117 Million Assets

Rochester Telephone Corp.
40% Preferred
Not Available

Philadelphia Suburban Water Co.
10% Preferred
9.5% Preferred
$5.25 Million Assets

Florida Power Corp.
5.8% Preferred
$31.7 Million Assets

Panhandle Eastern Pipe Line Co.
5.8% Common
$67.8 Million Assets

Iowa Illinois Gas & Electric Co.
7.5% Preferred
$16.5 Million Assets

Pennsylvania Electric Co.
10% Preferred
$23.8 Million Assets

General Telephone Co. of Michigan
20% Preferred
Not Available

Gulf States Utilities Co.
1 Director
$31.0 Million Assets

Consolidated Edison of N.Y.,
Inc.
7% Preferred
1 Director
$274 Million Assets

Total $3.939 Billion Assets

Puerto Rico Telephone Co.
23.8% Preferred
13.4% Preferred
Not Available

Long Island Lighting Co.
5.8% Common
$51.2 Million Assets

Columbia Gas System, Inc.
1 Director
$85 Million Assets

Atchison Topeka & Santa Fe Railway Co.
1 Director
$22.8 Million Assets

Central Louisiana Electric Co.
6% Common
$11.9 Million Assets

Montana Power Co.
5% Preferred
$141 Million Assets

Paper and Paper Products

Hudson Pulp & Paper Corp.
15.2% Common
5.3% Preferred
27.6% Preferred
$29.0 Million Assets

Northern Pacific Railway Co.
1 Director
$104 Million Assets

American Airlines, Inc.
7.5% Common
1 Director
$301 Million Assets

New York State Electric & Gas Co.
11.9% Preferred
$29.1 Million Assets

Laclede Gas Co.
6.3% Preferred
$15.9 Million Assets

American Telephone & Telegraph
1 Director
$2.936 Billion Assets

Scott Paper Co.
1 Director
18.4% Preferred
$171.0 Million Assets

United Airlines, Inc.
8.2% Common
$472 Million Assets

mon

Longview Fibre Co.
5.1% Common
$33.6 Million Assets

U.S. Plywood-Champion Papers Inc.
9.8% Common
$334 Million Assets

Canadian Pacific Railway Co.
1 Director
$195 Million Assets

Pennsylvania Railroad
7.2% Common
1 Director
$271 Million Assets

United States Lines
1 Director
$36.3 Million Assets

n Assets

aroid orp.
Common

Union Camp
2 Directors
$83.4 Million Assets

P. H. Glatfelter Co.
5.3% Common
$10.3 Million Assets

Southern Pacific Co.
1 Director
$23.9 Million Assets

TWA, Inc.
7.4% Common
$303 Million Assets

Consolidated Freightways, Inc.
9.4% Common
$67.5 Million Assets

n Assets

Million Assets

Total Assets $661.3 Million

Total $2.217 Billion Assets

agers are becoming less reticent to assert their power in an aggressive way. Many mutual funds, for example, have publicly taken sides in control contests in the last several months. This trend is likely to be accelerated as the institutions assume even larger positions in corporate finance.

Financial Power and Public Accountability

The unmistakable fact is that, with institutions in control of influential blocks of stock in major corporations, there is a basic risk that our biggest companies can be made to dance the tune of a plutocracy of bank and investment managers who are effectively sheltered from view, let alone having any meaningful notion of public accountability. Moreover, to the extent that the institutions make no effort to throw their weight around, corporate management is left free to do pretty much as it pleases. Either way, the result is that a small group of men—whether they happen to be labeled bank managers, mutual fund advisers, or company officers—remain in control of enterprises of great significance in the economy of the United States, not to mention other nations. Whatever the exact situation, the allocation of effective authority in our biggest corporations leaves the public on the outside trying to look in, and often finding the corporate walls opaque.

The typical corporation has become not only a huge, rapidly diversifying international business empire, but a force that is breaking down old industrial lines and spreading broadly throughout the economy. Its basic character has fundamentally changed. So too has the pattern of corporate control and investment been revolutionized with the growth of financial institutions, bank-influenced if not controlled, which are rapidly replacing individuals as direct investors. The corporate scene has been drastically revised in recent years—in so many ways that old modes of thought make it impossible for businessmen or the public to appreciate fully the likely implications. Clearly, though, the worlds of business have changed and new reactions and new policies are necessary to cope with the challenges of the new business universe.

Before dealing with these basic policy issues, several of the other dimensions of change must be considered. For what is happening, simultaneously, is that while business is undergoing profound alteration, so also is the larger social, technical, and economic environment within which it functions being recast.

PART II

The New Business Constituency

CHAPTER 5

The Postindustrial State

Vast in size and wealth, diversified in their product and geographic orientation, reasonably secure in their preeminent place in the industrial hierarchy, and tightly interwoven with the banking and financial community, the big American corporations have become a world onto themselves. Yet to show the modern corporation in its fullest dimensions we must examine both the dynamic inner worlds of contemporary business and the growing variety of institutions which are beginning to impinge on the traditional business sector.

Corporations, however large, are not lifeless, artificial creatures. They are given substance by the humans who control their affairs— by their employees, managers, and that expanding band of technocrats who are assuming strategic places of power within all modern enterprises. Yet each of these groups is presently undergoing profound change—in their composition, values, and demands—which are so far-reaching in their implications that we must be aware of the problems and inner tensions they create for the giant corporations which occupy such a crucial place in all our lives.

Whatever one wants to call it—the "postindustrial society" or the "service society"—the United States has become the first country in the history of the world in which most of the employed population is *not* involved in the production of food, clothing, houses, and other tangible goods. Indeed, virtually all of our growth in jobs since the end of World War II has come in the service-government sector. Today just about two thirds of our employment is in the service-government area and by 1975 it will reach 70 percent. Meanwhile the goods producing industries (manufacturing, construction, and mining) will continue to decline, with their proportion of total employment falling from the present 35 percent to about 30 percent by the mid-seventies. Keep in mind that in 1930, which really isn't very long ago (about 60 percent of today's population was then alive), these proportions were just about reversed, with two thirds of the employed labor force then engaged in the traditional types of work—in farming or factories producing autos, steel, or other goods. A silent revolution has taken place.

As in so many aspects of economic development, America is leading the way into a service state. Other countries will be at this point, but not for at least one or more decades. In Great Britain, for example, nearly 60 percent of employment is still in farming and manufacture. For France the proportion is near two thirds and in Greece, to cite a still-developing though hardly backward nation, the figure is close to 80 percent (we were at this stage in the 1880s). How the United States and its business leaders cope with the problems that the transition from a goods to a service society inevitably creates thus will constitute an example of immense practical importance to the entire developing world.

Expansion in the Service-Government Sector

The explosive expansion in the service-government sector has many implications for business and the economy as a whole. In aggregative dollar terms it means that many types of concerns are experiencing faster growth than firms engaged in manufacturing and in other goods industries. The service-government slice of the GNP is getting bigger, almost entirely at the expense of manufacturing. Services (government included) now account for almost

40 percent of the GNP compared with close to 30 percent in 1929. Even this understates their sharp expansion for it fails explicitly to take into account the role of government as an increasingly important economic factor.

In 1929 governments at all levels—Federal, state and local— purchased only about 11 percent of the nation's output of goods and services. Today government purchases exceed 20 percent, with the most rapid recent gains coming in the state-local area. The service-government sector directly accounts for a growing proportion of economic activity and exerts a powerful influence on the composition of the entire economy. Government, for example, is less interested, economically speaking, in the purchase of automobiles than it is in the provision of education or health care. Its much heavier expenditures for the latter functions help explain why from 1950 to 1960 the *increase* in employment in education and in health services was greater than the *total* employment in auto manufacturing or primary metals in *either* year. Today government and services account for twice as many man-hours as manufacturing and mining.

While job opportunities in the service sector have been increasing markedly in recent years, they have varied considerably by type of business. The best index for comparison is growth in employment. It shows that while the service category grew rapidly overall, the trade, recreation, restaurant, hotel, and personal service categories fared poorly compared with banks, business services (research most notably), education, and medical care. It is particularly significant to note the character of the last three groups for they are suggestive of a significant new development—the rise of the nonprofit organizations. Their growth has coincided with the accelerating expansion of the service sector, and especially the education, health, research, and business service subcategories.

Rise of the Nonprofits

Who or what are these nonprofit organizations that have sprung up in such great numbers throughout the educational, research, health, and other portions of the service sector? It is a markedly heterogeneous family, defying simple categorization, but it includes at least all of the following: charitable foundations, hospitals, group health associations; colleges and universities; credit unions and mutual insurance companies; quasi-public transportation authorities; community chests; community action and neighborhood legal groups; and nonprofit research organizations. It would include "things" as diverse as Harvard University, Blue Cross, the New Jersey Turnpike Authority, the Ford Foundation, and the Stanford Research Institute.

Such a list tells quite a bit about the nonprofits. First, they are unlike such profit-seeking corporations as Texaco, Chrysler, General Electric in that they do not have shareholders who own stock and are entitled to vote for a board of directors. They may have "members" (Blue Cross), or alumni and students (Harvard), or they may have a self-perpetuating board of trustees or governors (Stanford Research Institute), or they may be vaguely responsive to some outside group of political officials (New Jersey Turnpike). In no case, though, are they responsive to an "owner." Who, for example, "owns" Harvard or Blue Cross? That makes them unique and underscores the enormous power held by their managing officers. Still, their distinctiveness is largely a question of degree, for, as discussed earlier, it is true more in theory than in reality to say that the 1.3 million stockholders of General Motors actually "own" that vast international corporation in the sense that they exert meaningful control over its operations.

Second, while the nonprofits perform a great variety of activities, they are concentrated in the service-governmental area. They rarely make or sell goods; typically they provide only services, with heavy emphasis on "thinking" and health. This puts them apart from most of the country's biggest companies, but not all, for there are a number of profit-seeking corporations that also are engaged principally in the provision of services. Insurance companies are but one example. Nonetheless, it is true that nonprofit organizations effectively dominate the educational and health fields and occupy a very large position in research and business consultation. This point leads to a third feature. The nonprofits often are in direct competition with profit-making private firms. The Stanford Research Institute is a major nonprofit organization, handling thousands of projects for government and business and with annual revenues exceeding $55 million. SRI is a very big operation indeed, but it is under no compulsion or necessity to make a profit. Yet it (and others similarly situated, like Battelle Memorial Institute and Illinois Institute of Technology Research Institute in Chicago) competes directly with profit-seeking research organizations like A. D. Little or Planning Research Corporation, in much the same way Blue Cross competes with Aetna or John Hancock for the health insurance dollar. Thus the nonprofits not only complement business, they compete as well.

The Diverse Service Industries

Companies that offer services, whether on a profit or nonprofit basis, can do more than offer assistance or competition to companies engaged in what we traditionally think of when we speak of "business." In health care, for example, nonprofit organizations —like hospitals and Blue Cross—dominate a market that is growing more rapidly than any other in the United States. Approximately three million are now directly employed in health services, more even than in education. Expenditures for health and medical care amount to more than 6 percent of the GNP, or roughly $50 billion. Already the nonprofits are beginning to come into direct competition with established for-profit insurers, equipment suppliers, and other enterprises which are involved in some way with medical care. Right now there are more than 160 million Americans who have some form of hospitalization insurance. In 1940 the number was around twelve million and in 1945 it was still only thirty-two millon. Today, the biggest of the medical insurers is Blue Cross-Blue Shield, with more than sixty-five million members and annual income nearing $5 billion.

Vast though it is in the scale of its operations, Blue Cross is only one among a number of participants in the fragmented health-care field. Indeed, medical service ideally illustrates what can take place when a common problem is viewed piece by piece rather than as a single system. The growing dissatisfaction with the balkanization that presently exists in medical care strongly suggests that fundamental changes in its organization are likely to occur in the near future—no doubt opening up great new markets for corporations that can handle all of the associated problems on a systematic basis. Right now there are many loosely coordinated participants in medical care. At the most immediate personal level are the doctors, of whom only about two thirds are in practice (this percentage is shrinking as more medical specialists go into research and other fields). Then there are the drug companies, aiming pointedly at the doctor and investing a large piece of their sales dollar in inducing him to prescribe their brands of drugs. The government is also involved, at all levels, through research (the National Institutes of Health finance about 80 percent of all the medical and drug research done in this country), hospital construction, support of medical education, operation of medical centers, provision of health care (as through the Veterans Administration, Public Health Service, and local welfare agencies). Lastly, nonprofit organizations operate most of the nation's hospitals and train virtually all of our skilled medical personnel.

This quick survey of medical care shows the complex interplay of participants and reveals the considerable extent to which profit-seeking business firms, governments, and not-for-profit organizations function alongside one another in dealing with a common set of problems. Not only does it demonstrate the futility in thinking of the economy in terms of two neatly defined worlds, one "public" and one "private" (and profit seeking), but it points out the ways in which distinctive institutions, some seeking profit for their "owners," some carrying out "governmental" responsibilities, others performing identifiable tasks but not "for profit," can work together, even though our political-economic mythology might suggest this would be impossible.

The complex mixture of participants in health care points the way to similar relationships that are emerging in the provision of other kinds of services for the public. Education is one example. So too is legal service, where steps are now being taken to provide legal service on a prepaid group basis, just as medical care is provided by the Group Health Association in Washington or the

Kaiser Institutes on the West Coast. Organizations are springing up all over the country—many on a nonprofit basis—to provide insurance, on a voluntary group basis, for life, fire, and auto coverage. In a similar vein, at least one labor union has worked out an arrangement by which a nonprofit firm, controlled by the union, buys cars and leases them at cost to its members. The stellar example of what might spread throughout the economy, however, is provided by the American Farm Bureau Federation. With almost two million members (only half of them farmers), its family of businesses has assets approaching $2 billion. It sells insurance, gasoline, fertilizer, and auto supplies; operates a mutual fund; runs a complex of dairies; provides veterinary and accounting services; rents cars and trucks; and leases real estate. It is a pure conglomerate and a business of immense scale, but it is also operated as a "nonprofit" cooperative and may well suggest the kind of enterprise that could become an increasingly active rival of "for-profit" businesses in providing services in return for the consumer dollar.

Research Organizations: The New Engine of Change

One further distinguishing feature lies in the nature of many of the nonprofits' principal function as a source of change. Their job is to develop ideas, to devise new approaches, to concoct different techniques. Simply put, they are inherently a threat to the status quo, and that is both good and bad for business for it can mean obsolescence for a firm just as it can also lead to new products and bigger profits. It is their qualitative rather than their quantitative impact that makes the nonprofits such an important new factor in the economy.

If you lump in government (and government is obviously a close relative because of its equally diffuse "ownership" base and the kinds of functions it performs), the nonprofits account for more than a third of U.S. employment and account for more than 25 percent of the GNP. More significantly, they employ two out of three professional and scientific workers, directly or through the work they generate. Excepting universities (of which more in Chapter 7), there are now over six hundred nonprofit organizations engaged strictly in scientific activities, plus another seven thousand that deal in a wide range of consultative activities not purely technical in character, spending more than $600 million a year. It is the nonprofits along with the universities which have become the prime movers in basic and applied research. They hold a position as the very center of scientific change, as a stimulus, exploiter, and adapter, that is of the utmost long-term economic consequence.

Independent research organizations are unquestionably one of the key arrivals on the business scene in the last two decades. Their role is peculiarly postindustrial because of their stress on the use and exploitation of brainpower. Usually small, numbering a few skilled scientists and engineers, they are heavily centered in a few geographic regions, on the West Coast, around Washington, and along Route 128 in the Boston technological complex. Their particular specialization varies, but all are engaged in the discovery of knowledge and its systematic application to known or as yet undefined business problems. Their contribution to business lies in the organized, systematic application of individual scientific brainpower to problem solving. Put differently, their primary mission is technical change, to speed it up and broaden its impact.

Some of these organizations have been essentially government appendages, spawned by the Federal Government—especially the Department of Defense—and sustained by its money. RAND and the Institute for Defense Analyses are in this category. So too is the Aerospace Corporation, a weird enterprise that was incorporated in California in 1960 by officials of the Pentagon to serve as an "independent" research arm of the Air Force. Some research institutions, however, have never been strongly tied to the government and do a much greater percentage of their work for business. A. D. Little, Booz-Allen, and EBS, among the profit-seeking firms, and Stanford Research, among the nonprofits, belong in this group. So, too, does Battelle, but with a significant qualification. It manages the Atomic Energy Commission's big Pacific Northwest Laboratory at Hanford, Washington, for an annual fee of about $20 million.

There are other distinctions, too, between the research institutions. Many, probably most, are linked in one way or another to universities. In fact, some were founded by or with the active participation of one or more schools. Illinois Institute of Technology Research Institute in Chicago fits this description, as does the Research Triangle Institute in North Carolina and the Spindletop Research Center in Kentucky. Others were founded by businessmen but consciously placed under the awning of a major university. Stanford Research is the prime illustration and the Graduate Research Center of the Southwest in Dallas is a more recent example. These linkups between campus, research, and business are an exceptionally important development in the recent history of the American economy.

The nation's research institutions—growing in number and in their degree of technical sophistication and acceptability to business—typify the way that the software-emphasis service industries can drastically affect the more traditional industrial sectors. In essence, they change the chemistry of industry, accelerating the movement of technological blood from the brain through the rest of the economic system. The results have been most noticeable in the aircraft, electronics, and computer companies. Pressed by government and attracted by new public-sector markets the aerospace firms, in particular, have totally accommodated their enterprises to the kind of systems engineering that is a hallmark of the independent research organizations. Systems applications, sophisticated problem definition and solution, computer applications, PERT (Program Evaluation Review Technique), and all the rest of the new technological and managerial tools have been put to wide use in the development of intercontinental ballistic missiles, the Polaris submarine weapons system, military aircraft development, and space exploration techniques. Those same approaches are now not only applied in civilian aircraft development (the SST, the jumbo jets, and the air bus), but they have been widely diffused throughout the business community. Terms like "systems engineering," "computer simulation," and "PERT" were not in common business usage fifteen years ago. Today they are a standard part of the business vocabulary—but beyond that, they have been ingrained in the daily operations of most corporations. With the aid and under the pressure of the research community, business has entered a new, far more technical, much more sophisticated era. It is only suggestive of what can happen as the emphasis on service and software is intensified.

What this review shows is that in our postindustrial economy, with its growing emphasis on service, the conditions are ripe for all sorts of new arrangements to provide the software—education, health care, insurance, organized "thought"—that people and business want. Profit-seeking firms can and will help meet this demand. But services and software are functionally distinctive from goods production and permit government and strange "things" like non-profit organizations to compete with at least equal effectiveness. For business this means a new world—a world of unique external challenges and immense opportunities if a firm is sufficiently creative and flexible to adapt to the changing times. In a sense it's a new economic game we're playing, with many new players.

CHAPTER 6

Workers, Managers, and
the Changing Worlds of Business

Just as the external worlds of business are changing, so too is the
modern enterprise changing internally. Increased size coupled with
extensive geographic and product diversification alone would create
managerial challenges of great magnitude. But other forces have
also been at work to complicate even more the affairs of the modern firm. Most importantly the human quotient, the complex of
workers, technicians, foremen, and managers themselves, is changing markedly. Better educated, performing different kinds of tasks,
possessed of a distinctive outlook on their careers and their relationship to the firm, and far more sophisticated in their skills and
perspective of the place of business in the social order, they present
a completely distinct assembly of humans, one which will severely
try the ability of managers to harmonize and use for the fulfillment
of accepted economic goals. In fact, it may well be that corporate
executives, who once cursed the labor unions, will look back
fondly at their encounters with organized labor as far simpler than
coping with their far more heterogeneous work forces of the last
third of the twentieth century. This chapter looks at two closely
related issues: the changing labor force and its impact on the

union movement and at the problems of management in the big, diversified contemporary corporation.

Decline of the Labor Union

The nation's labor unions are on the decline and number in their ranks a steadily diminishing proportion of the labor force. In itself that is a fact of great economic and political importance. The factors that explain it, though, are of even more significance. In 1930, back in the pre-New Deal days, fewer than 12 percent of nonfarm employees were enrolled in labor unions. By 1939, helped along immensely by the Wagner Act and other legislation, the unions, with aggressive organizational drives in key manufacturing industries, boosted their membership share close to 30 percent. Slower but still substantial gains were made during the war and by 1945 nearly 36 percent of the nonagricultural labor force was union enrolled. No one knew it then, but that was the pinnacle of union success. Since the end of the war, the unions have seen their share of civilian employment shrink steadily, narrowing in almost every year. In the mid-fifties it was about 33 percent. Now it is approaching 25 percent, and every statistical sign shows that the decline has continued, picking up speed downhill. Today's eighteen million union members are no greater in number than they were a decade ago despite the fact that there are now more than ten million additional nonfarm workers.

The relative decline in labor union membership disguises considerable shifts within the labor movement. The older manufacturing-mining-rail brotherhood group is rapidly losing strength, with its enrollment declining even in absolute terms. As a result, the AFL-CIO, once the backbone of the organized labor movement, has been losing ground to unaffiliated unions (the Teamsters are one, but there are others—particularly in government employment). The withdrawal of the Auto Workers from its ranks in 1968 weakens it even more. The best-known and once the biggest unions, like the United Steel Workers and the United Mine Workers, have been supplanted by those unions which represent workers in the more rapidly growing industries, like chemicals, paper products, and utilities. As a group, the industrial labor unions have been far outdistanced in enrollment by unions of employees in trade establishments (retail department stores and supermarket chains), finance, and particularly in government. Between 1956 and 1966 alone, when total union membership fell from 18.5 million to only about 17 million, government union membership—Federal, state, local—rose sharply from 915,000 to 1.5 million. Looked at in very sweeping terms it is evident that the old industrial unions are on the decline and that power in the union movement, as reflected in membership, is decidedly shifting to the government-services-software sector, a feature that parallels the developments noted in the preceding chapter.

Several facts help explain the important changes taking place in labor (and also offer useful comment about the changes taking place throughout the economy). Historically, the unions found most of their members in heavy industry (metals, autos, and the like), mining, transportation (primarily among rail workers), and in construction. But these economic sectors have grown only slowly during the postwar period and, where their output rose, productivity gains reduced the need for additional workers. Fifty percent more steel, for example, is being produced with barely 10 percent more production workers than ten years ago. As well, there has been a shift in the location of industry away from the big cities of the North and East and into the smaller, less labor-sympathetic communities of the South and West. Moreover, the more rapidly growing industries—like chemicals, electronics, and petroleum—present a less favorable atmosphere for union gains. There are fewer workers relative to output (reflecting a high proportion of capital to labor) and such unions as do exist are often not centrally coordinated and are more susceptible to managerial manipulation (a charge often made, with some accuracy, in the chemical and electrical goods cases). Too, many high-growth companies are small in size and more difficult to organize. Significantly, of more than seven thousand representation elections held in 1968, unions lost in 43 percent. Of those elections won, the average number of members gained was only seventy; in elections lost by the unions the number of employees was usually bigger, averaging more than eighty. Today, in sharp contrast to the great union victories of the 1930s in steel and autos, half the organizing "triumphs" of AFL-CIO unions cover less than fifty workers.

Effects of Corporate Diversification

One other development weakening the position of the nation's labor unions has been the trend in industry to product and geographic diversification. Through mergers, and in other ways, companies have broadened their interests to such an extent that no single union has jurisdiction over more than a small percentage of the firm's employees. Take ITT as an illustration. A labor dispute with Sheraton Hotels, or Avis, or Continental Baking, or with any of a number of its family of domestic and foreign subsidiaries involves a separate union. It is likely to be impractical, tactically unwise, and perhaps unlawful to strike the entire parent corporation to resolve a dispute with any of these subsidiaries. Yet if pressure cannot be brought to bear on the entire corporate complex, the parent enterprise can accept a work stoppage until the local union membership finds its resources depleted and gives up the battle.

Much the same situation exists with the big international enterprises. A strike initiated in 1967 by the Mine, Mill & Smelter Workers against the four major U.S. copper producers was largely unsuccessful because the companies simply increased their foreign copper production and imported it for sale domestically. The union was no more successful in bringing pressure on management than if it had struck only half of their domestic mines. A union clearly can be effective only if it can shut down all of the sources of revenue of the company with which it is negotiating. Yet this is nearly impossible when one is dealing with a widely diverse international enterprise with facilities in a dozen or more countries and activities in half a dozen distinct product markets. The unions have recognized their plight and are taking steps to establish coordinated bargaining units composed of all the unions representing workers for a single corporation.

International Metalworkers Federation unions representing

workers at the world's four largest auto manufacturers—three American and one German (Volkswagen)—have taken steps to create worldwide councils for each corporation. So far these efforts show no particular success, largely, no doubt, because the interests of the various unions and their members are so widely disparate. Still they indicate how the unions are trying to adapt to changed business operations and suggest the new kinds of forces with which business will have to cope in the future.

The Changing Employment Mix

Also weakening the unions have been a number of changes in the composition of employment, the kinds of jobs and workers involved. Unskilled blue-collar workers, historically the backbone of the labor movement, are declining in number, with their place taken by highly trained white-collar workers. In 1947, blue-collar employees made up 41 percent of the civilian work force. Today, their share is down to 36 percent, with the reduction particularly noticeable among common laborers engaged in repetitive assembly-type operations. White-collar workers, by contrast, account for 45 percent of employment, up from 35 percent in 1947. By 1975 they will make up more than half the total. Significantly the greatest gains among the white-collar class are coming among professional and technical workers, not among managers or sales personnel.

The pronounced shift to white-collar employment has had a seriously deleterious effect on the labor unions for several reasons. Most white-collar workers are not organized to begin with (it is estimated that only about 10 percent belong to unions). The unions thus start at the bottom of the hill—and it is a long, steep climb. For one thing, many white-collar employees are women, reflecting the fact that almost 40 percent of all the workers in the United States are now women. Often employed only part-time and typically not the principal source of their families' income (if, indeed, income is their main reason for seeking employment), women have a pronounced aversion to union affiliation. Similarly, many white-collar workers, male as well as female, are in the professional and scientific category and are unreceptive to the traditional appeals of labor unions. For them, recognition of professional status is more important than better wages and improved working conditions. Some unions have succeeded in sharpening their appeals in such a way as to attract skilled members, as with actors, airline pilots, and newspaper reporters. By and large, however, the unions have been unable to establish rapport with the growing breed of white-collar specialists and thus have been falling behind a powerful new employment trend. This can mean that the managers of most companies will increasingly find themselves dealing with nonunionized employees who nonetheless possess credentials which, in their view, entitle them to professional respect and preferred economic status.

Quite conceivably these technocrats will ally in new organizations, perhaps not even bearing the name "union," that will make demands on management no less aggressively than those once presented by blue-collar industrial trade unions. What kinds of demands might these be? A hint may be obtained from the recent maneuvers of the unions which represent the nation's schoolteachers and social service workers. Increasingly militant (it would have been unthinkable a few years ago for a city's schoolteachers to go out on strike and close an entire school system), these unions want more than higher pay, better fringe benefits, and air conditioning in the classroom. That "something more" comes down to a recognition that teachers and social service workers are professionals who should be allowed as a matter of right to participate in the evolution of the policies and practices they are to implement. Teachers do not merely seek more money. They wish to be consulted, as a regular part of the decision-making process, about every aspect of educational policy in the school system of which they are a part. They want not simply to be asked for their opinions and comment, but to be centrally involved in the development of the curriculum, the design of the system's educational strategy, and the choice of the best ways to carry it out. Similarly, welfare workers are not just concerned with the volume of their caseload, but seek to participate in the establishment of overall welfare policy. The New York City Social Service Employees Union, for example, once demanded that the welfare agency give relief clients grants for clothing and allowances for telephone service.

What the teachers, welfare personnel, and other similar professionals demand is recognition of their status and a role in the process by which decisions are made in the institutions they serve. Translate this into its industrial counterpart and you can anticipate that at some near-future date it could lead to a demand by a company's professional and technical personnel—meaning most of its employees—for a voice, and a big voice at that, in decisions which management has traditionally regarded as its own prerogative. In the past, industrial unions were really not vitally concerned with basic company policy as long as wages, fringe benefits, hours, and working conditions were adequate, but that is only one objective of the new professional classes. They demand more, much more, specifically a right to a voice equal to that of management in setting the firm's basic policies.

What this could come to mean within the corporate framework is suggested by the growing insistence of the various professional groups, scientists, engineers, executives, among others, upon preservation of their professional status. To take a specific case, suppose that an engineer working on the development of a new auto model feels that its safety has not been fully established, but is unable to persuade his supervisors that the design should be tested further. Should he have a formalized opportunity to adjust his "grievance" in the same way that a union member may have recourse to administrative machinery to adjust a dispute over his compensation? For the engineer, in terms of his own professional code of ethics, his grievance may be at least as important (and even more so to the public) as is the issue of wages to a worker on an assembly line.

Looking not far ahead, it seems quite reasonable to anticipate that engineers, scientists, and other technologists will soon begin to insist on a legally protected right to a public hearing on significant intracorporate disputes which they feel are of broad public and professional consequence rather than be obligated either to "go along" or to quit their jobs. Indeed some professional organizations are already seriously considering this point, and it may suggest the unusual character of future employment relations. What is evident is that in the transition from an old-style industrial society to the new technological order, it is no longer possible to separate the workers from the managers. Today a company's employees fall along a continuum in which there is a large bulge of technocrats—specialists in finance, researchers, computer programmers—at the point where a clear gap once divided the laboring and executive classes.

The New Worlds of the Business Executive

Just as there have been fundamental changes within the ranks of organized labor, brought about by the shift from an industrial to a service state, the worlds of management have been profoundly affected by the new business environment. The trend to widespread corporate diversification, conjoined with the growing significance of technology, accentuated by universities and independent research organizations, has radically altered the conditions in which the modern executive must work. It is this fascinating interplay between manager and enterprise that is likely to affect, not just the corporate official, but the firm's whole scheme of relationships with the society.

Of the many new faces of business which have presented themselves in the last two decades, none is more important from a managerial standpoint than the big highly diversified firm. With its dozens of separate product divisions and with facilities spread around the globe, it presents a great challenge to management. And it is a challenge that has been happily, excitedly accepted. Direction of a sprawling business empire has become the current counterpart to the problems of mass production faced and overcome earlier in this century by the likes of Henry Ford and Andrew Carnegie. Theirs was a job of production—of learning how to combine the necessary ingredients to make autos and steel in large quantities at low cost. Today's challenge is no less difficult, but it essentially involves organization—the blending of unrelated units into a single profitable economic enterprise.

Modern managerial responsibilities assume their most awesome proportions in a conglomerate like Litton Industries, ITT, or Textron. The answer, say the conglomerate proponents, lies in planned decentralization. In Litton, for an outstanding example, each of some eighty division managers is responsible for making a profit and managing the sale of his products. Divisions may even be pitted against one another, as in the auto industry, in a kind of shadow-competition that serves as a substitute for the uninhibited market rivalry characteristic of classical economic theory. Kaiser Industries brags that its nine major subsidiaries are urged "to beat the other's brains out" in a struggle that, says one company officer, "tightens and toughens." Compared constantly on sales, profit, and investment performance, the feudal barons are kept under close scrutiny by the king and his immediate ministers of state.

By no means, of course, is the notion of decentralization confined to the recognized conglomerates. Since the 1920s and the pioneering days of Alfred P. Sloan, General Motors has relied on this principle as "a basic and universally valid concept of order." Production is planned and carried out by a diffuse line organization, backed up and coordinated by a number of functional "service staffs" specializing in law, finance, and public relations, among other affairs. Overseeing the entire GM complex are two key committees composed, in part, of the top corporate officers in the "line" and "service staff" groups. A similar structure is found at Standard Oil of New Jersey. Responsibility and authority are widely diffused, both functionally and geographically. Its Humble Oil subsidiary handles the goliath's U.S. affairs, Imperial Oil rules in Canada, Esso Standard Eastern takes care of things in Asia and Australasia, Esso Africa handles that continent just as Esso Inter-American does in South and Central America and the Caribbean. Other subsidiaries specialize in oil production, chemicals, and transportation. Topping it off is a staff concerned with long-range planning, finance, and investment. It's all quite neat, at least on paper.

In actual practice the diversified corporation experiences severe internal strains that constantly threaten to tear the organization apart. Encouraging rivalry between subsidiaries or divisions can just as easily weaken the firm as toughen its fiber. Decentralization of authority can free the individual baron to act in a manner that is debilitating for the enterprise as a whole. While the synergistic concept tells us that the total may be greater than the sum of its parts, it is also true that the parts affect the final sum. Further, while it may be true that distance lends enchantment, the gulf that separates the central management group from the line elements can lead to the same kind of trouble that has historically afflicted vast political empires. Looked at from the other direction, the extent to which the top executives are able to exert effective control over a loosely joined enterprise affects the psychology, the esprit de corps, of the firm. Decentralization of authority cannot be readily combined with forceful central staff direction in such vital functional areas as finance, investment policy, and "forward" planning. But this means dictation "from the top."

The two concepts—decentralization and centralization—are at odds and there are few magicians who can keep them in the delicate balance that is required for maximum performance. Uncommon executive genius is required, and few executives have it, far fewer than those who claim it. Still, though, the computer and the other tools of management help by making it possible continually to take the pulse of a diversified giant and monitor the performance of its scattered parts. The institution of a carefully refined management information system can yield the flow of data that assists a central staff in exercising effective control over the entire complex. The conglomerates have yet to prove, however, that they are susceptible to efficient direction and control. The operational results of Litton and other far-flung corporate empires are distinctly ambiguous. Their stock-market performance, even in brighter periods, can be as readily attributed to financial sleight-of-hand as to anything more substantial. All things considered, the conglomerate may prove itself to be a foe not susceptible to conquest even by the shrewdest Harvard Business School graduate.

Science and the Sophistication of Management

While the new managerial tools may make it possible, if nonetheless difficult, to direct a far-flung enterprise, they also represent a formidable executive challenge. Computers, for example, are a powerful instrument of managerial control, *if* one speaks the language of cybernetics. The few managers who do so form the emerging business elite. But most executives matured in an earlier day and converse in a less technical style that is rapidly being outmoded under the imposition of technology. Science has burst its laboratory bounds and is stalking the executive corridors. Managers who are now in their fifties, and even their forties, were schooled in the traditional ways of corporate finance, sales, engineering, and law. But that day has passed and today the business manager who is "with it" speaks and acts in a far more technical style that is less verbal (and general) than mathematical (and precise) in character.

If you do not quite fully appreciate the pronounced shift in a technique that has taken place in barely a decade in business, and think you are conversant with industry just because you read the *Wall Street Journal,* try your hand at defining the following: The Delphi technique—morphological projections—relevance tree theory—time-independent contextual mapping—extrapolation of time-series on a phenomenological basis—iteration through synopsis—and probabilistic exploratory forecasting. Far-out theory, known to only a few academicians? Hardly. All of these concepts and approaches are key parts of modern technological forecasting, widely used by businesses in Europe, North America, and Japan. Their definitions are less important than their implications—for management itself (how many senior executives really understand these highly mathematical, analytical, and projective styles?), for business organization (these techniques approach problems in functional terms, disregarding established product or divisional lines and thus threatening the status quo), and for government policies (how relevant, set against this backdrop, is a body of law tailored to older economic concepts?).

The sophisticated modern styles of business management undermine established economic notions, and they also create important cultural and intellectual gaps between the humans who make up the corporate family. Two splits are particularly evident. One can be seen between the scientists and the nonscientific managerial class. As firms increase their expenditures for research (and they are doing so at a rapid rate), scientists come to occupy a central role within the executive group. As their research endeavors begin to pay off in higher sales and bigger profits for the firm, their position assumes even greater strength. However, as C. P. Snow depicted so skillfully in his *Two Cultures,** the nonscientific generalists who still hold the reigns of power within most institutions are typically unable to close the knowledge gap that separates them from the scientific clique. At best there is mutual suspicion, at worst there is bureaucratic warfare. It will take years and, more than that, far better education, to bridge this divide.

There is a second point of strain within the modern business, one that is defined largely by age differences. The young college graduates being absorbed into the enterprise today possess different skills and depict a style remarkably out of keeping with their elders in the firm. For one thing, and this is noticeably true of the business school graduates, they are far more conversant with the new scientific-mathematical managerial techniques. The University of Chicago Graduate Business School, for example, requires extensive course-work in advanced mathematics, including sets, functions, vectors, and Lagrange multipliers, as well as linear and dynamic programming. Other business schools have a similar requirement. Each year nearly eight thousand graduates with this sort of intensive training in mathematics and econometrics are being fed into business.

The attitudes of the current college graduate about the society, the economic order, and the place of the company in it are very different. Most students today are suspicious of business and question its values. A 1969 *Fortune* survey of American youths aged eighteen–twenty-four revealed that 40 percent are disdainful of "careerist" values, with one in five harboring what many people regard as distinctly radical views. While these beliefs are keeping many intelligent college students from accepting careers with business (fewer than 5 percent of the members of one recent Harvard graduating class had taken jobs with business by the time of grad-

* *The Two Cultures and the Scientific Revolution* (Cambridge: 1959).

uation), even those young people who do join the executive intern ranks of major corporations harbor a cynicism about business that is clearly out of tune with company officials for whom business is a cherished and honorable way of life. When one not atypical college student was asked which of the established values held by the older generation he did not accept, he replied: "The lot. Work hard. Get along in the corporation. Keep your nose clean and maybe you'll get a home in the suburbs, a key to the executive washroom, and two cars." That attitude is bound to complicate even more the internal affairs of the nation's corporate enterprises, for the younger generation, even if neatly dressed in suitable garb, is going to challenge many of the basic assumptions of senior company officers. It may be a refreshing experience for executives, but it will not be an easy one.

Throughout the work force there is a clear trend to better education which, from another standpoint, will create tensions within any big enterprise. In 1952, only 8 percent of the workers had graduated from college and only another 43 percent had high school diplomas. By 1965, little more than a decade later, 12 percent of the labor force were college graduates and another 58 percent had completed high school. This trend to more highly educated workers is particularly noticeable among the young. Today most employees under the age of thirty have completed some college while workers over the age of fifty-five averaged little more than ten years of schooling. By 1975, more than a fifth of workers in the twenty-five–thirty-four age bracket will hold a college degree, but proportionately less than half as many among those in the fifty-five–sixty-four age group. The work force, then, is becoming far better educated, a fact that will affect employers and labor unions alike. The implications can be better appreciated when it is recalled that workers in the thirty-five–forty-five age category—the usual time for appointing middle management positions—are now in short supply because of the low birth rate of the 1930s. Indeed by the mid-1970s the male population in this age range will decline by more than one million. As a result younger employees are being moved quickly into junior executive openings. From the company's standpoint, this not only fills a need but it makes full use of their employment force at a time when technology imposes new demands on employees. Right now nearly 10 percent of the foremen in American plants are college graduates.

The accelerated upward movement through the executive ranks of young people, establishing them firmly within the executive ranks far more quickly than has ever been true before, places additional pressures on the human strands of the corporate structure. The younger generation, as noted earlier, is simply different from that born in the 1920s and before: better educated, more scientific, considerably more sensitive to the role of the individual in the society, and less convinced of the inherent virtue of The Firm. This makes them less susceptible to old styles of executive training and a less certain quality in any company's development.

Managerial Professionalism

In assaying the changing human dimensions of the big, diversified corporation, one is struck by the growing professionalism within the ranks of business executives and technologists. Increasingly, for a host of reasons, corporate officials take on trappings of a sort commonly associated with law or medicine. Men are more likely to think of themselves as professional corporate managers than as executives of a particular firm. This process has already taken place in higher education. Faculty members view themselves as sociologists, economists, or political scientists, whose career development takes place within those professional specialties. A typical professor's relationships with the institution that happens at the moment to be his employer are generally accepted, by both the individual and the university, as highly transitory. One moves "up" in his profession commonly by moving "on" to another campus.

This same process is beginning to take shape in the business community. One reason is advanced education. A quarter of the top two executives of each of the 100 largest U.S. corporations now hold advanced degrees (that proportion is up by half just since 1955). A degree from one of the major graduate business schools stamps the holder as a professional manager, whose status is independent of any particular employer. Another factor relates back to the self-confidence—the near-mystique—of those who manage the conglomerates. By their own theory they are convinced they can run any company with which they happen to be affiliated. This attitude, coupled with the experience actually obtained in overseeing unrelated enterprises, impels them frequently to move on to other challenges. Since the Korean War executive turnover is up five times, mostly among the younger college-trained managers, the "mobiocentrics" as they have been called. A long list of officials have left Litton Industries and taken on presidencies of other conglomerates, generating a high rate of executive turnover which is accepted by all concerned as refreshing. For these men, and dozens of others like them throughout corporate America, the old notion that a responsible official stays with his company, rising through the ranks and wearing the indelible badge of Ford or IBM or du Pont, is quaint and out of tune with a world of skilled scientific business management. It is not that the new executive is any less interested in or dedicated to the success of the company that employs him; rather it is that he sees himself as a specialist whose skills and growth are in no way necessarily associated with any particular enterprise.

This is true not only of top-level executives but of other technologists. A good systems engineer, research physicist, capital budget analyst, or production supervisor is beginning to develop the same outlook. This is a development of immense significance to private corporations and the public. It means an end to the colorful chief executive whose identity became almost interchangeable with "his" company and a transition to more professional, less spectacular officers. In the airline industry, for example, the first generation of leaders is passing from the scene, succeeded by little-known experts—competent but colorless men in the vein essentially of senior partners in the typical big-city law firm. At American Airlines, C. R. Smith, whose career spanned thirty years, has given way to an ex-Wall Street lawyer. Pan Am's Juan Trippe, who for three decades saw his role as extending the American flag around the globe through air transportation, has retired. Eddie Rickenbacker has departed from Eastern. "Pat" Patterson has gone from United. At National Airlines, the reins have passed from the founder and air pioneer, L. B. Maytag, to his college-educated son. One can find essentially this same pattern throughout the economy. The "pros" are taking over.

The spread of managerial professionalism creates grave new problems for U.S. business. It takes on special significance because of the features discussed in earlier chapters—the growing financial power of the modern corporation, widespread diversification, and the consolidation of effective power in the hands of management. The latter point—with its emphasis on the fact that corporate officers and financial institutions, not stockholders, actually control the affairs of a big public corporation is now seen as considerably more complex than it may at first have appeared. With corporate managers holding the reins of widely diversified, global firms, but conceiving of themselves essentially as professionals, what are the rules—the standards—with which these men are to be governed in their use of the immense power they possess? As well, how are those *within* the corporation—especially its multitudinous family of technocrats and middle-level executives—to be protected from encroachment on their legitimate interests? Given the big corporation's central role in the economy, these questions are of crucial public importance, yet they have not been squarely confronted by businessmen or government officials in their assessment of corporate behavior in the American economy.

CHAPTER 7

Business and Higher Education: The Emerging Alliance

"There are few earthly things more beautiful than a University."
—*John Masefield*

"Universities are inhuman places. They're service stations for the establishment that mold people to fit into cogs in our cold-war, mechanized, IBM society."
—*Bruce Kahn,* former president of the Student Government Council at the University of Michigan

If you compare the quotes above, you can tell a great deal about what's been going on in the world of American higher education. Masefield was writing at a time when the campus was still an idyllic preserve, sheltered from the world, a place for contemplation and a symbol of the search for truth. As an enclave of thought rather than action, the university was far removed from the harsh, pragmatic concerns of man. Its contacts with business and government were extremely limited, involving little more than a reflection of the process by which students become alumni, workers, and financial contributors.

How things have changed! The university is now on the front line of controversy, as Bruce Kahn's remark, typical of the reactions of many "radical" student leaders, makes so very clear. Deeply involved with the problems of government and business the campus has become a nerve center of scientific and social change. Higher education has evolved into a big business and has cultivated close working partnerships with both the corporate and governmental sectors. Its constituency has expanded enormously and students and faculty have forged new associations with so many people and institutions off campus that it is literally impossible to separate the modern university from the rest of the "things" that make up our society. Today's university resembles a widely diversified nonprofit conglomerate more closely than any other organism on the contemporary scene.

The Campus's New Business Image

The relevance of the university to business is threefold. First, it is itself in business and competes for government research contracts and other sources of revenue. Second, it is a new partner of business in attacking many sorts of problems, particularly those of a scientific nature. Third, it is an engine of change—it creates and impels the forces that continually alter the world in which business must carry out its affairs. For all of these reasons, and many in between, the campus has assumed an increasingly important place *in* the corporate world.

The typical contemporary university clearly is not the idyllized center of learning located on the sleepy campus in the quiet, small town. Rather it is a big factory that in a not uncommon case offers instruction for undergraduates and graduate students (most of whom teach, forming a key element in the "faculty"), provides a base for professors who actually spend more time doing off-campus consulting work for business than they do in the classroom, carries out research for and in cooperation with business, conducts a large amount of research under contract with the government, and manages a Federally owned scientific facility. Cal Tech, for example, runs the Jet Propulsion Lab for the National Aeronautics and Space Administration (for an annual fee of $200 million), Johns Hopkins University operates the Navy Applied Physics Lab, and MIT directs the Air Force Lincoln Lab at Cambridge, Massachusetts. These are not little laboratories on the edge of the campus. They are big businesses in their own right, with hundreds of employees and annual budgets of $100 million and up.

Universities not only run research centers for the government, but they often have a direct interest in an independent research facility that is physically and functionally linked to the campus. Stanford Research Institute is a good example. Set up by a group of businessmen shortly after the war, its board of directors is effectively controlled by the university board of trustees. Stanford receives substantial income from SRI in return for the University blessing. In North Carolina, three universities share with a number of businesses a dominant interest in the Research Triangle Institute. At Minneapolis, the North-Star Center is linked similarly to the University of Minnesota and to that city's business community. Comparable research centers, tying campus to business, exist in Pittsburgh, San Antonio, Lexington, Dallas, and elsewhere around the country.

As universities have plunged into the hectic world of research and business cooperation, their financial base has radically changed. Once the campus primarily depended for revenue on tuition and the generosity of concerned alumni and assorted benefactors. State universities received substantial additional amounts from their legislatures. Today all this has changed. No longer is a big school dependent primarily on any one of these traditional sources of income. Instead the Federal Government has assumed the dominant role. At the University of Chicago, where the annual budget exceeds $200 million, income from the Federal Government, mostly for research, provides two thirds of the total. Tuition and student fees provide less than 10 percent, and endowment income, for what is a very rich school, makes up less than 5 percent. At Harvard the Federal stake is not quite so large, yet it still provides 40 percent of the university's income, more important than any other source, greater than endowment income and gifts combined.

The vast significance of Federal funds is true of every major university, even state institutions. The University of Michigan, for example, gets as much money from Washington as it does from the State Capitol at Lansing to help it cope with a budget that now approaches $200 million a year. Farther west, the University of California—with its ten separate campuses, 85,000 students, and budget of $600 million—obtains nearly 30 percent of its dollars from the Federal treasury in spite of vast aid from the State of California.

The Ties That Bind

Just as the universities have turned to Washington for financial sustenance, so too have they established new, more intricate ties with business. Some involve the university directly, some its faculty, but the most interesting are those that bind the campus and its constituency to the immediate off-campus environment. Most often the cord that binds is research, with brainpower as its inner core. Ann Arbor, home base of the University of Michigan and once a small town of quiet elm-shaded streets lined with fraternity and sorority houses, claims it is the "research center of the Midwest." In the mid-fifties there was only one private research firm in town, employing fewer than twenty workers. Now there are at least fifty research firms, with more than three thousand employees on their payrolls.

The key reason is the scientific resources made available by the University. Bolstered by more than $50 million yearly in Federal research contracts and grants, U. of M. has some of the finest research installations and facilities ever built. It is especially strong in electronics, nuclear power, the exotic outer reaches of chemistry, and high-energy physics. Its faculty is world renowned and it produces more Ph.D.'s than any other university in America (40 percent of its thirty thousand enrollment is in the graduate and professional schools). This complex of facilities and skilled manpower makes Ann Arbor one of the nation's best climates for research and development, as favorable to the scientist as Aspen is to the skier. Let Dr. Harold Katz, a major company research director, explain why:

> Today the environment of a professional man's job is almost as important as the job itself, and for the scientist, Ann Arbor is ideal. It offers the University of Michigan. A researcher can use its facilities for advanced study. He can call on its staff for expert consultation. He can employ its students in professional training on a part time basis and groom them for bigger responsibilities

later on. There is ample opportunity to meet men of other disciplines, which not only is important because of the emphasis on the inter-disciplinary approach to problems in the new technology but is stimulating socially. With all of this to offer, we've got men coming here from New York and California.

In exploiting its vast physical and human resources for the good of business, the University has hardly been passive. Its Institute of Science and Technology, operated by the College of Engineering, is aimed specifically at harnessing the talents of the engineering faculty to the needs of industry. A Bureau of Business Research and a Bureau of Industrial Relations provide additional skills, as does the Institute of Social Research, one of the richest deposits of economists, statisticians, and social scientists. Through these special centers, and on their own, hundreds of U. of M. professors regularly engage in extensive consultation with industrial firms around the country.

The Profit Quest

Universities have often turned their research into profits, very big profits indeed. Indiana University earns $100,000 a year from Procter & Gamble for a license on a University-developed stannous fluoride compound that is used in Crest toothpaste. Rutgers University's Research and Educational Foundation has earned over $12 million from the development of streptomycin. The University of Wisconsin Alumni Research Foundation has collected more than $40 million in patent royalties, mainly stemming from the synthesis of vitamin D. MIT was paid $13 million by IBM for rights to an MIT-developed magnetic memory device for use in computers. Stanford University has received more than $2 million in return for assistance it provided to the Varian brothers in their early microwave experiments. That aid led to the invention of the klystron tube, a key electronics component.

With the distinct search for profits uppermost in the institutional mind, several universities have turned their attention to the management of such diverse enterprises as real estate (Columbia University real estate holdings in New York City are estimated to have a value of $300 million), a supplemental airline, a timber forest, publishing house, a spaghetti-macaroni factory (controlled by New York University), and, of course, divers sports-entertainment emporia. One well-known church-connected college in the Southwest secretively works hand in glove with a group of Texas oil speculators in a complex legal maneuver that cuts their taxable income and yields the school a portion of the taxes thus evaded.

The thrust of the campus into business goes beyond the mutual accommodation of the needs and desires of each. Often those on the campus plunge aggressively into business, not content with the rewards of consultation. Sometimes professors establish manufacturing firms, but more commonly they form their own research partnerships or corporations. One such firm, the Conductron Corporation, was founded in 1960 by a group of twenty-five University of Michigan scientists led by Professor Keeve M. Siegel who then headed the University's radiation laboratory. Helped along in its early days by a University subcontract, today the company, which specializes in the esoteric outer reaches of electronics, has facilities that spread from Ann Arbor to California, Massachusetts, and Texas. Quite properly Conductron attributes its growth to its ability "to enjoy the adjacent facilities and services of the University of Michigan." When Siegel sold out his controlling interest to McDonnell-Douglas, the aircraft company, he took his reported profit of $5 million and started another firm.

In a similar manner campus intellectuals have seized the business ring and established numerous advisory services around the fringe of many major campuses. At Cambridge, Massachusetts, for example, a group of Harvard-MIT economists have formed Charles River Associates and, nearby, Harvard Business School professors were instrumental in founding United Research and Harbridge House. These concerns are deeply engaged in research and advisory services for business and for the government (their corporate status, incidentally, permits the owners to charge higher fees, in effect, than they could lawfully receive as individual consultants with the Federal Government). At the University of Texas a group of professors organized Tracor, Inc., to work on defense systems. Its annual revenue is now $50 million.

Just as the university professor has shifted his attention from the classroom and the lab to the industrial firm and government agency, so too has business increased its ties with the campus. When, as an instance, the auto industry, under criticism from Ralph Nader and Congressional investigating committees, decided to improve its public image in the safety field, it huddled under the protective canopy of a university. In 1965 Ford, General Motors, and Chrysler contributed $10 million to establish the Highway Safety Research Institute at the University of Michigan's North Campus. With some additional financial aid from the Federal Government, it reflects the character of so many other business-campus-government hybrids. Of its fifty senior research staff members, fifteen are members of the U. of M. teaching faculty and several others instruct part-time. With industry financing the Institute's physical structure and also its staff and research, there has in effect been a coalescence of higher education and business that is a radical departure from the older notion of the university as an independent seeker of truth, beholden to no one.

In the past the university was relied upon to serve as a social critic, insulated from the kinds of pressures that inevitably dictate accommodation in business and government. Today that independence is rapidly being lost as the universities join with industry and government in mutually appealing endeavors. One should not be quick to conclude that this is necessarily bad, but its newness outmodes our older notions of the way the society is to function. We have long depended on a system of social checks and balances in which corporations, labor unions, government, and institutions of higher learning operated as constraints on one another. That countervailance has been very markedly eroded, and we must begin the deliberate search for new ways to harness coalesced private power with the public interest. It is a search that is only beginning, and slowly at that. It remains an open question whether it will progress far enough, fast enough, to avoid the creation of an education-scientific-industrial state that may be so elitist in nature that it is democratically unacceptable.

For many reasons our major universities have increasingly taken on the character of businesses. With huge budgets and large numbers of employees and students, they have assumed the character of any large enterprise, complete with a covey of vice presidents and diverse management specialists. Their enormous scientific capacity and rich human resources have made them natural allies of business and government. As their expenses have soared (Michigan's budget rose four times from 1951 to 1966, Yale forecasts its will double between 1966 and 1976), their propensity to accept grants and contracts from these sources has understandably increased. The lure of money has gone hand in hand with the desire of students and faculty to be "relevant" to the world beyond the campus. For the engineer and the physical scientist, this has often meant research for government or business and for the social scientist and lawyer it has implied deeper involvement in grappling with the assorted problems of a complex, urbanized world. The result is that the typical university is actively engaged in three areas—teaching, research, and public service—in alliance with business, government, and assorted "outside" institutions. Government and business have turned to the universities for the specialized knowledge they require, and the universities have reciprocated with their own demands for outside participation. In the process the worlds of higher learning, business, and government have been fundamentally changed, blended in a distinctive institutional concoction.

The Uneasy Relationship

While corporations have been willing, indeed anxious, to retain the advisory services of a university laboratory or a professor, they have tried to isolate themselves from the strong winds of ideological change that are now blowing across the nation's campuses. For most companies the university is still treated as a place that serves as a depositary of experts to be called upon as needed. Reflecting this primitive outlook, unrestricted corporate gifts to colleges remain ridiculously small, amounting now to less than half a billion dollars a year (or less than half of 1 percent of their disposable income). And when gifts are made, they are often burdened with restrictions that are designed primarily to keep recipients from getting involved in anything "controversial." Bethlehem Steel has gone so far as to insist on a "body for a buck"—rewarding colleges with a grant of $4,000 for each live graduate hired by the company as a management trainee. This sort of attitude reflects a view of the campus that is no less astigmatic than the view of business held by many students and professors.

Most companies have tried to buy only what they want from the nation's universities and have tried to remain aloof from the rest of the campus milieu. It can't be done. As users of faculty and campus labs and as employers in ever greater numbers of college graduates, business inevitably will become drawn even more into the world of higher education. It will be affected at least as much as the university. It may be good for both, but it will be a harsh experience for there is nothing more revolutionary than a new idea, and business is likely to find that it can be as thoroughly changed by association with the humans who make up a university as it is by the new technology.

A partnership has been forged between campus and company that alters the posture of both participants. The effects can be substantial for they not only compromise the universi y, making it and its faculty to some considerable degree beholden to business, but also affecting business by subjecting it to a different sort of outside force than has heretofore been brought to bear on the corporate community.

PART III

Business's New Economic– Technological Environment

CHAPTER 8

The Economic Prospect

At the same time that business enterprises are changing radically in their size and extent of diversification and in the nature and character of their constituency, the complete environment in which business must function is also being transformed through surging currents of economic and technological change. In a very real sense the chemistry of the American economy is being fundamentally altered, with the result that long-established firms—and often whole industries—are being rendered obsolete, engulfed by the swirling forces of the new economy. One of these forces is economic growth itself, setting a pace which not every company is proving itself able to maintain. The other force is technology, and in the long run the scientific revolution may be much the more powerful.

The inner tensions of an economy climbing toward a trillion dollars develop strains that constantly threaten to destroy the foundations of any business whose management falls behind the extremely rapid pace of economic expansion. But merely to run is not enough, for technology, propelled furiously by multi-billion-dollar research expenditures, is constantly altering the ingredients that make up the economy. While the twin forces of economic growth and technological change create large business opportunities, they also represent a potent, continuing threat to the very survival of any modern company. This chapter probes the issue of economic growth, the following chapter takes up the closely related subject of the technological revolution.

For a host of reasons the changes in the economic environment are of the utmost practical importance in assessing the dynamics of contemporary business. Fundamental economic growth is essential if we are to make full use of our physical and human resources. A slowdown in our rate of economic growth would not just be "bad for business," but it would create serious problems of unemployment and further aggravate the disease of poverty that afflicts a fifth of our population. In a very real sense, then, steady, rapid economic growth is as vital as it is financially rewarding to all segments of the American society.

For all of its importance, however, economic growth presents many tough challenges. Given the present size of the economy —with our Gross National Product (GNP) of over $900 billion— likely average annual growth of 4.5 percent means we will cross the trillion-dollar mark in the early seventies. By 2000 the GNP will eclipse $3 trillion (even after allowing for inflation). The absolute scale of this growth, what it implies (indeed, requires) for the overhead service industries (like energy, communications, transportation, and finance), in manufacturing, and in international trade, is certain to strain severely our economic, political, and managerial capacity to mobilize the necessary resources and to sustain the momentum of unprecedented economic expansion. In ten years the United States will be adding about $50 billion annually to its output of goods and services. Since the figure today is "only" about $35 billion, our net annual GNP increment, in real terms, will be nearly half again as big as it is now. By 2000 the *annual increment* (in then-current dollars) will be close to $300 billion! That's larger than our *entire* GNP was in 1950 and approximates the aggregate present GNP of *all* the countries in Asia and Africa. Even if there was no change at all in the composition of the economy, the rate and scale of economic growth in the United States would have great significance for business.

But again, like a spinning kaleidoscope of change, other forces are also at work. Two principal factors must be taken into account. First, steady economic growth is by no means assured, nor can it even be assumed on the basis of recent U.S. experience. Significant ups and downs can occur, and only by anticipating and compensating for them can a desirable rate of growth be maintained. Fluctuations in business investment and personal consumption, as well as in the Federal net budget position, represent powerful destabilizing forces that can substantially inhibit economic growth. Big as it is, the American economy, with all of its *potential* for steady upward growth, is terribly sensitive and requires careful, sophisticated management and understanding, by those in business as well as in government. Second, the composition of the economy, in all its sectors, is certain to undergo fundamental change in the upcoming third of the twentieth century. There will be important shifts between industries and between regions and areas within regions. Several established industries will experience a sharp decline in their relative economic importance, others will accelerate their expansion, and whole new industries will emerge—partly as the result of mergers and conglomerate amalgamation and partly as the consequence of the new technology.

Other developments can be foreseen. The trend to internationalization of business activity will become even more noticeable. World trade will expand rapidly, but the worldwide production of goods by global corporations will grow even faster. In a decade it will make far more sense to talk of the world economy than of the U.S. economy. Government expenditures are also showing the signs of basic alteration. State and local governments will continue to be the largest source of public spending, so much so that their outlays for education, welfare, transportation, and other high-demand purposes may outdistance their revenue-raising capacity to such an extent that new forms of Federal assistance will be essential. Government outlays themselves are growing substantially, but, more significantly, their character is changing, with increasing emphasis on social or other programs designed to improve the quality of life and of man's environment. Sharply expanded outlays for education, water and air pollution, recreation, and health care are inevitable. Additional billions will be paid out to individuals, businesses, and other units of government as grants to aid in the maintenance of family well-being and community values.

Think about these developments and it quickly becomes evident why the pace of economic growth and the composition of the U.S. economy of the seventies, and indeed of the rest of this century, are crucial to business survival. No well-run corporation, no institution, can shut its eyes to all these emerging issues for they dictate not simply its investment, production, and financial plans but the substance of its very existence. Business, government, universities, everyone plans ahead these days, systematically attempting to forecast future economic trends. Indeed it is said that the chief executives of most major companies now think more about the future than they do about the present. And well they might, for the decisions made today will shape a company's performance ten, twenty, even thirty years, ahead. A new factory may take a year to design, as much as two years to construct, and it may have a life-span of twenty-five years, all of which means that it will be supplying goods and generating profits (or losses) in the 1990s.

Plans for investment in everything from machine tools and transportation equipment to office space must realistically anticipate the company's role in meeting the demands imposed by the markets of the 1970s, 1980s, and beyond. For corporations dependent on natural resources (oil, coal, copper, bauxite), the search for reserves to be drawn upon in the twenty-first century is already underway. Manufacturers of consumer goods no less than makers of items of investment capital must peer ahead, trying to gauge the desires of the customers of the next decade and to create the productive capacity in time to meet those needs. Whatever the exact situation, all organizations now plan, carefully and with a true sense of urgency, with their gaze spanning

CHART 4
The Postwar U.S. Economy, 1947–1967

GROSS NATIONAL PRODUCT OR EXPENDITURE

Billions of dollars

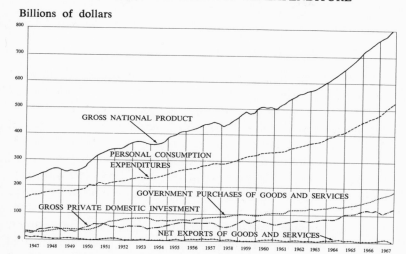

Source of data: U.S. Department of Commerce.

THE BASIC STATISTICS
(Billions of dollars)

Year	Total gross national product	Personal consumption expenditures	Gross private domestic investment	Net exports of goods and services	Government purchases of goods and services				
					Total	Federal			State and local
						Total	National defense	Other	
1947	231.3	160.7	34.0	11.5	25.1	12.5	9.1	3.5	12.6
1948	257.6	173.6	46.0	6.4	31.6	16.5	10.7	5.8	15.0
1949	256.5	176.8	35.7	6.1	37.8	20.1	13.3	6.8	17.7
1950	284.8	191.0	54.1	1.8	37.9	18.4	14.1	4.3	19.5
1951	328.4	206.3	59.3	3.7	59.1	37.7	33.6	4.1	21.5
1952	345.5	216.7	51.9	2.2	74.7	51.8	45.9	5.9	22.9
1953	364.6	230.0	52.6	.4	81.6	57.0	48.7	8.4	24.6
1954	364.8	236.5	51.7	1.8	74.8	47.4	41.2	6.2	27.4
1955	398.0	254.4	67.4	2.0	74.2	44.1	38.6	5.5	30.1
1956	419.2	266.7	70.0	4.0	73.6	45.6	40.3	5.3	33.0
1957	441.1	281.4	67.8	5.7	86.1	49.5	44.2	5.3	36.6
1958	447.3	290.1	60.9	2.2	94.2	53.6	45.9	7.7	40.6
1959	433.7	311.2	75.3	.1	97.0	53.7	46.0	7.6	43.3
1960	503.7	325.2	74.8	4.0	99.6	53.5	44.9	8.6	46.1
1961	520.1	335.2	71.7	5.6	107.6	57.4	47.8	9.6	50.2
1962	560.3	355.1	83.0	5.1	117.1	63.4	51.6	11.8	53.7
1963	590.5	375.0	87.1	5.9	122.5	64.2	50.8	13.5	58.2
1964	632.4	401.2	94.0	8.5	128.7	65.2	50.0	15.2	63.5
1965	683.9	433.1	107.4	6.9	136.4	66.8	50.1	16.7	69.6
1966	743.3	455.9	118.0	5.1	154.3	77.0	60.5	16.5	77.2
1967	785.1	491.6	112.1	5.0	176.3	89.9	72.6	17.3	86.4

Source of data: U.S. Department of Commerce.

the remainder of the twentieth century. Viewed in these terms the significance of the long-term economic outlook becomes all the clearer.

The Components of Economic Growth

To put the issues in perspective, one should first look backward and consider, if only briefly, the basic factors that have shaped recent U.S. economic growth. Since the end of World War II the American economy has grown at a startling rate, with annual GNP doubling in barely two decades—up from $231 billion in 1947 to $785 billion in 1967 and over $900 billion in 1969. Chart 4 has the details. Although population rose from 150 million to more than 200 million, per capita personal income has gone up more than 50 percent. Even with rising prices and taxes fully taken into account, just about everyone—even the poorest among us—is far better off than he was twenty years ago. Business shared handsomely in this wealth, selling more, earning more profits, and adding more each year to its investment in plant and equipment. Government, too, has grown rapidly, largely because of the necessity to satisfy the public desire for improved education, better health, and relief from the pressures and insecurity of an urbanized, distraught world. The cornucopia that is our economy has gotten so much bigger so quickly that it has allowed the United States to do many things simultaneously: to improve our individual standard of living, to expand business sales, to enrich the public sector, and to play an active role in international affairs.

What has been the key to the spectacular U.S. economic performance in the last twenty years? The basic explanations are the standard underpinnings to the expansion of any economic order. Looked at generally, between 1948 and 1969 the economy grew at an average annual rate of about 4 percent, so that by the end of the period we were adding more than $30 billion a year to our output of goods and services. This growth stemmed from a combination of two essential ingredients: man-hours and productivity. Start with the latter. In the years 1948–1969 the average annual increase in output per man-hour ("productivity," as it is usually defined) amounted to 3 percent. Of course, those in the labor force have tended to work fewer hours per week (the decline has not been as large as is commonly believed—with average weekly hours having declined by less than half of 1 percent annually in the postwar span of years). But this has been offset by an increase in population and in the number of workers.

Putting both factors together—more workers employed fewer hours per week—meant an average annual increase in man-hours of 1 percent from 1948 to 1969. With productivity up 3 percent, this explains the 4 percent increase in the growth of the economy. It does so, of course, only in very general terms. The increase in productivity is itself the product of many forces—a better educated and trained labor force, more capital investment by business, a superior infrastructure (transportation, communications, utilities, and public services), and research that yields new techniques and products. All of these elements, some obvious, some subtle, have combined to produce a remarkable period of economic growth.

Yet, good as it has been, the U.S. economy has recorded serious instability and been unable to provide full employment opportunities or eradicate widespread unemployment. For most of the 1950s the economy was in a recession that inhibited business and drove unemployment well above 7 percent. In less than two decades the United States, supposedly among the most sophisticated of national economic managers, experienced three serious recessions and operated on a skim-milk diet of economic growth. By contrast, in the 1960–1969 period the GNP rose steeply, at nearly a 5 percent rate that about represents the maximum now attainable. This has cut unemployment drastically, well below 4 percent until the anti-inflation measures began to slow the economy late in 1969. Nonetheless, three million people are out of work and a sixth of young Negroes cannot find jobs. Nor has it meant an end of poverty. Today nearly thirty million people live in poverty, including nearly 20 percent of all those under the age of eighteen. An additional fifteen million live so close to the poverty line that it is self-deceptive to think of them as other than poor. While our economic performance thus has been impressive in the last two decades, it has hardly cured the problem of poverty nor assured us of sustained high-level economic growth. It behooves us, then, from a practical standpoint, to peer into the future and attempt to identify the principal features on the economic landscape.

The Economy: A Look Ahead

What is likely to happen to the economy in the years immediately ahead, to say 1975? No one can be certain of the details, but we can be reasonably confident of the general outline. Most of the people who will then be alive have already been born. And most key economic variables tend to change only slowly over time. Productivity, for example, should continue to increase at an annual rate of 3 percent, just as it has during the last two decades. What of man-hours? That depends, in part, on population. Here there is a certain degree of unpredictability because of the prevalence of birth-control devices and drugs and, even more, on the propensity of married couples to use them to avoid conception. Significant though these factors are, they have little short-term impact and, over the long run, lose relative importance because of the sheer absolute size of the population that will be alive.

Given these considerations, the projection of a U.S. population of about 220 million in 1975 can be made with considerable confidence. This is fifteen million more people than at present, a fact itself of considerable importance, for the spending of each American will average out to more than $3,500 a year by the mid-seventies. Those fifteen million additional people will be ringing up $50 billion annually on business cash registers. In spite of a slightly shorter work week, the much bigger labor force of the seventies will continue to increase total employment hours, by approximately 1.5 percent a year. Combining productivity gains (of 3 percent a year) and increased man-hours, the economy should grow at an annual average rate of 4.5 percent.

These statistics may seem rather bland, of more interest to the technical economist than to the man of business, but they take on great practical significance when translated into sales, profits, and wages. Table 3 contains the highlights, comparing the American economy of 1969 with that of 1975. Consumers will be spending

TABLE 3
Projected Growth of the U.S. Economy to 1975
($ in millions)

Item	1969* 1975** (current $)		1969* 1975** (1958 $)	
GNP	$925	$1,310	$727	$960
Personal Consumption	573	816	466	631
Durable goods	91	126	86	125
Nondurable goods	242	316	199	253
Services	240	375	181	254
Gross Private Domestic Investment	137	201	111	151
Nonresidential investment	98	113	81	91
Residential structures	33	73	24	48
Change in business inventories	7	16	6	12
Net Exports of Goods and Services	2	11	—.5	9
Government Purchases of Goods and Services	213	282	150	170
Federal	101	99	76	64
State and local	112	183	74	105

* 1969 figures are seasonally adjusted second quarterly totals at annual rates.

** The 1975 projection was prepared by the staff of the Joint Congressional Economic Committee, in cooperation with the Department of Commerce. The figures presented assume a 4.5 percent annual rate of growth in real GNP and unemployment of 3 percent.

Note: Figures may not add to totals due to rounding.

$35 billion more in 1975 for automobiles, appliances, furniture, and other durables than they did in 1969; $74 billion more for items like food, cigarettes, and clothing; and over $135 billion more for services. Government outlays and capital investment will add still more billions in sales for those businesses sufficiently farsighted to expand their plant capacity to keep up with booming demand.

The lustiness of the American economy in the 1970s, important as it is to business, cannot be allowed, however, to disguise the significant changes in its composition. As noted earlier the civilian labor force will increase from its present eighty million to ninety million by 1975. The distribution of this gain tells a great deal about the mix of the economy and of employment. Reflecting the intensification of the shift (noted in Chapter 5) from a goods to a service-software economy, two thirds of the new jobs to be created between now and 1977 will come in just two sectors: services and government. Older key industrial categories, like transportation and manufacturing, will add only a very few jobs.

Paralleling this change in emphasis is a further pronounced shift among occupational groupings of employment. Throughout the postwar years the number of farm workers and unskilled laborers has sharply and continually declined. This process will proceed even further in the years immediately ahead, accentuated by a broad decline among all categories of blue-collar production employees. Even sales workers will find that their share of employment will not increase in the next decade. Where, then, will the gains come? Primarily among professional (including scientific), managerial, and service workers. It is worth stressing, once again, that this projection is fully consistent with the transition from a goods to a tertiary economy.

Important though changes in the employment mix are, in the future as in the past most gains in output are expected to come from increased productivity rather than from additional man-hours. A portion of this gain is attributable to increased capital investment by business. In 1948, for example, capital stocks (structures and equipment) per worker in manufacturing figured out to $6,600. By 1966 they totaled $9,500. That rate of increase, which averaged less than 1 percent a year from 1948 to 1966, should accelerate considerably in the next decade, nearing 3 percent. Annual fixed-capital investment by business, factories, machine tools and the like, has already risen from $47 billion in 1960 to nearly $100 billion. By 1975 it should amount to at least $115 billion (and some economists feel it may go as high as $140 billion), reflecting a substantial further expansion in capital per unit of labor. It is this factor, embodying all of the ingredients of mass production and automation, that largely explains the continuing sharp gains in productivity.

Yet it is not only because of the use of more capital equipment— harvesting machines, diesel locomotives, coal mining machines, computers, etc.—that productivity has steadily accelerated in the last several years. For one thing, workers today are better educated. They can be more easily trained to use much more complex equipment and can efficiently perform a wider range of intricate operations. Today the typical worker has completed high school, and a fourth of all workers have finished at least one year of college. Complementing this high quality work force is the mammoth research effort mounted in America in the last fifteen years. In 1970 we will spend more than 3 percent of our GNP on research, an amount in proportion not even closely approximated in any other country in the world. With over $25 billion a year now being spent to develop new products and new techniques, it is hardly surprising that a significant portion of this effort has paid off in the form of more efficient equipment and organizational techniques.

Add it all up, a healthier, better educated and trained work force, extensive research, and more improved capital equipment, and you have the explanation for the rapid growth in productivity forecast to continue into the future. It is the key to the expansion of the U.S. economy. But while a growing labor force and productivity gains make economic expansion possible, they do not insure it will take place. Supply does *not* provide its own demand, contrary to the teachings of the nineteenth century economist Jean Baptiste Say, who tried to convince us of as much. At any given moment in time supply equals demand, but this is just a truism for what is not purchased is said to be "bought" for inventory investment. What is much more important is the dynamic interplay between the forces of supply and demand, for it is this process which determines the rate of growth and cyclical stability of an economy. Having already looked at the ingredients of potential output, we should now examine the elements of demand.

Consumption, Investment: Expansion but with Uncertainty

Viewed summarily, the principal components of demand are consumption (the purchases of goods and services by families and individuals), government expenditures, investment (which may take the form of business purchases of new equipment or family acquisitions of housing), and net trade exports. Of these ingredients unquestionably the most sizable is consumption. It is the major market for business as a whole, accounting for 60 percent of the GNP. In 1969 as Table 3 shows, personal consumption totaled approximately $573 billion, with $242 billion spent for nondurables, $240 billion for services, and $91 billion for durable goods. For the future, indications are that consumers will not only continue to be the backbone of the economy, but will increase their purchases even more rapidly than they have in the recent past. While per capita personal consumption should rise at an annual rate close to 5 percent, purchases of services, significantly, will rise even more sharply so that they will be about 50 percent above their 1967 levels by 1975. With disposable per capita income likely to increase 70 percent by 1975, consumers will be spending over $800 billion in 1975. The sharp expansion in consumer outlays for goods and especially for services that is anticipated in the future signifies a sharp upward trend to higher family incomes.

If America was affluent in the sixties, it will surely be super-affluent—almost regal—in the seventies and beyond. By 1975, predicts *Fortune,* average family income after Federal taxes will be close to $10,000 (calculated in 1967 dollars). In 1959 less than a fifth of family units in the United States had incomes of $10,000 and over, but real disposable incomes then began to climb steeply —advancing by 43 percent in the next eight years. Still, despite this income explosion, only a third of the nation's families were in the $10,000-plus class by 1967. The fact that in 1975 more than half the families in the country will be in the five-figure category will mean a major shift in the things that are purchased. Most of the additional income will be "discretionary" in character; it need not be spent for the necessities of life, food and clothing and shelter.

Statistics about the spending patterns of the affluent $10,000-and-over families show that they are much more inclined to travel, entertain at home, seek out entertainment beyond the home, buy more cars (we are rapidly moving beyond the two-car home and, if auto purchases continue at their current rates, by the end of the century there will be an average of three cars per family), spend far more on education of their children (and themselves, for the number of adults seeking part-time education is astonishing: as many adults now are enrolled in some kind of class in the Los Angeles area as there are full-time younger students), read more books, drink more liquor, invest more discriminately (a factor that helps explain the mutual fund boom noted in Chapter 4) and, of course, spend much more on what are usually regarded as luxuries (furs, jewelry, silver, antiques, art). Just one little sign: there are now over eight million recreational boats on U.S. lakes and rivers and their number rises at a rate of more than four thousand a week. The yacht, once the symbol of the rich, has been captured by the proletariat. Consumers, then, with their soaring incomes, will remain the key force in the economy, but as their incomes rise their pattern of spending will change—opening up vast new opportunities for the American business community.

While consumption is the single biggest element in the economy, it still only accounts for three fifths of what is produced each year by an economy that is growing at a rate of nearly $50 billion annually. Of the two other major components, investment, in business facilities and in housing, presently accounts for over $120 billion a year or about a seventh of the GNP. Its sheer size is of obvious importance, but in dealing with investment we are also confronted with a highly unstable element of aggregate demand. Businesses can, and do, suddenly revise their spending plans in the light of their assessment of future prospects. Families do the same, being even more sensitive to fluctuations in the price of money with which to finance home purchases. Over the longer run, however, these short-term cyclical considerations can be discounted and the more basic underlying forces that dictate capital investment can be given basic attention.

Currently business investment in plant and equipment is valued at about $15,000 per worker, reflecting a steady increase in the proportion of capital per unit of labor. This upward movement is certain to continue and by 1975 it is estimated that the value of capital per worker will amount to nearly $17,000. Even though it is anticipated that there will be a continued upward improvement in capital productivity—more goods produced per dollar invested —rising prices of capital goods could well increase the business investment share of the GNP from its present level of 10 percent.

A similar upward relative shift is likely to take place in the case of residential housing. Recently it has accounted for slightly over 3 percent of the GNP, but probably this will rise over the next ten years to a level approximating 4 percent. If these forecasts are reasonably accurate, and they are deeply rooted in economic analysis and cross-checked against other components and historical trends, they mean that housing investment, which totaled $33 billion in 1968, should soar above $70 billion by 1975.

In the early and mid-1960s there were about 1.5 million new private housing starts a year, but by the mid-1970s it is likely that there will be 2 million housing starts a year, with a value more than twice that in the early sixties. The reason lies in the bulge in the formation of new households that will be in evidence in the years immediately ahead. Conservative forecasts predict that household formations will increase from an annual average of 900,000 in the period 1961–1965 to an average of 1.1 million in the 1966–1970 period and 1.3 million between 1971 and 1975. As a consequence, in the ten years from 1966 to 1975, the number of family households will have swelled from 58 million to 70 million. With nearly 700,000 residential units "disappearing" each year because of demolition (for highway construction and urban renewal) or conversion to other purposes, the demand for new residential housing construction is certain to rise far above the levels observed in the last few years.

Government's Big Role

The final major component of demand, and in certain respects the fastest growing in percentage terms, is government expenditures for goods and services. Recently government outlays have amounted to over 20 percent of the GNP. That is itself significant, of course, but it hides from view two other facets of government's role in the economy. First, it takes into account only the direct purchases by government of goods and services. It makes no allowance for transfer payments—money paid out, usually to individuals, for social security, workman's compensation, and retirement pensions. The recipients spend virtually all of this money for their needs, but in the strange world of government income accounting it appears as an element of consumption rather than a government payment. This fact has much significance. Currently a fourth of Federal Government expenditures take the form of transfer payments (that's up from 21 percent in 1955). By 1975 it is expected that transfer payments will account for just about a third of all Federal expenditures, with much of this increase caused by higher social security and Medicare payments. In fact, if transfer payments, grants in aid (paid out to the states), and interest on the debt are put aside, barely half of all Federal expenditures take the form of direct purchases of goods and services.

The second point to be noted is that state and local government outlays have been rising far more rapidly than Federal outlays in the last decade and are certain to show this same steep rate of growth in the next ten years. In 1955 state and local units of government accounted for only a third of all government expenditures in the United States. Federal funds made up the remainder and were clearly dominant. Since then Federal programs, as a whole, have grown much more slowly than state-local programs. The result is that state and local government now account for more than 40 percent of all public expenditures and by 1975 their proportion of the total will be close to 50 percent.

If it ever was, surely it is erroneous to think of "government" as if it were a Washington-based monolith. It isn't. Governmental functions have been widely decentralized and the state capital, the school district, and the city hall are equally important participants along with the White House and Capitol Hill. Between 1968 and 1975 state-local expenditures are expected to soar from less than $112 billion to more than $180 billion, while Federal expenditures go up by only 10 to 20 percent (depending on defense needs). In 1968 state and local government spent approximately $43 billion for education, up from $12 billion in 1955. By 1977 education will call for more than $70 billion in state-local support plus another $9 billion in Federal grants. Health and hospitals cost the states less than $3 billion in 1955. By 1975 these functions will cost nearly $20 billion. Highways and other transportation needs required state and local expenditures of only $6 billion in 1955, but by 1975 the price tag will exceed $25 billion.

The amount of government expenditures is not only going to keep pace with the enormous future growth of the economy, but their mix will change radically. There will be an accompanying shift in emphasis from Washington to the states and local communities, and far greater stress on what can be denominated simply as social functions like education and health care. This will have diverse ramifications for business, but with sales opportunities likely to be greater in the education-health-community improvement area than in the older defense-space sectors, important new opportunities and challenges are opened up for business to participate profitably in confronting and solving "public" problems.

The slums of the nation's cities—with their terrible evidence of neglect and their festering sores manifested in bad housing, inadequate schools, and crowded and outmoded hospitals—are the most vivid example. Nelson Rockefeller, for one, estimates that in the coming decade we must invest $150 billion in the rebuilding of our cities. But there are many problems that affect just about everyone, in every area of the country. Congested transportation (more than $10 billion must be spent for airports and airways alone in the next five years), contaminated air, polluted water, antiquated law enforcement—here are but four categories of problems which have received too little attention and whose correction will require huge government expenditures and call for substantial business participation.

The Economic Outlook Summed Up

If the forces of potential supply (size of the labor force, man-hours worked, productivity) and potential demand (consumption, investment, government) are matched up, the American economy appears likely to grow at a relatively rapid rate of about 4.5 percent a year, at least until 1975. No one, of course, can guarantee that the economy will in fact measure up to its potential. In the last twenty years our growth averaged only 4 percent a year, largely because of the sluggish pace experienced in the last half of the 1950s. But the signs for the future are more encouraging and the rapid growth of the 1960s (averaging better than 4.5 percent annually) may point the way. There are other bases for optimism. An expected step-up in man-hours, attributable to a more rapidly growing labor force, provides one good reason to think that a 4.5 percent rate of expansion is easily within our reach, given continued growth in productivity. The primary areas of uncertainty are on the demand side. Will investment, in housing and business capital equipment, grow rapidly and steadily enough? Will consumers maintain a high rate of purchases or will they divert a bigger share of their rising incomes to savings? Will government maintain a rate of increase in its spending so that, in conjunction with its tax programs, it does not constitute a fiscal brake on economic growth? These are serious questions for which there can be no sure responses, but the discussion in this chapter suggests that there is good reason to believe that answers can and will be found. The future, though, is never free from the mists of unpredictability. That is just one of the facts of business life, but it cannot be allowed to divert the executive decision-maker from trying to shrink the range within which he must guess.

Most of our discussion so far in this chapter has focused on the year 1975, but we should look beyond that terminal date and peer ahead to 2000. In doing so the basic ingredients indicate that continued growth at about the same rate of 4.5 percent a year can be expected through the rest of the century. Chart 5 sums up the results, comparing the 1975 forecast with that for 2000. It shows that in 2000 the GNP will exceed $2.7 trillion (expressed in 1958 dollars, as are the comparable figures for 1975 and 1968). By the end of the century a labor force of 129 million will be working an average thirty-three hours a week. It will be a supersuperaffluent economy, with each civilian employee turning out $21,000 worth

CHART 5
Projected U.S. Economic Growth 1967–2000
Selected Key Indicia

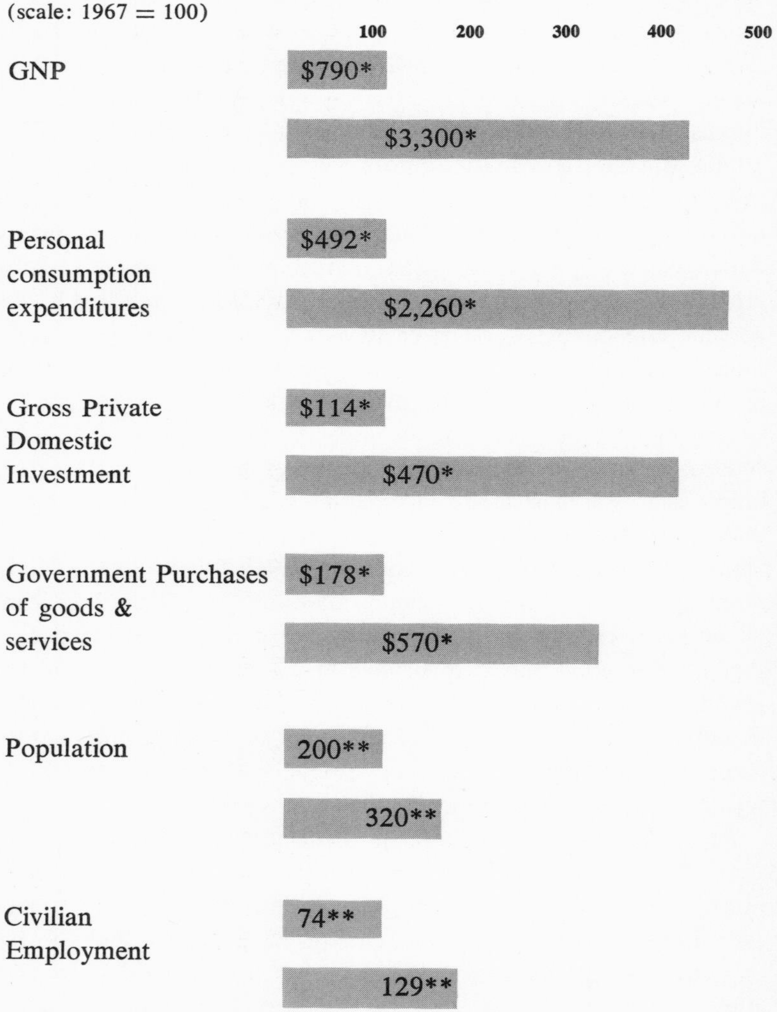

(scale: 1967 = 100)

	100	200	300	400	500

GNP
- $790*
- $3,300*

Personal consumption expenditures
- $492*
- $2,260*

Gross Private Domestic Investment
- $114*
- $470*

Government Purchases of goods & services
- $178*
- $570*

Population
- 200**
- 320**

Civilian Employment
- 74**
- 129**

* 1967 dollars in billions
** in millions

Sources: 1967 data from Department of Commerce; projections based on forecasts of the National Planning Association and Herman Kahn & Anthony J. Wiener, *The Year 2000,* Macmillan, New York, 1967, tables XXVI–XXVIII.

of goods and services a year and earning an average family income in excess of $20,000.

What all of this means to business is almost incredible growth throughout the rest of the century. By 1975 alone the typical firm will have to add 35 percent to its sales capacity and in barely three decades it will have to plan to nearly quadruple its present scale. For many enterprises, of course, the rate of growth will be even faster—much faster—and it will be a severe test of managerial adaptability that many firms will not pass satisfactorily, for rapid growth, a tough enough challenge, is being combined simultaneously with other changes that radically alter the social, political, and economic environment. Science—manifested in a veritable technological revolution—is a particularly potent force for change.

CHAPTER 9

The Scientific Explosion

The revolution that is taking place in American business has been caused by many forces—some noted in earlier chapters—but none is more important or more far-reaching in its implications than science. Since the end of the war billions of dollars have been spent for research and development in the United States in a deliberate effort to accelerate the pace of technological change. That objective has been realized in a way and to a degree that has fundamentally altered relationships between business, government, and academia at the same time that it has greatly speeded up the life cycle of technological evolution. More than anything else, research has turned business and government into partners with each other and with the universities, a development with such far-reaching political and social implications that it is now possible only to appreciate some of them. Equally important, intense research activity of the kind carried out in the last two decades is certain to create instability in business, hastening the creation of new products and processes and the destruction of the old.

Science, of course, has always been a powerful source of change.

What is different now is the vastly increased support being given research by the government, business, and nonprofit sectors, working in close alliance. Research is at the very center of contemporary industrial and public activity, a force whose value is regarded as essential to success in a technological world although feared because of its inherent propensity to compel unanticipated and unsettling changes in the status quo. Increasingly, therefore, the leaders of business and government are providing more support to research, but trying, too, to organize and manage it so that it will not get out of hand. Yet science by its nature is inherently unpredictable; it cannot be controlled as if no more were involved than the manufacture of steel or autos. It is like marriage: modern business cannot get along without extensive involvement in research and development, but it cannot get along easily with the unsettling effects either.

Business Looks to Its Technological Future

Recognizing the unavoidability and gravity of science-induced technical change, most major business firms have established high-level units within their organizations or hired outsiders to maintain a "lookout" for the future and attempt to anticipate scientific developments that are relevant to their long-term economic interests. Though these efforts are almost entirely postwar in time, they have spread widely and have become highly sophisticated in their operational characteristics. At the end of the war not more than 20 percent of American companies attempted systematic forecasts beyond a three-year time horizon. Today more than 90 percent do. Some six hundred medium and large-sized U.S. corporations have established a special technological forecasting function within their central management staff. They spend at least $100 million a year in an effort to assess research trends and predict developments likely to take place five, ten, or even thirty years distant.

To do this businesses employ a wide variety of constantly expanding techniques and retain the consultative services of independent think tanks like RAND, Hudson Institute, Abt Associates, and others noted in Chapters 5 and 7. More than a hundred different approaches currently are being used in technological forecasting. They range from the Delphi technique (which involves bringing together a large number of experts in an attempt to produce a consensus of their intuitions) to relevance tree approaches, morphology, time-independent contextual mapping, and other mathematical models that call upon the operational research and systems analysis styles which have been so highly refined in advanced military decision-making. The details are not central to the present discussion, but it is pertinent to realize just how few people, even those in top company and government positions, are really familiar with these new scientific forecasting techniques. It is this fact that makes many executives extremely uneasy when they ponder the secular ramifications of research.

For the traditional corporate manager, educated in the arts and trained in law, sales, or finance, the burgeoning realm of science—with its peculiar language and specialized techniques—is a land of mystery. Its power concededly is great (that, of course, is one key reason for concern), but its future meaning is unclear. This is exactly why so many companies have plunged deeply into technological forecasting, for it provides some perspective on what lies over the horizon and makes it possible to plan. Still, though, the contours of the future are changing so quickly and so fundamentally under the pressure of our multibillion-dollar research expenditures that no one can be very certain about what lies beyond the day after tomorrow. The pace of scientific advance is not only accelerating but its direction is not subject to precise definition. Surely, however, it will outmode several industries as we know them today, rendering many big enterprises obsolete and substituting new firms which have proven to be better adapted to the changing environment of modern technology.

To understand the pulsating forces emanating from the hyper-emphasis on research in the United States, one must gain an appreciation of both the rising dollar commitment to research and the complex array of participants that finance and conduct scientific research.

The Current State of R&D

Research and development (R&D) in the United States now involves annual expenditures—from all sources, public and private—of over $25 billion, making it not only a major item of economic consequence but one of unusual social and political importance as well. Yet large-scale, highly organized research is largely a new force in our experience, one whose implications we have not come fully to appreciate. This is not surprising considering the speed with which research has swelled to its present proportions.

Until the 1950s our national outlays for research were relatively insignificant, but since 1953 expenditures for R&D have skyrocketed, advancing by more than six times and trebling their share of the GNP. R&D now represents one of the most dynamic forces in the entire economy. In the past decade and a half, while the GNP was doubling, research support soared by more than 400 percent. By contrast with the prewar period the data stand out even more sharply. Expenditures amounted to a mere $166 million in 1930 and to only $345 million in 1945. Even during the war years average annual research was only $600 million.

Before World War II, disbursements for R&D never exceeded one half of 1 percent of the GNP. Even by 1948 the ratio was still below 1 percent, a mark above which it did not rise until 1952. Since then, however, research has commanded a clearly rising proportion of the nation's output of goods and services, with the result that research now accounts for more than 3 percent of the GNP. No other country in the world even closely approximates this relative level of research effort. Only England spends more than 2 percent.

In 1954 expenditures for research in the United States amounted to something over $5 billion. In the next four years they doubled, rising at a rate of more than a billion dollars a year. By 1965 they had doubled again. Some idea of the rapidity of the growth can be gained by looking back to a projection made in 1959 by Dexter

Keezer, the highly respected McGraw-Hill economist. At that time he predicted that by 1969 research would amount to $22 billion, with $12 billion of this originating with the government. Many thought his projection excessively generous. In fact, however, the government spent $12 billion in fiscal 1963, equaling Keezer's carefully formulated ten-year projection in less than half that period of time.

Government's Dominant Role

What explains this enormous expansion in American research and development? Many factors, but chief among them is the Federal Government. Its multibillion-dollar research programs—particularly in defense, space, and nuclear energy—have been the principal source of growth. In the fiscal years 1958 through 1969, propelled by urgent defense assignments (most notably the development and perfection of aircraft, electronic systems, intercontinental and intermediate-range ballistic missile systems) and inspired by the Russian Sputnik space accomplishment, the government spent $125 billion in massive defense, space, and atomic research undertakings unprecedented in the history of science. Today, as Table 4 shows, the Federal Government provides nearly 70 percent of all the money used in the performance of research. As a consequence domestic research has in a very real sense been "nationalized." Currently government R&D expenditures amount to around $18 billion. Representing 10 percent of the Federal administrative budget, this huge sum exceeds what the government spent for research in *all* the years from the time of the Revolution through the end of World War II. Currently we spend more for this function in a single *day* than we did in any one *year* before the Second World War military buildup commenced. The reason lies essentially in the programs of the Department of Defense, the National Aeronautics & Space Administration, and the Atomic Energy Commission. Between them, they account for four fifths of all Federal research activity, pointing up the strong mission orientation of much government research support. Indeed, about 70 percent of all Federal research expenditures are for "development"

TABLE 4
Who Puts Up the Money, Who Does the Work
($ in millions)

PERFORMERS

SOURCES	Federal Government	Industry	Universities and Colleges PROPER	Universities and Colleges FEDERAL CONTRACT RESEARCH CENTERS	Other Nonprofit Institutions	Total	Percent Distribution, Sources
Federal Government	$3,500	$9,100	$1,600	$700	$660	$15,560	62
Industry	—	8,200	60	—	70	8,330	33
Universities and Colleges	—	—	840	—	—	840	3
Other Nonprofit Institutions	—	—	100	—	170	270	1
Total	$3,500	$17,300	$2,600	$700	$900	$25,000	100
Percent distribution, Performers	14	69	10	3	4	100	

(the translation of the known into products or processes) and only 30 percent reflect any form of "research" at all. A modest 10 percent of the government's outlays is for "basic research" (scientific investigation undertaken purely for the advancement of knowledge).

While public funds now form the backbone of the country's R&D, it is critical to recognize that most of this money is paid out to others for the actual performance of research. What is involved, in short, is a massive transfer of funds from the Treasury to universities, nonprofit organizations, and especially industry. As a consequence, while Federal agencies *fund* about 60 percent of U.S. research, they *conduct* less than 15 percent of the work. Conversely, industrial firms carry out 70 percent of all the research that is done, but provide only a third of the financial support; Federal money fills the gap—and it is a gap that now approximates $9 billion a year. The same is true of other research performers. The universities conduct 10 percent of our R&D, but finance barely 2 percent.

It is this huge shift of funds that is vital to understanding the character of contemporary research. It vividly depicts the role of the Federal Government in shaping virtually every aspect of scientific inquiry in the United States. Yet while government funds shape much of our research, they do not control it entirely and exert their influence only in partnership with the intellectual and financial contributions of private firms, universities, and nonprofit entities. It is a subtle balance, with each partner playing a role in determining the outcome.

The Government-Business Alliance

The characteristics of present-day research in the United States can best be seen by taking a close look at industry, which performs 70 percent of the nation's R&D. In 1968 this meant that private for-profit enterprises spent an estimated $17 billion for R&D, five times as much as in 1953 and $5 billion more than as recently as 1963. Over half of these industrial research expenditures are financed by the Federal Government. Equally striking, some 165,000 of the 359,000 scientists and engineers employed by private enterprise are supported by Federal contracts. Indeed, of the 570,000 professional scientists and engineers engaged in research work in the United States, 469,000, fully 82 percent, are Federally supported. The commanding role of the government is clear, although it is receding somewhat in importance. Company-financed research is now growing more rapidly, increasing by an average of over 10 percent a year since 1963.

Reflecting the mix of Federal support, the picture changes dramatically from industry to industry. With matters of defense, space, and nuclear energy occupying the forefront of government attention in recent years, not surprisingly the industries carrying out the biggest R&D programs are in aircraft/missiles, and electrical/communications equipment. These two industries account for nearly 60 percent of all the research done by private companies. The explanation lies largely in the fact that Federal research emphasis is focused so heavily on these product areas, involving, as they do, the development of hardware and associated systems for purposes of both defense and space exploration. Hidden within these figures are the classified requirements of the CIA and its even more capital-intensive mate, the National Security Agency, totaling an estimated $2 billion a year. The picture, then, is one of considerable concentration of research among industries (with just two representing three fifths of all research done by industry) and in terms of financial support (with Federal money paying for over half of all the research performed in industry).

In an important sense, therefore, R&D in the United States is narrowly based, with most of the work done by a mere handful of industries heavily dependent on Federal support. It is truncated in another sense, too, namely in the character of the research performed by industry. According to the most recent available data, 75 percent of all the R&D done by industry is for development, not research at all. Basic research accounts for a slim 4 percent, with the rest, a fifth, accounted for by applied research. Put differently, three out of every four dollars spent by industry involves the translation of known research results into new or improved products or processes.

Most businessmen view basic research, of the kind carried out at the Bell Labs, as esoteric and impractical. They want a quick payoff. One survey of industrial firms engaged in research found that 39 percent of the respondents expected their outlays to generate earnings at least equal to the cost of the research in less than three years; 91 percent of the firms questioned expected a full payoff in less than five years. Most companies, it is quite evident, are interested basically in new products and product improvements and in ways to reduce costs. Perhaps, though, this outlook is changing, albeit slowly. Between 1957 and 1967 industrial firms doubled their overall R&D performance, but their support of basic research increased somewhat more, by 125 percent. It remains true, however, that over 95 percent of all R&D conducted by industry consists either of development (which alone represents over 75 percent) or applied research.

Industry-Supported Research

While Federal money sets the pace in several industrial sectors, it is also true that in most U.S. industries the great bulk of research is financed by the companies themselves. In 1969 private firms did nearly $18 billion of R&D and financed almost half of the work from their own earnings. As Table 5 reveals, however, except for aircraft and parts and electrical and communications equipment, companies in other industries paid for the bulk of the research they performed, with the actual percentage varying from two thirds (as in optical equipment and scientific instruments) to near 100 percent (as in the primary metals industry, where there is practically no Federal research interest). For *most* companies in *most* industries, therefore, the role of Federal research funds is extremely limited. Thus it is important to assess private research funding patterns to get a complete picture of the nation's scientific activity.

Until the mid-fifties Federal money supported less than half the research done by industry. Then the balance swung. Now it is swinging back once again as the growth of Federal research expenditures slows somewhat and companies increase their own research outlays. Each year since 1964 the private industrial sector has increased its research outlays more than has the government, reflecting a new, sharpened corporate awareness of the importance of research in determining its own future. Viewed another way, as a proportion of net sales, company R&D funds increased by over a third in the decade ending in 1969 and now amount to more than 2 percent of manufacturers' revenue. Reflecting U.S. industry's sharply expanded research commitment, nearly 400,000 scientists and engineers are employed as researchers in industry, a gain of 150,000 over 1958.

Why some U.S. industries give much more attention of research and development than others is subject to no simple explanation. The aircraft and missile industry does 35 percent of all the R&D performed in American industry, yet it accounts for less than 3 percent of the total value added by the country's manufacturers. Similarly, electrical equipment and communication firms do about another quarter of the country's research, but they provide barely 10 percent of the amount added by manufacture. The two industries, then, account for nearly 60 percent of the country's entire research effort even though they represent only about an eighth of total value added in manufacturing. At the other pole, a number of industries, like textiles, food processing, paper, rubber products, and primary metals, which are of major consequence in the private sector, do only a very small amount of the nation's R&D, roughly not over a tenth of the total.

While companies in some industries devote a considerably greater proportion of their resources to research than others, it is also unmistakable that industry as a whole is substantially increasing its research spending. From 1961 to 1968 industry research expenditures nearly doubled, rising well above the $8 billion level. Moreover, the rate of increase has turned significantly upward in the more recent years. Industry is spending a much larger fraction of its sales dollar for research than was the case in the early 1960s.

The Research Commitment: Implications and Prospects

While it is evident that not all firms in all industries have made the same commitment to technological research, American business

TABLE 5

Funds for Performance of Research and Development, by Industry and Source, 1957, 1965, 1966
($ in millions)

Industry	Total			Federal			Company		
	1957	1965	1966	1957	1965	1966	1957	1965	1966
TOTAL	$7,731	$14,185	$15,541	$4,335	$7,740	$8,287	$3,396	$6,445	$7,254
Food and kindred products	74	151	166	*	1	1	74	150	165
Textiles and apparel	15	38	42	1	**	**	14	**	**
Lumber, wood products, and furniture	14	12	14	—	**	**	14	**	**
Paper and allied products	35	77	85	*	—	—	35	77	85
Chemicals and allied products	705	1,390	1,515	89	191	191	616	1,198	1,324
Industrial chemicals	503	932	1,016	80	148	159	423	784	857
Drugs and medicines	104	274	304	*	**	**	104	**	**
Other chemicals	98	184	194	9	**	**	89	**	**
Petroleum refining and extraction	211	434	441	11	69	56	200	364	385
Rubber products	107	166	182	37	25	25	70	141	156
Stone, clay, and glass products	69	117	131	**	4	6	**	113	125
Primary metals	108	213	228	5	8	7	103	205	221
Primary ferrous products	64	128	137	1	1	2	63	127	136
Nonferrous and other metal products	44	85	91	4	7	6	40	78	85

Fabricated metal products	135	145	164	38	15	16	97	129	148
Machinery	669	1,128	1,301	272	267	343	397	800	958
Electrical equipment and communication	1,804	3,168	3,570	1,196	1,963	2,161	608	1,206	1,409
Communication equipment and electronic components	748	1,918	2,126	518	1,241	1,332	230	677	795
Other electrical equipment	1,056	1,250	1,443	678	721	829	378	529	614
Motor vehicles and other transportation equipment	707	1,223	1,321	190	325	345	517	898	976
Aircraft and missiles	2,574	5,098	5,446	2,275	4,476	4,690	299	622	756
Professional and scientific instruments	249	383	444	109	126	143	140	257	301
Scientific and mechanical measuring instruments	139	76	90	80	19	23	59	57	66
Optical, surgical, photographic, and other instruments	110	308	355	29	107	120	81	200	235
Nonmanufacturing industries	93	443	490	74	267	298	19	176	193

* Less than $0.5 million.

** Not separately available but included in total.

Source: National Science Foundation.

investment in research is nonetheless of elephantine proportions, far exceeding the amount of research conducted or financed by business in any other country. Moreover, the vast research programs being carried out in some industries, like electronics, have pervasive consequences for businesses in all sectors. The same is true of research in chemistry, drugs, and instrumentation, not to mention aircraft, where the results broadly benefit the society by making available better products and more efficient processes. Whether they jump or are pulled in, today's business enterprises simply cannot stay out of the research milieu. Rapid technological change, propelled by the billion-dollar support of government and industry, appears to be the primary distinguishing characteristic of the U.S. in the last half of this century. How the research revolution can affect business is looked at in several selected cases in the succeeding chapter.

CHAPTER 10

Industry and
the Technological Revolution

"We live in an age iv wondhers."

—*Mr. Dooley*

Computers, Communication, Cybernation

If we have passed through the industrial age, as suggested earlier in this book, then certainly we have entered the age of cybernation. The postwar development and widespread use of the computer, electronics, and automated control systems, joined together through communications, introduces, says the economist-philosopher Kenneth E. Boulding, "a new gear into the evolutionary process." The computer, in all its wondrous forms, is an extension of the human mind in the way that a tool or even an automobile is an extension of the human body. By linking computers together, wherever located on the face of the earth, you achieve what Marshall McLuhan calls an "all-at-once" environment—a sort of global village. To appreciate the computer, and to sense its impact, it is essential to view it in these grand terms—to realize that it is more than a high-speed adding machine or data retriever.

In the last twenty years the computer has become a near-synonym for industrialization. The value of general-purpose computer installations in 1962 was $4 billion; in 1965 it was $8 billion; in 1968, $14 billion; and by 1972 their value will amount to an estimated $30 billion. Two decades of development have increased computer speed by a million times and reduced equipment size a thousandfold. Machines that could print only 150 lines a minute in 1947 now spew out more than a thousand lines a minute. In all of these respects future computer technology is certain to make even greater gains. Experts predict that in the last third of this century computer speed will increase ten thousand times while cost and unit size will continue to decline steeply. This would mean that in comparison with a present-day computer, a year-2000 unit would be 10,000 times faster, one ten-thousandth as big, and cost one one-hundred-thousandth as much per unit of output.

What is likely to permit this continued advance in technology? One key explanation lies in the components used in computer manufacture. Much of the progress made in the last two decades is attributable to the substitution of transistors and microintegrated circuits for the older vacuum tubes and wiring that made up a machine's innards. A comparable improvement is on the near-horizon, so-called large-scale integration (sometimes referred to as LSI in the trade jargon). Today an integrated circuit will have about twenty transistors, diodes, and related resistors and components mounted on a chip of silicon one thirty-second to one eighth of an inch square. LSI circuits, however, may have from three to one thousand times as many components in the same space. Some engineers believe that in the early seventies it may be possible to array 100,000 transistors on an inch-and-a-half diameter wafer. The shoe-box-sized computer is just around the corner. Costs will fall too. Presently the price of an integrated circuit works out to from 20 to 50 cents per computational function it will perform. LSI circuits should cut this to a penny per function by 1970.

Though the prospects of further gains in computer technology are astounding, even greater accomplishments lie just over the horizon. The key is the laser (an acronym for "light amplification through stimulated emission of radiation"), or the use of coherent light. Creating the sharpest, purest, and most intense light beam known to man, the laser can be used in all sorts of ways. It can cut a hole through a diamond in minutes, dig a tunnel through the earth subsurface, reattach loose retinas in the human eye, or rejoin vessels in the heart. From the standpoint of computers and communications the laser has very special properties. By using lasers to etch a microscopic circuit pattern on a silicon wafer, the principle of LSI can be extended to a point where 1.5 million transistors can be arrayed in an inch-and-a-half diameter. By using the laser in the production of other computer subsystems (like the memory unit), supercomputers can be built in perhaps just a decade—small, reliable, extremely fast, and very low in cost.

Although computer size, speed reliability, and cost will be greatly improved through future predictable technological advances, actually the most important gains will come in the ways computers are put to use. It is in the fuller exploitation of the computer, coupled with its vastly improved characteristics and the prospect of large-scale computer interconnection, that its revolutionary potential will be felt.

To date computer applications have drawn largely, though not entirely, on their relevant speed and memory properties. For banks, credit, and reservation operations this has meant widespread adoption. In industry computers have been employed to manage repetitive production processes, though on what is really only a very limited basis except in telephone communications where computers handle most high-speed switching functions. In certain research-topical areas, the ability of computers, when properly programmed, to simulate the behavior of an identified system has been put to rather considerable use. Computer models of the economy, for example, have helped in projecting rates of growth and in providing clues to problem areas. In all of these applications the potential of the computer has been tested and proven, but in comparison with future uses the past record hardly even represents the equivalent of the tip of the iceberg. Eventually, says industrialist Simon Ramo, computers will permit "a totally controlled national economy in which all of the information needed to run businesses will be made in the right place at the right time to assure maximum efficiency and the smoothest optimum relationship of all elements of the economy."

Take any of the principal types of application and one has little trouble in forecasting large-scale computer involvement in diverse problem situations. By 1975 over half, and perhaps 75 percent, of all computers in the United States will be linked via communications facilities. Thousands of these computers will be internationally connected, either through underseas cables or communications satellites. As an intensely practical matter, this means that just about all the information stored in computers (and it will be virtually unlimited, ranging from general physical and technical phenomena to details about individuals) will be retrievable almost anywhere by almost anyone with access to a computer terminal. This will necessitate the creation of computer-information "utilities" that will serve either as large data banks or as "brokers" between information sources. In more specific terms this prospect holds immense value for every decision-maker. For the businessman, government aide, doctor, lawyer, scholar, or student, the near-instantaneous availability of information can lead to more complete understanding of complex issues and improve the quality of choice at the same time that it speeds up the decision process. It may even permit the elimination of the individual "expert" by automating what we now regard as judgment. Medical diagnosis and many types of legal problems (as in the tax area) can be analyzed through use of the computer.

Computers can also be exploited far more widely in managing production-inventory processes. A great deal of office work that is still handled manually could be automated through computer adaptation. Libraries can be extensively automated, with remote information retrieval and instant copying and transmission of materials. Foreign languages can be acceptably translated by computer (some of this is already done by the CIA), although the need for this function to be performed will probably decline as computer "language" *itself* becomes an international tongue, understandable to a technical elite in the industrialized countries of the world. In education the computer can be the fulcrum for new learning techniques that offer a student many of the advantages of individual instruction. From a political standpoint the computer, coupled with access by home telephone, could permit automated voting on specific issues. It is quite feasible technically to think that individual citizens could come to constitute a modern town hall, voting, not just for candidates, but directly on major questions that in an earlier and perhaps more "primitive" day had to be resolved by elected representatives in a local, state, or Federal legislature.

Transportation presents one area in which the computer could be more extensively used. Automated air traffic control can make more efficient use of the airspace, speeding up the movement of aircraft in congested areas and increasing safety. In large cities the street network can be remotely managed through electronic devices coordinated by a computer, which would issue orders to street signals and even individual vehicles that would make maximum efficient use of the city road system. Such a technique increases street efficiency by at least 30 percent, cutting down on congestion and travel time. High-speed automated rapid transit in heavily populated cities could be fully operational by the early 1970s and, between cities, automated highways and trains promise to make travel much faster, safer, and considerably more enjoyable.

Perhaps the greatest impact of the computer-communications revolution is in the trade-credit field. It is feasible, and probable, that within twenty years most retail sales will be made remotely, by phone, with payment recorded instantly on a bank computer (and with purchases recorded simultaneously on the seller's inventory computer and on the goods producer's planning computer). Currency is likely to become an unusual means of accomplishing even a routine sales transaction. Even today more than $40 billion of retail goods are sold by catalog to suburban housewives who simply telephone their orders. A Sears executive sums it up, saying that "it's entirely possible that the telephone will do the same thing that the automobile did to shopping habits. The next step beyond bringing the stores closer to the home is to bring the stores into the home."

In its capacity to expand one's range of experience and to raise our standard of living, the computer-communications revolution is a valuable contribution to twentieth century civilization. At the same time, however, it poses risks that we have not previously encountered. The accessibility to detailed information about individual persons poses a serious challenge to privacy, which can be met only if one recognizes the potential of computer technology. From another, equally pragmatic standpoint, computer communications represent such a new and powerful tool for business and government decision-making that only those executives and firms who understand and can converse with the machines can reasonably expect to keep pace with the emerging new era of electronics technology.

Polymeric Marvels

Physical products such as wood, leather, cotton, wool, oils, the paper this book is printed on, consist of large molecules, each comprised of many identical units of matter. These molecules have come to be known as *"poly"* (many) *"meros"* (units), with the parts, or building blocks, denominated monomers. The natural organic polymers, on which so much of life depends, include such basic compounds as cellulose, starch, and resins. Until well into the twentieth century and the development of such magnificent analytical gear as the electron microscope and the ultracentrifuge, the natural polymers defied attempts to understand their molecular composition. That secret has been unlocked and with the discovery that the giant polymeric molecules are made up of a large number of repeating units linked in chains of various shapes, it became possible to synthesize monomers and construct diverse polymers. The practical result: cheap, adaptable new raw materials commonly known as plastics, artificial fibers, adhesives, and synthetic rubbers.

With the synthesis of polymers, chemistry had unleashed a whole new industry whose incredible past growth is matched only by its potential future expansion. The production of polymers in the United States has risen more than a thousand times since 1930, more than for any other major material. Annual production in the U.S. of polyethylene, the most widely used plastic (bread bags, milk cartons, squeeze bottles), is close to four billion pounds. Vinyl production (floor covering, most notably) is near the three billion pound mark, and polystyrene (toys and housewares) amounts to 2.5 billion pounds. In terms of cubic feet rather than pounds, a better measure because of plastics' light weight, polymer use has surpassed aluminum and copper and is approaching that of steel and cement. Susceptible to adaptation in everything from tires, furniture, and clothing to the packaging of food and related products, the polymers—cellophane, wrapping films, polyethylene, nylon, butyl, synthetic leathers (like Corfam), and man-made fibers like Dacron and Mylar—have the potential for replacing most natural materials and other substances in common use, including metals. The reason lies in their relatively low cost of manufacture coupled with their adaptability to use in a great variety of circumstances. They are light in weight, cheaply transported, easily installed on a mass production basis, and resistant to corrosion and moisture. All of these characteristics help explain their rocketing sales growth.

If the polymers are to continue their conquest of materials markets, however, they must be better adapted for structural purposes, for use in building construction and in the manufacture of such things as autos, trucks, and boats. Is this a realistic possibility? The answer is yes, and it is what makes the outlook for polymers so bright. It is also what will make materials a battleground for interindustry warfare as established companies attempt to fight off new entrants.

To strengthen polymers and to make them usable as structural materials, several of their properties must be improved. In rigidity, elasticity, tensile strength, heat and corrosion resistance, considerable gains must be made. Each imposes a heavy burden on scientists, but the technological prospects are exceptionally encouraging. One technique involves crystallization of polymers. Through chemical manipulation, the polymeric chains can be induced to line up in parallel and form crystallites. The number and regular spacing of the individual chains gives considerable rigidity and improves heat resistance. By linking the chains together through chemical means (such as by adding sulfur) the structure can be made very strong. One product developed this way is ebonite, strong, with high temperature resistance, and as completely insoluble as it is unswellable. By strengthening the chains themselves (by, say, adding methyl to carbon atoms, the foundation of Lucite), very hard, tough polymers can be developed. By combining these techniques —crystallization, cross-linking, and chain stiffening—polymers with sufficient strength and temperature resistance to make them usable in buildings, vehicles, and even jet engines can be produced in large quantities at costs that will make them attractive substitutes for steels and other metals, and perhaps superior in certain essential properties.

Polymer prospects are so attractive that they must frankly be conceded to be revolutionary in their economic impact. However, other materials also will be put to much wider use in the future than is now true. Titanium is one. Although it is still relatively expensive, titanium technology has taken great strides in the last decade and its price, relative to that of steel and aluminum, is falling sharply. Its physical properties suggest that by the end of the century, and perhaps earlier, titanium will be the base for relatively low-cost, lightweight structural alloys. As the "steel" of the next century it will, in alloy form, be particularly well suited for weight-sensitive structures such as bridges, towers, surface vehicles, and perhaps aircraft. Lower in cost and equally important materials newcomers are glass-fiber-reinforced resins and other composites that are of medium strength and available at less than the cost of titanium, but with sufficient distinctive qualities so as to make them more attractive than polymers.

Clearly, the physical shape and composition of the world of the future—what we wear, use, live in, and even what we eat—is going to be sharply different from that of today. This will most dramatically affect materials producers, but it will inevitably influence every segment of industry, affecting what is produced and how it is manufactured. Along with the omnipresent computer and its communications network, the marvelous materials of tomorrow will mark a new phase in man's economic revolution. But medical scientists are also learning more about man himself—his physiology, body chemistry, and mental system.

Microbiology and Medical Science

As one surveys the future of medical research, the changes which can be anticipated—and their sweeping character and implications—are so dramatic as to be nearly incredible. No other area of modern science holds as much hope for major accomplishment as health. The drastic curtailment of disease, cancer, most notably, is one anticipated accomplishment, but the new breakthroughs go much further and hold out to man the prospect of manipulating his own behavior and significantly influencing the lives of future generations. Doctors, chemists, and engineers will share in this upcoming medical adventure, opening up broad new vistas to business exploitation.

Many of tomorrow's medical gains will come through microbiology, representing the dual contributions of chemists and biologists in their promising quest for knowledge about basic life processes. Scientists have at last developed the means to peer into the cell, the basic building block of all life, and determine its composition and the way it carries out its functions.

The cell is much like a chemical factory. Small, almost minuscule by our standards, but massive in its output, it manufactures proteins out of amino acids, thus creating and enlarging its "life" just as it also molds its own distinctiveness. It has now been discovered that a single key chemical compound, deoxyribonucleic acid (DNA, as it has come to be called), is, in essence, the blueprint for protein manufacture. DNA calls the signals to which chromosomes, located in the nucleus of cells, respond. By controlling cell replication, DNA also determines the process by which amino acids are formed into protein within the living cell.

All of this sounds pretty complex to a layman, and it is, but its human significance is incalculable. The scientist who understands DNA and its composition can synthesize it in the laboratory and perform experiments that expand our knowledge of the reasons why the human cell becomes cancerous, or otherwise deviant. With that knowledge, the medical technologist is in a position to develop counteragents that may restore a cell's normal function. What this opens up is not only the possibility of curtailing cancer but of checking or curing diabetes and other genetic diseases. The rewards are self-evident.

With the synthesis of DNA and the discovery of the basic ingredients of life itself, the doors are opened to much more, though, than the curtailment of disease. The knowledge needed to synthesize DNA, and thus to build defenses against cell-attacking viruses, is also the knowledge that permits the very creation of life and its calculated manipulation. Cells determine physical and mental condition and through chemical means they can be altered in ways that allow, within very narrow limits, the shaping of human physiology and psychology. Our ignorance in this area of science is still immense, but the discoveries made to date—and they are truly fundamental in character—lay a solid foundation for early, continuing, and lengthy strides into medical realms that will place man in a position by the end of the century where he can play an active role in determining and shaping the nature of his own existence. With the ability to manipulate the genetic structure, man will be able to prolong his life significantly, influence human behavior (perhaps reducing the maladjustment of the criminal psychopath), slow down or substantially mitigate the consequences of aging, and even determine the sex of unborn offspring.

While all of this portrays a greatly expanded role for industry in the health business, it also raises the most sensitive and intransigent kind of ethical questions concerning the propriety of using our advancing technological know-how in dealing with matters that so vitally affect the human family. We lack a set of standards to guide our own behavior. Here, again, we must face one of the toughest challenges in our technological evolution—namely, the criteria to be employed, by government, business, and individual scientists and doctors, in exercising their power and technical skill.

The problem is complicated further by the prospects posed by bioengineering—the transplantation of human organs and their synthesis. Not only are liver, lung, and heart transplants certain to become commonplace in the future, if they have not already become so (as they have in the case of kidneys), but it will become increasingly feasible to manufacture synthetic organs and to use them as replacements for "natural" components which have malfunctioned or become diseased. The polymers are peculiarly well adapted to this purpose because of their strength, light weight, and ease of adaptation. But this prospect, clearly defined though it is, creates many difficult problems. Kidney transplants, for example, are extremely costly and kidney machines, which are available in much smaller quantities than the demand would justify, are even more so. Only an eighth of those persons suffering from chronic uremia now receive the treatment (transplantation or dialysis) that could save their lives. How is such treatment to be rationed among those in need? Is ability to pay to be the only guide? If not, what rule is to govern: age, "value" to the society (should a Senator be preferred to a high school teacher?), or what? And, whatever the standard, who should apply it—a medical practitioner, the hospital that services the substitute organ or life-giving machine, the government? The answers are hardly easy, but they underscore the difficulties inherent in our unleashing of the secrets of human biology and emphasize that while medical science will open up vast new markets for business, it will also create serious problems.

The Consequences of Technical Change

The effects of modern science on business—spurred on by our huge, multibillion-dollar public and private research programs—fundamentally change many dimensions of the worlds of business, opening up large new markets at the same time they threaten to tear down well-established industrial positions. Viewed against the backdrop of the kinds of changes described earlier—changes in the size and diversity of corporate America, the business constituency, and the economy—technological breakthroughs of the significance of those noted in this chapter are truly revolutionary in their economic and social consequences. The next chapter assesses their overall impact on the economy and the composition of American industry.

CHAPTER 11

Science, Business,
and the New Economy

As one looks back at the developments that have taken place in American industry during the postwar years, the role of technology in altering the composition of the economy is immediately apparent —and indicative of what present-day research holds in store for the future. Consider a few anecdotal highlights: soap flakes, once the only form of laundry cleaning agent, have been all but completely replaced by detergents. The glass milk bottle is not far from being a museum piece, relegated there by coated-paper cartons. The newsreel has vanished, overcome by the assault of television. Television itself has vitally affected entertainment, for a while sending movies into decline, but now making extensive use of movies (new as well as old). Seventy-eight rpm, monaural phonograph records are collectors' items, replaced by long-play stereo discs. Fountain pens are becoming rare (their sales fell by a third in the last decade, as sales of ballpoint pens quadrupled). Wringer-washers have been nearly completely replaced by automatic laundry equipment. Unpackaged, unprepared foods are now uncommon. Propeller-driven commercial aircraft are in about the same class as steam locomotives. The list could be extended (and you can add your own examples), but the key point to grasp is that as a consequence of past research efforts, many basic changes in products and processes have taken place. The effects, on individual enterprises as well as entire industries, are readily apparent and will continue to be felt—even more sharply—as ongoing research is translated into specific applications.

The New Materials: A Study in Change

Materials—the "stuff" with which we build, clothe ourselves, and wrap our wares—are a splendid example, depicting the large technologically induced changes that can take place in the space of only a few years. What has happened is that several new types of materials have been developed, with cost and physical advantages that often have made them superior to older products. Conversely, established materials have been refined so that they are being used in novel ways. In food packaging, for example, plastics and new types of paper products are being substituted for glass and metal containers. Not only has the milk bottle given way to the paper carton, the steel (tin-coated) can has lost ground to aluminum. Metal and glass containers have met increasing competition from plastics (pickles, vegetables, and other edibles can be packed in moistureproof polyethylene plastic bags), and the waxpaper bread wrapper has been widely replaced by divers "see-through" plastics. Similarly, in clothing natural fibers have lost position to synthetic substances. Leather hides for shoes are being replaced by Corfam and other porous synthetics just as a number of artificial fibers were found to be good substitutes in clothing for wool and cotton. By the mid-seventies, one manufacturer predicts synthetics will be used in the production of more than 70 percent of all new shoes.

Turn to construction. Less glass may be used today in packaging, but more glass is now employed in building construction. Less steel is used, but some types of steel—the strong, lightweight varieties—are in far greater demand. Less brick is sold, but more cement. Throughout modern buildings new products are in wide application—floor and ceiling tile, wallboard, wall and surface coverings. The older materials have either been replaced or been changed in composition and character.

In interior walls, partitions, and floors, vinyl asbestos tile now accounts for a third of all plastics used in construction. Exterior applications show equally great promise. Polyvinyl chloride has established itself as an effective material for window sash, just as plastic siding and roofing have gained wide acceptance. Plastics also are being used as downspouts, insulation, counter tops, and wall covering, and plastic pipe is increasing in popularity for many applications.

Recognizing that materials are typically susceptible to many uses, what have been the net results of these various developments in materials applications? For steel and all nonferrous metals other than aluminum the picture is clear: they have lost substantial ground to their rivals. Glass also has slipped in usage, relative to its competitors, with most of its decline having come in packaging; in construction glass has found new applications. Aluminum has greatly increased its position, as also has cement. The greatest gainers, however, have been the synthetic polymeric materials— plastics and artificial fibers. In two decades plastics and synthetics increased by over 50 percent as a component of final demand as reflected in the GNP. By the same measure of relative contribution to final output, wood, steel, nonferrous metals, and nonfood agricultural products (principally hides) actually declined in usage. The technologically new clearly were eroding the position of the old, compelling accommodation or decline.

The Research Crucible

What has taken place in materials naturally is occurring elsewhere in the economy, presenting a sharp challenge to business firms either to get in tune with the research revolution or to risk obsolescence. A few firms are orchestrating the beat. Several have picked up the tune, but many companies are still struggling to pick up the tempo and a few (more than would care to admit it and many more than realize it) have yet failed to appreciate the harsh new scientific environment in which they must survive. "The earth is not a resting place," the philosopher René Dubos has cautioned, but not all corporate executives have learned that lesson.

Some enterprises, however, have taken an aggressive, creative posture in this technological era. The Burroughs Corporation, for example, was just a producer of adding machines and cash registers as late as the 1950s. Then it grabbed the ring and plunged into the bustling world of electronics. Now it is a rapidly growing global producer of computers and associated equipment, poised on the very frontier of electronics research and favored with a bright, fast-growth future. Similarly, Ford Motor, recognizing that forecasts of auto sales offer comparatively limited prospects of earnings growth, has diversified into electronics and other fields. Its rapidly expanding research staff is working on electro-luminescence, cryogenics, and nuclear magnetic resonance. Two broad areas characterize its research program: material sciences and basic energy storage and energy conversion techniques.

Many firms, though, have been remarkably reticent to plunge into the technological surf. The reason is not altogether clear, but a close look at the behavior of big corporations strongly indicates that they are often hostile to new ideas or sharp deviations from their established ways. For example, it was not one of the large American steel companies, like U.S. Steel or Bethlehem, but one of the smallest, McLouth, that first put to use in the 1950s the new basic oxygen process. It cuts costs and greatly increases steel-making efficiency, but it represented such a seemingly radical innovation that none of the giant steel corporations could change their accustomed ways to adapt it to their operations. The case illustrates that for most firms, especially those that are big and firmly entrenched in a dominant position in an established market, technological innovation is looked upon more as foe than friend. Some large companies can adapt to the world of rapid scientific change, and even accelerate and mold it, but many, misled by the strength of their present position, cannot. To cope with the research revolution and to exploit its potential is as much a question of attitude and organizational adaptibility as it is of wealth or presumed technical competence.

What is apparent as one peers into the technological future is that in the remainder of this century there will be major advances in many fields that will powerfully reshape the content and outer contours of the economy. The types of sophisticated technological forecasting noted in the preceding chapter have helped sharpen our awareness of what these revolutionary forces are most likely to be and thus help us form a judgment as to their likely implications. What we must anticipate, it deserves to be emphasized, is not simply a large number of minor technical improvements but rather fundamental innovations—basic new concepts—that can completely alter our established ways of thinking about the world in which we live.

New Sources of Energy: Impact on the Older Industries

Resources typify these forces of change. To serve the demands of a world which already has more than three billion inhabitants and which by 2000 will have a population of nearly seven billion, our presently known sources of energy and food will no doubt prove inadequate. Additional supplies must be found to permit the pace of economic expansion essential to a better standard of living and the avoidance of global disaster. Water, energy, raw materials, food: all must be produced in greater quantities to satisfy a burgeoning world economy. With our existing knowledge and present technology we could not realistically hope to meet this demand, but fortunately research prospects promise important new advances that should allow us to keep pace with man's growing needs. Significantly, however, the resources technology of the future differs significantly from that to which we are accustomed.

A quick preview suggests some of the changes we can reasonably expect. Perhaps most notably, extensive exploitation of the oceans (and the ocean floor) will be common within less than two decades. This will provide important new mineral resources (oil is perhaps the most obvious example, but other minerals, particularly the more valuable kinds like molybdenum and platinum, will also be ocean-mined) and yield immense quantities of food. "Aquaculture" or intensive sea-farming will be routine by the end of the century, accounting for perhaps 20 percent of the world's food supply. The food problem will be assailed from another direction, too. By 1990 the production of synthetic protein in large quantities will be economically feasible and popularly accepted (laboratory experiments are already well advanced).

Energy requirements for a world whose aggregate economic output will swell four times by the end of the century will be satisfied in ways no less unique than in food production. The thirst for water, already severe in many parts of the world, will no doubt be quenched through large-scale desalinization. In the 1970s this should become commercially competitive with most other forms of water supply, especially when linked with nuclear reactors. Not later than 1980 nuclear electricity generation costs will be competitive with other fuel sources in nearly all parts of the country. Thereafter, and especially with the introduction of breeder reactors (which produce more fissionable material than they burn), nuclear power may well become the major source of electric power supply throughout the world, supplanting fossil fuels, oil, and even hydrogeneration. Some seventy-five nuclear plants are on order or under construction in the U.S., with a combined capacity equal to about one fifth of the nation's present electrical generating capacity. Given the improvements which have been made in the efficiency of long-distance transmission of electricity (much power used in New York City is now "shipped" from Niagara Falls and even Newfoundland), it is probable that massive nuclear plants, located immediately adjacent to the oceans, will supply the bulk of the world's electricity and simultaneously desalinate hundreds of millions of gallons of water a day.

For other energy requirements, particularly transportation, it seems probable that many present power sources will be in far less extensive use by the next century. The fuel cell is one major alternative form of energy, but there may be others—like steam engines or improved batteries—which offer low cost and minimize air contamination. The latter is an objective of growing importance as the numbers of individually owned vehicles increases: at recent rates of purchase there would be nearly three hundred million automobiles in the United States by the year 2000, nearly three times the present number.

With these radical shifts in the character of our energy resources, only a farsighted and quick-footed company can maintain a position it now occupies (which is one good reason why the big oil companies are, as pointed out in Chapter 3, excitedly moving into other forms of energy). There is another consequence too. As sources of energy become more portable and flexible, like the fuel cell, and as it becomes feasible to obtain demineralized water in areas now presumed arid, it is reasonable to expect that business enterprises will establish facilities in regions of the United States and around the globe that are now automatically rejected.

Overall Effects on Industry

The much bigger U.S. economy of the future, then, will be far different from that of the present, something which will radically affect all segments of business just as it will also profoundly affect workers and government officials. For a host of reasons—many stemming from the rapid pace of technological change induced by our massive postwar investment in research and development—the composition of the American economy is being fundamentally changed. Whole industrial sectors, once dominant, are dwindling in importance—agriculture is one, mining is another. Industries within key economic sectors are giving way to newer arrivals, as exemplified by the erosion of railroad passenger service through market penetration by air transportation. Many new industries, as with plastics and synthetic fibers, are displacing older product industries. In the process many companies, unable to adapt to a changing technology and new market circumstances, are losing ground to more aggressive firms better tuned to the dynamics of the late twentieth century. These same forces are altering the character of employment and affecting the present location of industry within states, regions, and metropolitan areas. An economic revolution is underway and no one is to be spared its impact.

Many major sectors of the economy are certain to reflect the continued expansion of the service area at the expense of goods production and agriculture. As a share of the GNP agriculture will fall to 2.5 percent by 1977, down from 3.1 percent in 1966. Reflecting continued rapid productivity gains, the farm share of civilian employment will parallel this downward course, but fall even more sharply and by 1977 account for less than 3 percent of total jobs (agriculture accounted for more than 7 percent of employment as recently as 1957). Manufacturing output is likely to lose some ground in its percentage contribution to the GNP, but most of the decline is likely to come in nondurables (especially in food products, textiles, and apparel). The relative significance of manufacturing and other goods-producing industries as a source of employment show marked signs of decline. By 1977 the manufacturing industries will account for less than a quarter of civilian employment (it was close to a third at the end of the war).

By contrast with the declining position of agriculture and goods production in the economy, the service sector will expand greatly, both in terms of its contribution to the GNP and in employment. Because of the problems associated with the valuation of certain types of service output (like that of government), this can be most easily seen in employment statistics. What these data show is that by 1977 nearly 70 percent of all civilian jobs will be in the service sector. Large gains will come both in government, especially at the state and local level, and in pure services (of the kind typically used by other businesses as well as those providing direct service to the consumer). Output will rise, absolutely and relatively, in transportation, communications and other utilities, and finance, but gains in productivity, from huge capital investment in computers and other labor-saving devices, will keep employment little more than in line with present levels. The general image, then, of the future economy is one characterized by a further decline in agriculture, a stabilization of manufacturing (with durable goods rising a trifle in relative significance while nondurables lose some ground), and a sharp expansion in services (including government).

These, of course, are broad trends and it is necessary to probe beneath the surface to gauge the vibrant currents of change likely to affect the economy of the seventies and beyond. Manufacturing is the prime subject for a closer look, largely because it is still so important as a source of jobs and contributor to the GNP. A look into the future shows that the subgroups that comprise manufacturing will experience striking adjustments, some falling far behind the economic pace, others spearheading the economic growth rush. Consider the metals and materials industries, for a good case in point. In the period 1970 to 1980 steel, often spoken of as if it were a perpetual "key" industry, will grow only slowly in sales—advancing by less than 2 percent a year, not even half the anticipated rate of growth in the economy as a whole. Copper will do little better, growing only 2.4 percent a year over the same period. But aluminum, a lighter, more versatile, and often cheaper metal, will grow at more than 5 percent a year (a pace it is likely to maintain until at least 1980). Plastics sales will increase still more rapidly, rising at over 6 percent a year. In actual sales dollars steel will still exceed aluminum and plastics by a considerable margin, but its lead will have been narrowed and it will find strong rivals in many markets which were viewed in the past as its exclusive preserve. In much the same way the metals producers will be losing markets to paper (for packaging and similar purposes) as well as to plastics and glass.

These surging forces of change will affect trade relationships between industries. The auto-bus-truck companies will be buying aluminum at a rate twice as fast as steel, furniture makers will be increasing their purchases of plastics at more than double the rate of aluminum (a fact of indirect consequence to oil producers because oil feed stocks are a key ingredient in plastics), and textile firms will be buying more synthetics from chemical makers like Eastman and Celanese than wool and cotton from farmers. Through this kind of network of changes the composition of the economy will be fundamentally altered.

Comparative Industrial Rates of Growth

To gain a more complete picture of the forces of revolution underway in the American economy, Table 6 compares those industries whose sales growth to 1980 will exceed—or fall below— the expected rate of growth of the economy.

The precise forecast rates of growth are less important than the

TABLE 6

Comparative Rates of Growth to 1980
for Selected Major U.S. Industries

Sales Growth *much below* growth in GNP	Sales Growth *somewhat below* growth in GNP	Sales Growth *about the same as* growth in GNP	Sales Growth *somewhat above* growth in GNP	Sales Growth *much above* growth in GNP
Steel	Agriculture	Textiles	Paper	Aluminum
Leather	Food & tobacco	Furniture	Printing &	Plastics
Copper	Fabricated metal	Petroleum	publishing	Computers
	products	refining	Instruments	
	Nonelectrical	Transportation	Communications	
	machinery	Glass	Utilities	
	Electrical	Lumber	Medical care	
	machinery	Motor vehicles	Optical &	
		Construction	photographic	
		Office supplies	equipment	
		Wholesale &		
		retail trade		

comparative orders of magnitude. What is readily seen are the significant differences likely to take place in the U.S. economic
order. Listed in the left-hand columns are less technologically
sophisticated, older manufacturing and service industries. In the
right columns are either the newer products or those which have
proven more versatile in use in industries which themselves are
growing rapidly (like lumber, extensively used in construction).

If one were to look inside the groupings noted in the table,
considerable differences in growth rates are evident. Transportation is a good example. In volume of freight and in passenger
miles transportation tends to expand at about the same rate as the
GNP. Since the economy will be nearly 50 percent bigger in ten
years than it now is—and four times bigger by the turn of the
century—that is a fact of considerable practical import. By the
mid-seventies it means there will be more than 150,000 aircraft
and nearly 120 million trucks and cars (up by about 20 million).
By 1973 there will be twice as much air traffic as there was as
recently as 1967 and by 1975 an average of more than a million
people a *day* will board airliners for intercity transportation. As
the nation urbanizes—with more than 75 percent of our ex-

panding population in cities by 1975 and 85 percent by 2000 —and as the number of cars grows still more, the nation's transportation system, as we now know it, would simply collapse. New means for the movement of goods and people in and between cities must inevitably be devised and new systems of power developed if the country's needs for mobility are to be met—and met in a way that is socially acceptable (*e.g.,* not air polluting). The implications are especially disturbing for the makers of autos, trucks, and other forms of transportation equipment, not to mention the oil companies, but their concern for the future is rightly shared by many businesses whose growth rates are decelerating and whose future is clouded with uncertainty.

Table 6 also helps cast considerable light on the conglomerate merger movement. In looking back at Chapter 3 one will recall that many older, well-established firms are actively diversifying their interests. The reasons now become clearer. First, they are anxious to get a foothold in the faster-growing industries, and the quickest way to do so is by acquiring a going concern. U.S. Steel's moves into aluminum, Ford's interest in electronics, General Tire's entry into community antenna television, GE's moves into education and real estate, railroad purchases of chemical manufacturers—all exemplify steps from the slower toward the faster end of the industrial growth chart. Second, for the older, well-entrenched corporation—laden with assets and often with cash —conglomerate mergers represent prudent steps to diversify and broaden their financial base, thus gaining some insulation from the winds of technological and economic change.

The Composition of the New Economy

The shifts that are taking place in industry will have regional reverberations as well. Firms will continue their relative withdrawal from the Northeast, Plains, and Great Lakes areas and concentrate more on their investment in factories and distribution facilities in the Southeast and in the West. Population will follow a similar trend and as this process of widespread geographic industrialization proceeds, the inequality in personal income that has long characterized the United States will be narrowed considerably. In 1950, for example, individuals living in the Southeastern states had incomes which averaged barely two thirds of those for the nation as a whole. By 1975 incomes in that region will approximate 80 percent of the national average. Similarly, the relatively wealthier areas will find their position eroded. Incomes in the Middle Atlantic states were nearly 20 percent higher than those for the entire country in 1950, but by 1975 they will be only about 10 percent higher.

As industrialization, population, and income tend to become more evenly distributed throughout the United States in future years, so too will economic activity come to be diffused somewhat more widely within urban regions. True, more people will live in cities—75 percent by 1975, 85 percent by 2000. But many of these "cities" will be comparatively small—sometimes the suburbs of major city hubs, often no more than the satellites of big cities that may be twenty-five to one hundred miles distant. By the end of the century a quarter of our total national population (about eighty million persons) will live in the Washington-Boston corridor complex. Another 15 percent will dwell along the California coast from San Diego to San Francisco. Twelve percent will reside in a central belt running eastward from Chicago to Detroit, Toledo, Cleveland, Pittsburgh, and Buffalo. Yet while more than half of the 320 million Americans will live in these densely populated corridor complexes, the fastest growing counties within each belt will be, not these containing the biggest cities, but rather those which presently are of moderate size, in the fifty thousand to three hundred thousand population category.

Bolstering this trend to diffusion of business activity is the flight of industry from central cities to suburban fringe locations which has been going on feverishly, for more than half of all the new jobs created in urban areas have been connected with suburban business establishments. Jobs created in central business districts have not been of the same type as those which have been exported. Unskilled, blue-collar employment has been suburbanized while professional and clerical jobs have been increased in number in the core city business districts. Slum dwellers have been seriously affected as a result, typically being compelled to follow employment out into the suburbs—something which is extremely difficult for the poor who are heavily dependent on public transportation. One further consequence of this economic diffusion is that traffic patterns within major metropolitan areas have become increasingly complex. In some cities nearly as many people now commute outward to jobs from the central city as travel inward from the suburbs; many others travel laterally, skirting the central city along belt roadways, like Route 128 in Boston or Interstate 495 in Washington, that ring the area. These patterns of movement have accentuated the demand for the kind of highly mobile transportation provided by the auto, truck, and bus.

The dynamic interplay of all these indicia of change will cause fundamental shifts in the relative importance of industries and their interrelationships, alter the patterns of employment, and accentuate the trends in the shift of industry between and within geographic regions. The result will bring about a veritable revolution in the American economy that will confront businessmen with harsh new realities to which accommodation will be as difficult as it is inevitable.

The radical transformation of the environment in which business must function is of major consequence in any assessment of the future of American industry. No less significant, however, are the new relationships taking shape between government and business.

PART IV

The New Partnership

CHAPTER 12

The Role of Antitrust

To understand the changing relationships between government and business, one must comprehend the place of antitrust in our scheme of political affairs. To identify its role, in theory and actuality, is indispensable to an appreciation of the new forms government's policeman role is assuming.

Ours is supposed to be a free enterprise economy, with prices and output determined by the uninhibited interplay of rival sellers fighting for the customer's dollar. Given a sufficiently large number of sellers and buyers, the arrangement works as well in practice as it does in the mathematics of classical economics. Spurred on by the lure of profits, business organizers assemble capital and labor into productive organizations that compete aggressively in price and, in the process, reduce costs to the minimum possible level. Not only does their rivalry automatically allocate scarce resources, but it keeps a stern check on the power of any particular buyer or seller. As such, the enterprise system is optimally efficient and for that reason alone is of incalculable value, as even the Russians and their fellow Marxists of East Europe are now openly admitting. But it provides a great bonus by distributing power widely, thus maintaining the conditions of democracy. Whatever we call it—free enterprise, a price or market system, or just plain old capitalism—it is a wonderful mechanism, satisfying our political desires as effectively as our economic.

Free enterprise economics, however, are extremely sensitive and a variety of disturbances can yield distasteful social and economic consequences. The most serious disease is "power"—the ability of a seller or a small group of sellers working together to influence what goes on in the market. Add this feature and the system breaks down, no longer a reliable allocator or a protector of democracy. Power can, of course, take many forms. It may wear the mantle of a monopolist—a single seller that dominates the market, controlling price and regulating output in the manner of a royal monarch. General Electric long has held such a position in the sale of light bulbs, GM in the production of diesel locomotives, Western Electric in telephone equipment. It also may consist of a group of supposedly competing sellers acting together in a conspiracy to rig the market for their own advantage. The big oil companies, steel manufacturers, electrical goods suppliers—and the small-corner gasoline service stations, druggists, and auto glass repairers—have been convicted, sometimes repeatedly, of having collusively fixed prices.

In essentially the same way large companies, few in number, big in relative size, have inhibited competition by tacitly coordinating their pricing decisions. Copper, auto, cigarette, and aluminum prices reveal precisely this sort of conscious interdependence, as was noted in Chapter 2. In each case the rival sellers have succeeded in gaining power over price and have freed themselves from the "tyranny" of the market. For them it has usually meant increased profits and shelter from the harshness of competition. For the public it has meant higher prices and, less obviously, a case in which their suppliers have acquired a sufficiently big share of the nation's wealth so that they can exert, in one way or another, a disproportionate influence over the political process.

Antitrust Laws: The Original Purpose

It is the threat posed by power to competition—to the free enterprise system itself—that is the declared enemy of our antitrust legislation. For three quarters of a century Federal antitrust laws have by their terms forbidden situations or behavior which is likely to interfere with the free functioning of competitive markets. First came the Sherman Act of 1890 (named after an Ohio Senator whose position as a committee chairman gave him strategic importance out of all proportion to his contribution to the measure) which forbids monopolization and diverse restraints of trade. Later, spurred on by Woodrow Wilson, Congress created the Federal Trade Commission and adopted the Clayton Act with the aim of nipping incipient anticompetitive behavior in the bud. Mergers which threaten to lessen competition were thus forbidden along with several types of marketing and distribution arrangements. The merger provision, however, was so easily circumvented that it was largely meaningless, and it was not until 1950, with the enactment of the Celler-Kefauver amendment, that mergers were effectively proscribed when they threaten to create monopoly or lessen competition.

Backed up by a torrent of litigation—something which has made antitrust one of the more active and lucrative fields of legal practice—the antitrust laws, in all their comparative verbal simplicity, have expressed a philosophy toward the economy that has looked askance at concentrations of private economic power. This notion, with its enormous ideological significance, has not always been clearly articulated nor fully appreciated by lawmakers, but it is at the core of antitrust. It assumes that the market will act as an efficient, impersonal allocator of our resources if it is protected by government from debilitating influences. The basic theory is that this limited exercise of governmental authority will preclude the necessity for the sort of detailed regulatory intervention, like price controls, that may be unavoidable if the economy comes under the control of a handful of giant enterprises. In short, antitrust aims at preserving the core of the free enterprise system—the market—by constraining anticompetitive forces and practices. In a very critical sense nothing could be more "conservative." The theory of antitrust is or at least should be evident, but the more practical matter concerns the way it has been translated into actual government policy.

Antitrust: Tough on Cartel Practices

Often businessmen speak of antitrust as if it were an omniscient intruding presence in their corporate lives, a kind of Big Brother peering over their executive shoulders. In a sense it is just that, but it is important to identify precisely the real role it plays in contemporary business behavior. In some respects antitrust is a vital shaping force, in others it is little more than a symbol—a "charade" as John Kenneth Galbraith called it in one of his typically colorful oversimplifications.

The law as it pertains to price-fixing, bid rigging, and market allocation illustrates where antitrust has worked quite well, forbidding kinds of behavior that are inimical to the sound operation of an economy and that stultify technological progress and inhibit innovation. It has been clear for at least sixty years that, if competing companies get together and agree on the prices they will charge or the bids they will submit, they are subject to criminal punishment. The clarity of the law on this point is not open to question, as the high officials of General Electric and other heavy electrical goods manufacturers found out in 1960 when their clandestine price-fixing activities were discovered. Some went to prison, all were fined heavily, and their employers were penalized and subjected to large multimillion-dollar lawsuits by customers they had overcharged. The nation's principal manufacturers of plumbing equipment and fixtures experienced the same fate in 1969 when found guilty of price-fixing.

American law as it pertains to price-fixing and other cartel-like behavior stands in sharp contrast to the situation which prevailed in Europe and Japan for many years. At least until the end of World War II, most foreign countries tolerated, and sometimes strongly encouraged or actually compelled, types of collusive behavior that has long been criminally banned in this country. Nazi Germany strengthened the great cartels—I. G. Farben, Krupp, and the rest—and in 1933 actually made membership in their ranks compulsory. The United States, with the exception of a fortunately brief experience under NRA in the early New Deal days, has been spared such a calamity. This is not to say its record is without some blemishes, for certain government policies run counter to the principle of competition. Government restrictions on the production of certain farm commodities (tobacco and sugar are two examples), state "fair trade" laws that constrain retail price competition in brand-name products, the inhibition of competition in transportation and other "regulated" industries, oil import quotas, and U.S. participation in various international price-fixing arrangements in transportation and agriculture are illustrative of policies that are anticompetitive in their purpose and effect. On the whole, however, the American position of hostility to cartel practices has been commendable. Insistence on competition—with all the rigor to which it subjects business—has maintained the pressure to cut costs, reduce prices, and introduce innovations. It has contributed greatly to the country's economic progress and, in the process, it has also kept competitors from forming the kind of tightly knit alliances that could threaten democracy itself.

Antitrust: Soft on Concentration

In sharp contrast with what historically must be viewed as a tough, unyielding, and reasonably effective anticartel policy, the ability of U.S. antitrust legislation to check the concentration of power in large monolithic corporate empires must be viewed as close to a failure. The situation, looking back over the last half century, was nearly as simple as this: if a group of half a dozen steel companies were to get together and fix prices, they would not only be hailed into court but would be fortunate to escape with fines and a badly tarnished public image. But if the same group were to merge, consolidating their affairs in a single corporation, they could successfully skirt the law, even though the result, in terms of their ability to control the price at which they could sell their product, would not differ significantly. Absurd, you say, but this is exactly the posture that was assumed by the law, as interpreted by the courts, until 1950.

Indeed in the 1920s several large companies were formed in exactly this way. Bethlehem Steel is one example, Republic Steel another. Looking even further back, most of the companies now ranked among the nation's biggest enterprises were created in exactly this manner, uniting anywhere from two to a dozen or more competing firms. The outstanding example, of course, is U.S. Steel, assembled in 1901 with a $1.4 billion capitalization by J. P. Morgan from the pieces of the Carnegie, National, and Federal steel companies. Though challenged in court in 1911, after nine years of litigation it emerged unscathed largely on the ground that it had gained control of "only" two thirds of the nation's steelmaking capacity.

The U.S. Steel colossus may be the best illustration of the comparative ease with which market-controlling enterprises could be consolidated, but it is merely one in a long list of corporate behemoths cemented together by financial wizards earlier in this century. Run your eye over this list of prominent companies formed under the same circumstances: General Electric, U.S. Rubber (now Uniroyal), Pittsburgh Plate Glass, National Biscuit, American Can, Eastman Kodak, International Harvester, du Pont, and International Nickel. Similarly, in the twenties a merger movement of great sweep took place, giving birth to Bethlehem and Republic Steel, noted earlier, and to Allied Chemical, General Foods, and National Dairy Products. While antitrust prosecution was moderately successful in assaulting a few big firms— like John D. Rockefeller's Standard Oil and James B. Duke's American Tobacco—the effect was to do little more than divide colossi into giants. American Tobacco, for example, was, like Gaul, divided into three independent firms which now share dominance of the cigarette industry.

At the time, therefore, when it counted most, American antitrust policy—as incorporated in Federal legislation, as enforced, and as interpreted by the courts—was unable to check the formation through merger of giant firms that have, with rare exception, maintained a preeminent position in the economy. There has, however, been a significant change in the pattern òf industrial concentration since the great trust-breeding days of the early 1900s. Then, as typified by U.S. Steel or Standard Oil, the quest was to gain absolute market dominance by a single firm. In more recent years these imperial objectives have been curtailed. But now the typical American industry is dominated not by a single producer but by a small group of companies. Together they may account for 80 percent or more of total output, but individually their shares may range from 15 to no more than perhaps 40 or 50 percent. Even General Motors, the giant among giants and a world superstate unto itself, accounts for barely half of our new auto sales. The picture in autos—or aluminum, copper, chemicals, cigarettes, petroleum, electrical equipment, and aircraft—is one, not of monopoly, but of oligopoly. Here power is shared and without the necessity of overt collusion, price identity is the general rule and competition takes the form of efforts to differentiate physically indistinguishable products through design and especially through advertising. Under the very nose of antitrust, U.S. industry has been thoroughly oligopolized and the share of productive wealth held by a relatively very few corporations, as noted in Chapter 2, has continued to increase.

Antitrust and Mergers

In pointing out the failure of antitrust to inhibit significantly the concentration of American industry, sight must not be lost of the post-1950 consequences of the antimerger law enacted that year by Congress. It put some teeth in what had been a paper tiger for the preceding forty years. While enforcement of the 1950 legislation has often been timid and desultory in Democratic as well as in Republican administrations, major cases have been initiated and important mergers have been halted. A good example was the 1953 effort by Bethlehem Steel, the nation's number two producer, to merge with Youngstown Sheet and Tube, the number five company. Carefully developed Justice Department evidence demonstrated that the two companies competed in the sale of many steel products. Federal Judge Edward Weinfeld concluded, in a landmark ruling, that the merger would lessen competition and forbade its consummation. If the same law and interpretation had prevailed fifty years before, the face of the U.S. industrial road map would be radically different from what it is.

What Judge Weinfeld declared in 1953 was reaffirmed in later decisions by the Supreme Court. Speaking for the Court in 1966 Justice Hugo Black put the tribunal's full weight behind Congress' presumed desire to arrest the trend to "the concentration of economic power in the hands of a few." That year the Court banned a merger between two Los Angeles supermarket chains, Von's and Shopping Bag, which between them accounted for less than 8 percent of the city's retail grocery sales.

The Von's case vividly demonstrated the Supreme Court's marked willingness, indeed eagerness, to halt virtually all mergers between competing sellers. But it also spotlights two of the great anomalies of antitrust—anomalies that point up its limited practical relevance to our present-day economy. The first concerns conglomerate mergers. Since 1960 more than 80 percent of all the major mergers that have taken place have been of the conglomerate variety, yet this category of mergers has received strikingly little, only spasmodic attention from the antitrust enforcement agencies. Out of over a hundred cases brought by the government to restrain mergers in this period, only about a dozen involved anything that even vaguely resembles a conglomerate acquisition. Why is this? The basic reason is that those who were responsible for antitrust enforcement, like Donald F. Turner, who was Assistant Attorney General in charge of the Justice Department's Antitrust Division during the Johnson Administration and part of the Kennedy Administration, believed that the antitrust laws now in force do not reach most conglomerate mergers. They argued that those statutes prohibit only mergers which lessen competition and that as a result the consolidation of firms which neither compete nor are linked together in a supplier-customer relationship are generally beyond the reach of present law.

With the coming of the Nixon Administration, however, there were developments pointing to a markedly more expansive interpretation of the law as it applies to mergers. The new Assistant Attorney General for Antitrust, Richard W. McLaren, indicated that he felt the law was less clear than his predecessors in office had believed. While clarifying legislation might be desirable, he said, "the matter (of conglomerate mergers) is too pressing to wait." Shortly after taking office in 1969 he promised to bring cases challenging "purer types of conglomerate mergers than have been dealt with" so far. It did not take long for him to show what he had in mind. In April he filed a suit to block consummation of the LTV-Jones & Laughlin merger. Later similar action was taken to undo ITT's 1968 merger with the Canteen Corporation. The fate of these lawsuits, novel as they are, is far from clear. The LTV-Jones & Laughlin action, in particular, involves previously untested legal theories and may take years to wind its way through the courts. Meanwhile, of course, hundreds of big conglomerate mergers will be completed. The McLaren interpretation, hotly disputed by many lawyers, is unlikely, therefore, to slow significantly the present merger movement. Even where it is successful in blocking those conglomerate mergers that properly warrant legal attack, this new enforcement effort lacks a clear rationale and may lead to the suppression of mergers that have no adverse effect on competition and that threaten no significant increase in concentration in oligopolistic industries. Its real impact will be to shield large, well-entrenched companies, like Jones & Laughlin and B. F. Goodrich, from takeover by conglomerate outsiders like LTV and Northwest Industries.

The second anomaly stems from the fact that while the antitrust laws can presently be successfully used to prosecute price-fixing and block those few mergers between competitors that still take place, they are totally incapable of reducing the power of corporations whose size and market position are already established, reflecting consolidations or sheer internal growth, or both, that may have taken place over a span of forty or more years. Here is the crux of the problem of industrial concentration in America and here antitrust is impotent, a condition caused largely by political indifference and a desire for peaceful accommodation in the status quo.

Not only is the law inadequate to the challenge, but the firms themselves have, over the years, put down so many roots—gained such a large constituency—that a basic attack on their legitimacy is fraught with such potentially serious social and political consequences as to be thinkable to few but the purest antitrust ideologues. Consider any of a number of corporations. General Motors is one. With 735,000 employees, 1.3 million shareholders, thousands of suppliers, and plants in nearly every state (not to mention twenty-four foreign countries), thoughts of its dismemberment can hardly be taken seriously. Some people, of course, would think such action economically unwise anyway, but the fact that ways could be devised to "slim down" GM by compelling the divestiture of parts of its empire is unimportant because no Administration in the foreseeable future is likely to be willing to risk the political disturbance it would create. Like GM, a number of other companies have assumed such size and status that their existence must simply be accepted as a fact of our economic life and their legitimacy conceded. The best evidence of this is found in the absence of any fundamental "break-'em-up" challenge to any major corporation in the last two decades. For Kennedy and Johnson no less than Eisenhower and Truman, the corporate behemoths that roam American industry were too big, too dangerous prey.

Further evidence of this is found in the Johnson Administration's reaction to the report of a task force appointed by the President in December of 1967 to review government antitrust policy. Composed of a dozen academic economists, law school professors, and practicing lawyers, the task force submitted a secret report in July of 1968 to the White House. It recommended a wide-ranging antitrust program, bolstered by new legislation, to reduce levels of concentration in oligopolistic industries by dismembering such corporations as GM, IBM, and U.S. Steel. The proposals were regarded as so politically explosive that the report was not only suppressed but its existence was not even officially acknowledged. Of course, no action was taken to implement the program called for in the task force report.

When the report prepared by President Johnson's task force was finally made public, the Nixon Administration, interestingly, was reviewing, in rather desultory fashion, a report submitted by *its own* clandestine antitrust task force. Not only had the creation of this panel never been publicly announced, but the new Administration steadfastly refused officially even to admit its existence. Nonetheless, after months of secretiveness a copy of its extensive report was at last procured by outsiders and promptly inserted in the *Congressional Record*. The reasons for the report's suppression soon became evident for the committee, headed by economist George J. Stigler, made several policy pronouncements that were inferentially critical of the Nixon Administration's antitrust policies. The task force urged a reordering of antitrust priorities and recommended, among other things, "a policy of strict and unremitting scrutiny of the highly oligopolistic industries." Finding such advice both embarrassing and unpalatable, the White House elected to treat the task force report as confidential, just as the preceding Administration had done in the case of its antitrust task force. In doing so, both the Democratic and Republican administrations provided explicit evidence of their distaste for proposals that might lead to the substantial deconcentration of American industry.

The de facto irrelevance of antitrust to existing concentrations of power in the U.S. industry is reflected both in the lack of direct challenge to established corporate positions and also in the lack of concern displayed by members of Congress and the public generally in antitrust issues. At the turn of the century the trusts were a favorite whipping boy for cartoonists, editorialists, and politicians alike. In 1914 Woodrow Wilson could speak out sternly "against monopoly, against control, against the concentration of power in our economic development, against all those things that interfere with absolutely free enterprise."

That spirit has long since disappeared. Hardly a member of House or Senate can today be found who is seriously concerned on more than a fleeting basis with issues of antitrust. Such support as does exist is tinged with cynicism and an aura of futility. One United States Senator, for example, widely and accurately regarded as a champion of antitrust and the consumer, has quietly sponsored a bill that would allow farmers to form cartels and rig the prices of the products they sell to the housewife. When asked why he could support a measure that so squarely contradicts the competitive ideal he explained that it was seemingly the only way, "as things stand," to give the farmers comparable power to that possessed by the big food wholesalers and processors who buy most of our agricultural output. An honest, practical answer—and it tells a great deal about the actual role antitrust now plays in the American economy.

The New Styles of Business Regulation

With the decline of antitrust, emphasis in government policy is shifting from the curtailment or elimination of concentrated private economic power to the regulation of its possible abuse. In a way, of course, this represents only a modest deviation from the substance of past antitrust enforcement. Prosecution of price-fixing, bid rigging, and similar practices obviously is aimed at the punishment and suppression of obnoxious business behavior. To a great extent the main thrust of antitrust has been directed *against* socially and economically unacceptable conduct rather than *in favor of* the preservation of competitive markets. It has, put differently, been essentially negative rather than affirmative in its policy orientation. This may help explain why the law has viewed cartel-like behavior so harshly and acquiesced, with hardly an audible murmur of protest, in trends toward oligopoly and rising concentration in industry. The latter, of course, present no less a challenge to competition—the keystone of a free enterprise system—but they are less visible and considerably more subtle in their impact on the public. Theoretically this may be a difference difficult to accept, but to the legislator and the average citizen it is a perfectly intelligible and understandable distinction. Indeed, much of the history of antitrust in the United States can be told in terms no grander than these.

The present stress toward business simply on the constraint of abusive conduct is likely to guide the course of government business policy well into the future. The basic underlying reason is that the public and government officials, elected and otherwise, now accept the inevitability of bigness and concentration in U.S. business. It is here—and here to stay—but this, it is widely and loosely appreciated, does not mean it should be left completely free. Reflecting this view, Congress has enacted several pieces of legislation in recent years that subject business to some form of government regulation. Evidence of the safety and effectiveness of drugs must now be submitted for review. Automobiles and auto tires must conform to equipment and related safety standards designed to reduce the toll of deaths and serious injuries in motor vehicle accidents. A truth in packaging law requires sellers of consumer goods to comply with established packaging standards that are calculated to provide the consumer with information about product quality and quantity. Nineteen sixty-eight Federal legislation compels retailers to disclose the "true" rate of interest charged on credit transactions. Cigarette packages must carry a label proclaiming that "smoking may be hazardous to your health." An updated meat-inspection law subjects a much larger percentage of meat products to health examination.

This list of examples could be extended, but the crucial point to note is that while there is a growing amount of legislation designed to protect the public from the effects of detrimental business conduct, there has not been any challenge to the dominant market position held by the firms subject to regulation. General Motors now must install seat belts and other safety equipment in its cars and General Foods must disclose more information on its packages for the elucidation of housewives, but their dominant place in industry is implicitly accepted, beyond serious thought of challenge.

Acceptance of powerful, diversified corporations as controlling, and certainly highly influential, factors in virtually every key industry greatly constrains the role of antitrust but it does not eliminate the problem of conforming their selling behavior to the desire for reasonable price stability. The problem of keeping private pricing power in tune with this central objective of economic policy is one which the White House and Congress have only dimly and sporadically recognized. In the past we may have been able to avoid the issue, for competitive markets automatically police prices and avoid the need for direct government intervention. But where, as in the modern U.S. economy, most markets are no longer competitive and instead are controlled by oligopolists, the government must either take a hand in keeping prices in check or relinquish a sizable share of its authority to private enterprises. The choice is clear and unavoidable but it has been faced ambivalently and uncertainly. Presidents, like Senators and Representatives, have hesitated to meet the issue head-on, preferring to wait for particularly grievous instances of abuse of private pricing power.

John F. Kennedy's historic confrontation with the steel industry in 1962 shows the difficulty we have had in striking a balance between the quest of big business for higher profits and the public interest in reasonable prices. Rebelling against a proposed $6 a ton steel price hike, the President hastily mobilized the disparate forces of the Federal Government and carried out a momentarily successful counterattack that rolled back the price increase. In similar but less publicized encounters Lyndon Johnson "persuaded" the steel industry to rescind or modify price increases in 1965 and 1967; he also assailed price increases in the molybdenum, aluminum, auto, and copper industries.

There are several anomalies in the Kennedy-Johnson efforts at informal price control. First, they were only temporary scattered victories and provide no guidance, let alone a systematic means of price review. JFK won his bout with steel in 1962, but within a year the industry boosted prices on 75 percent of its products—with no White House opposition. Lyndon Johnson did little better. While Bethlehem withdrew a $5 a ton increase in 1965, in the face of his criticism, a $2.75 a ton increase posted only a few months later by U.S. Steel was termed "inconsequential" by the Administration.

Second, White House efforts to keep a check on prices have almost necessarily been uneven in coverage. Metals prices have been constantly in the spotlight, but other industries—construction, chemicals, electrical equipment—have avoided attention as have industries whose markets are regional in scope. Third, it has been difficult, and perhaps unfair, to criticize business for raising prices without also subjecting labor unions to similar pressure to keep wage demands in line with productivity gains. Contract settlements well above overall gains in productivity understandably generate a demand by management for an offsetting price increase.

Lastly, and perhaps most important, Presidential efforts to inhibit the exercise of private pricing power which is economically undesirable have been guided by few discernible standards. Not only have they been random and ad hoc, but they are unrelated to any identifiable set of rules. Promulgation of wage-price guidelines by the President's Council of Economic Advisers in 1966 come about as close to the articulation of standards as we have had, but their generality (seeking closer conformance between prices and wages and national productivity gains) and limited application in particular cases where Presidents opposed price increases fail to constitute a body of principles against which participants in the private sector can readily measure their conduct and by which government officials can consistently evaluate industrial-labor union price and wage performance. For all their deficiencies, however the wage-price guidelines provided some frame of reference and may, in fact, have helped keep prices relatively stable in spite of declining rates of unemployment and rapid economic growth. Regrettably, since 1967, the Annual Reports of the Council of Economic Advisers have contained little more than a vague plea for voluntary "restraint" by companies and unions in making their price-wage decisions. This, as is rather obvious, is no policy at all. And the Nixon Administration has made clear that it does not intend to exert any effort at all to constrain inflationary price or wage increases. For the time being—and that may be quite a while—we have no orderly means for checking powerful private elements in the economy and keeping their actions in harmony with larger economic objectives.

Measures have been proposed for the regular review of prices and wages. Some involve detailed regulation, in the mold of utility rates, others call for public hearings following notification of a price increase. Bills to establish these techniques have been introduced in the Congress, but the fact that none has come under serious consideration in several years suggests that there is little interest in this approach to the pricing problem. It savors too much of the days of OPA and runs counter to a basic tenet of American economic mythology that the government should not "interfere" in business decisions.

Concentrated Private Economic Power: The Public Challenge

In spite of the widespread antipathy to overt government economic regulation, many people nonetheless harbor a latent suspicion that our corporations and labor unions possess too much power for the public good. This fear of concentrated private economic power could be mobilized, given the right conditions. Businessmen are thus in a position where, by carelessly exercising the considerable power they possess, public price controls could be made politically acceptable, perhaps mandatory. The big modern corporation has considerable discretion in its pricing and marketing decisions. It can price in a way that yields very high profits—much higher than those which could be obtained under competition. Still, though, there are limits to its discretion beyond which the public will rebel. The pharmaceutical companies have begun to find this out by charging prices so high—and generating such enormous profits—that there are very real prospects of some form of indirect drug price regulation. Most companies, however, have not pushed their power this far and thus are likely to be assured continued freedom to price their wares much as they choose and in a manner that produces high profits.

For the near future the public may not like the effects of concentrated private power, but there is little it seems able to do about it, given the existing political and economic climate. Power has gravitated to the American corporate giants. They exercise it, with some restraint, but realize that their future lies in forming a partnership with a government which need not be greatly feared as a regulatory policeman.

CHAPTER 13

The Evolving Coalition

All of the ancient concepts of the relationship between government and business are being transformed. The crux of this revolution is that the old conflict is coming to an end and a new partnership is emerging. Highly pragmatic rather than the preconceived product of either government or business ideology, this new coalescence of power reflects many factors, not the least of which is the direct and expanding involvement of business in what traditionally have been regarded as government pursuits.

The new partners first joined in taking on the problems of defense, then space exploration. Now they are broadening their scope of attention and together are dealing with diverse civilian problems—in education, job training, housing, city renewal, and a host of others in a list that lengthens almost daily. Yet for all the intimacy of this newfound friendship, there are no firm criteria by which to assess it or to insure that it will lead necessarily to public advantage. By bringing together private economic power with political power, two sources of strength that have heretofore been regarded as checks on one another, the new partnership is challenging a basic tenet of American political life and raising perplexing questions for which we have no good answers.

The new partnership necessitates a thorough reexamination of our established economic and political doctrine. Up to now we have lived in a simpler world—where government could be thought of as a kind of economic policeman, enforcing rules laid down by legislators to keep the private sector operating in a manner that would promote the general welfare. The business of business was thought to be business, the business of government was government. But now the two are thoroughly entangled, in all sorts of ways and for all sorts of reasons. Clearly this undertaking represents a major challenge to the American society, as basic and as complex as any we have ever faced as a people. It may compel changes in our public institutions, for it pointedly draws into question the adequacy of our existing political system to deal with the manifestations of change. The new partnership quite literally can remold the society.

What has brought us to this vital juncture in business-government relationships? There is no simple answer, for what is involved is a variety of forces which have in quite subtle ways made allies —albeit cautious ones—out of what had once been foes. For one thing, the expansion of government spending (state and local as well as Federal) that has taken place in the last thirty years has made government a big customer of business, and big buyers always exert some significant degree of influence over a supplier. But the character of the government policies is even more important. For much of what the government purchases—in defense, of course, but for space exploration, education, highway construction, medical institutions—it is a monopsonist, buying most or all of the particular product in question. Only the Federal Government acquires missiles, nuclear submarines, and lunar landing capsules.

Today the executives of large enterprises are not only welcome at the White House but are deeply involved on a continuing though usually informal basis in the highest decision-making levels of the Executive Branch. Their opinions are solicited, their ideas invited, and their participation anticipated almost as a matter of course in a great realm of issues. The two-way exchange of senior personnel between government and business has vastly improved communication between the two sectors and implicitly reflects a new appreciation of the commonness of the problems confronting executives in managing big organizations, whether they happen to bear a "public" or "private" label. This new interdependence is still in a formative state, but it was encouraged to such a degree by Lyndon B. Johnson and accepted so heartily by so many businessmen that it appears almost certain to be a permanent feature of the American way for years to come.

It is also important to realize the new signs of interest in mobilizing the talents and resources of the private sector for an assault on our accumulated social disorders. For years it was accepted by most people that problems like job training, civil rights, lower income housing, city rejuvenation, education, and water pollution were properly the principal concern of "government," not business. By and large, Democrats thought this desirable, while Republicans questioned the need for government to "waste" any significant amount of tax funds in dealing with such matters. Now not only is it widely agreed that these problems must be confronted massively, and urgently, but there is a widespread belief that government should actively and deeply involve business in their resolution. For its part, business has more than responded to the overture; it is aggressively seeking an even greater role in dealing with our great social challenges.

While the new interdependence reflects the ever increasing areas of interest to U.S. business and government, an important development in itself, it also alters the character and significance of government's classic regulatory role. By no means, though, does it mark an end to the claims of many company officials that government is "interfering" in their firm's affairs. Such beliefs are likely never to end, for most businessmen seem compelled to express such opinions about government as if to establish their corporate manhood. It is the reality, not the words, however, which should concern us. But even the words tell us quite a bit about the changing attitudes of private executives. Thus the same George Champion, chairman of the Chase Manhattan Bank, who in 1965 assailed "the new trend toward government-by-guideline as one of the most insidious and dangerous on the national scene today," could in 1967 speak expansively of the glories of what he termed the "sociocommercial enterprise." This, he said, could be private business's way of solving problems of education, job training, and air-water pollution and would be "the first phase of development of an exciting and challenging new concept of the relationship between the public and private sectors of the American economy."

By and large today's business leaders accept government's legitimacy (much as they do that of the labor union, in contrast to their predecessors of the 1930s or even those of Taft-Hartley vintage) and concede that its policies and actions are an unavoidable part of their daily affairs. What they are now coming to is that by being *active* participants in public affairs they can enlarge their own sales and profits at the same time they expand their effective range of influence. *Fortune* admonishes that business, "unable to escape the growing influence of government, should in turn strive to expand *its* influence over government." What is evident, therefore, is a new aggressiveness in which business, now an accepted partner, aims to become much more than a silent associate.

This basic shift in attitude and accompanying formation of the new partnership tear at the very roots of our established political culture. This is especially so when there is underway simultaneously a pronounced trend to industrial-financing concentration and diversification of the kind noted in Chapters 2–4. "From this country's beginning," said Justice Hugo Black in a 1966 Supreme Court opinion, "there has been an abiding and widespread fear of the evils which flow from the concentration of economic power in the hands of a few." Indeed there has, but that attitude conflicts squarely with what is actually going on in the contemporary U.S. economy. The new partnership is emerging at the same time that a vast conglomerate merger movement concentrates a larger portion of our national wealth in the hands of a smaller group of corporations. The two forces accentuate each other, producing a unique brand of corporate state in which the government and private sectors threaten to coalesce in a way that could be antithetical to democracy itself. Countervailing forces—in industry, government, and even in organized labor—are meshing in power alliances that can signify the formation of an elitist group with the power to determine the course it wishes to follow quite independent of the customary processes of popular democratic participation.

Up to now American political pragmatism has maintained a wide dispersion of power among many contesting groups and institutions. Some efforts, admittedly rather timid, have been made through law to check the concentration of power; certainly this has been one of the declared objectives of antitrust. The new partnership runs counter to these postulates because it accepts, indeed encourages, the concentration of power in industry, government, and labor and aims to harness and synthesize their potential. It also changes the way government deals with the private sector, for, recognizing that private power can sometimes be abused, it substitutes informal methods of persuasion for a rule of law in the protection of the public interest.

The demise of government's role as a regulator of business and its tacit acceptance of the inevitability of big business reflect many factors (some of which were examined in the preceding chapter), but none is more important than the evolution of the new partnership. Today most executives of major corporations and most government officials have come to view themselves as allies who can accomplish much more by working together in common cause than by prolonging their age-old cold war. Their coalition assumes many distinctive forms and is bound together by relationships that range from shared undertakings (as in the development of defense systems and space vehicles and the management of job training centers) to exchanges of high-level personnel and financial contributions in support of Presidential and Congressional candidates. These bonds are increasing in number and tautness, promising to forge a permanent association of the public and private sectors that leaves only limited room for the exercise of government's historic role as policemen. The dynamics of this revolution warrant close review because of their basic political and economic consequences as well as their practical effects on business.

What are the forces that have led to the new partnership? For one thing—and it pervades most of the other answers—business has learned that government policy, even when formulated by a Democratic Administration, can insure a booming economy, with all that it means for sales, profits, and expanded opportunities. Following an eight-year period of Republican fiscal conservatism, which coincided with slow growth, stagnant profits, and rising unemployment, the assumption of power by the Democrats in 1961 signaled a sharp upturn in the economy. Between 1953 and 1960 the U.S. economy expanded at an annual rate less than half that experienced in the sixties under Kennedy and Johnson. After-tax corporate profits followed this sharp upward course. From 1953 to 1960 annual after-tax corporate profits rose from $20 to $27 billion, but in the next eight years they expanded to a yearly level of more than $50 billion. No practical businessman can ignore the results. A consciously expansionary government fiscal-monetary policy, with all it implies in the way of a bigger role for government, can yield a booming economy that is free from the sharp ups and downs that once characterized our economic experience.

By being congenial business has found that even Democratic rule can be financially rewarding. The Kennedy Administration authorized faster write-offs of capital equipment and provided a sizable tax credit to encourage investment, thus boosting company profits. Too, larger government spending—the supposed bête noire of "sound" economic thinkers—has meant billions of dollars' worth of sales for U.S. companies. Federal purchases of goods and services now are close to $100 billion, up $50 billion in a decade. State and local expenditures, buoyed up by Federal grants, have tripled in a dozen years. What governments spend on things they buy from business is much bigger than all of what consumers spend for durable goods and equals outlays for nondurable goods.

Many shadings and qualifications obviously could be introduced in considering each of these points, but the important meaning is that government is no longer viewed by business as a predominantly negative force. The modern view accurately sees government as a force for economic growth and as a customer with a near-insatiable appetite. Moreover, company policy makers see that through cooperation with government great new opportunities in serving public wants can be opened up.

The Military-Space-Research Complex

For firms in many industries government's multibillion-dollar expenditures for defense, space exploration, nuclear development, and other purposes constitute the great bulk of their sales. Currently the Defense Department is spending more than $30 billion a year for the procurement of goods and research (total Federal expenditures for national defense reached $80 billion in 1969, up because of Vietnam, from $50 billion in 1965). The National Aeronautics & Space Administration has spent nearly $30 billion in its space exploration and most of the money has gone to manufacturers like North American Aviation, Boeing, Chrysler and McDonnell Douglas. Indeed, more than half of NASA's "own" workers are supplied under contract by private firms. In another field, atomic energy, the Atomic Energy Commission funds nearly $2 billion a year in nuclear research, with much of the work done by General Electric and Westinghouse, the world's leading suppliers of nuclear reactors. Key AEC installations, like the Sandia Laboratory in New Mexico and the Oak Ridge Laboratory in Tennessee, are managed, for substantial fees, by Union Carbide, Westinghouse, and other corporations.

To gauge how crucial Federal funds are to the survival of companies in the defense-space industries, consider the experience of the aircraft companies. In the seven years from 1961 through 1967 Lockheed was awarded nearly $11 billion in defense contracts, equal to 88 percent of its total sales. General Dynamics has $9 billion in contracts making up two thirds of its gross receipts. For McDonnell Douglas ($8 billion from 1961 to 1967, 75 percent of its sales), Boeing ($7 billion and over half its revenue), Grumman (a major Navy supplier, with $2.5 billion, or 67 percent), and Ling-Temco-Vought (almost $8 billion, or 70 percent of its total sales) the story is essentially the same. For these companies, and for many others in fields like communications and electrical equipment, chemicals (all of Thiokol's sales are to the government), and ship construction, the Federal defense-space agencies are not just customers—they are the lifeline and guarantor of continued corporate existence.

Government's dominant position as buyer is accentuated in other ways. Military contracting practice, for example, has the effect of supplying defense firms with over half their fixed capital and with as much as 90 percent of their working capital. Right now, according to the General Accounting Office, there is more than $11 billion of Defense Department-owned buildings, machine tools, dies, electronic gear, test devices, and other equipment in contractors' possession, representing a valuable interest-free loan. As a result big defense firms are highly levered, in the financial sense, and typically earn bigger returns on their net investment than other manufacturers. In a recent three-year period the profits of a group of major defense-oriented corporations yielded a rate of return on net worth 75 percent higher than for a group of big civilian industrial firms. Viewing the matter in a larger perspective, and considering their close interdependence, it is quite literally impossible to separate the government as buyer from the big defense suppliers. They have been blended in a way that defies traditional concepts of public-private categorization. One writer has called it "an institutional monstrosity—a bastard form of socialism crossbred with a bastard form of capitalism."

The place of "private" firms in the performance of defense-space-nuclear missions can reach much beyond production or the performance of tasks defined by the government. Often they are called upon to assume responsibility for handling an entire problem—from initial assessment to final resolution. In 1954, for example, the United States ascertained that Russia had secretly begun intensive work on the development of intercontinental ballistic missiles and had made considerable progress, thus prospectively threatening American security. Confronted with this challenge, and having made the decision that we, too, should undertake a crash ICBM program, one might think that the Pentagon itself would have determined the kind and character of missiles it needed and hired private firms merely to produce the hardware. That is pretty much the way things were done in World War II when even the atomic bomb was perfected by persons serving on government payrolls. But things have changed.

Faced with the missile challenge the Air Force placed full responsibility for overall systems design and technical direction in an outside firm that directed and coordinated the work of a number of associate contractors. For this job Space Technology Laboratories, then a division of the Ramo-Wooldridge Corporation, was chosen. By deciding to act this way, the Air Force had effectively delegated the entire job of developing an ICBM system to STL, which literally became a staff arm of the Defense Department. It exercised such extensive control over a family of contractors that for all practical purposes it, not the government, was the manager of the entire Air Force ballistic missile program in its most crucial period.

The weapons-system concept, now extended to a number of other major defense undertakings, accentuates the quasi nationalization of defense procurement. It wraps a company in both public and private robes, rendering its status ambivalent and compelling a fundamental reappraisal of its means and ends. Guided, not by a quest for profit, for it is compensated by a fixed fee, a corporate systems manager is expected to act in much the same manner as would the government if it possessed the same technical skill. Yet its executives and specialists are not chosen in the same way as government officials and are not directly accountable to the public. This difference makes it as difficult to evaluate a system manager's performance as it is for the firm's managers to perceive clearly the dimensions of their own newly acquired social role. The significance and subtlety of this point becomes all the greater as industrial firms plunge into civilian areas like education and urban renewal.

Whether it be supervising large defense-space programs, running government research centers, or "thinking" for a Federal agency, industry has developed extensive ties with the Federal establishment. Dwight Eisenhower thought them sufficiently important, and disturbing, to warn, in his 1961 farewell address, of

> this conjunction of an immense military establishment and a large arms industry. . . . The total influence—economic, political, even spiritual—is felt in every city, every state house, every office of the Federal Government. . . . The potential for the disastrous rise of misplaced power exists and will persist. We must never let the weight of this combination endanger our liberties or democratic processes.

However acute the warning may have been (it was reportedly written by Malcolm C. Moos, now President of the University of Minnesota), it has had no discernible effect on the contours of political comment or action. If anything, the government-industry complex has become larger, more intertwined, and more potent. To be accurate we would now have to speak of the military-industrial-*research* complex. When President Eisenhower issued his cautionary remarks in January 1961 the Federal Government was spending about $9 billion a year for research and development. Today it is spending twice as much, with the bulk of the funds—about 60 percent—being paid to private industry for the performance of specified research assignments. An additional $2 billion a year is going to universities for similar purposes, especially basic research in medicine. Federal agencies provide three fourths of the support for research conducted on the nation's college campuses and more than half the funds used by companies in conducting research. All things considered, Federally supported scientific research has probably played as important a role in establishing ties between Washington and private industry, universities, and nonprofit organizations as defense and space procurement.

More Ties That Bind

Already underway, with more soon to follow, are a number of new government-supported programs which will still more deeply involve the U.S. business community. These emerging civilian programs will be discussed more in the next chapter, but they call for far more active corporate participation in their actual development at the same time they open up many billions of dollars in sales potential. A quick review shows why.

The physical renewal of our cities, on a scale commensurate with the scope of the problem (and the years of neglect), carries a price tag that can conservatively be put at $20 billion a year. The alleviation of air and water pollution is estimated to call for expenditures of $5 billion a year for at least fifteen years. Construction of new high-speed mass transit systems at an average cost of over $1 billion per installation could require $20 billion over the next ten years (Baltimore, Atlanta, Seattle, Washington, and Los Angeles have completed plans for such systems, and San Francisco has begun construction). Development of airports to serve air passenger traffic that is likely to grow at a rate of 15 percent a year (doubling, therefore, about every five years) will demand a minimum investment of $5 billion by 1975. Airways expenditures to control aircraft movement in the skies will be of like size. Better medical care, involving the creation of hundreds of neighborhood health centers and the construction of many new, highly automated hospitals, as well as expanded educational opportunities and job training, among other social needs, will necessitate still more billions in expenditures. All of this opens up vast new markets and constitutes, in the words of Chase Manhattan Bank chairman George Champion, "one of the great new economic frontiers of the future."

The flow of Federal funds which underlies existing and pending programs in the defense, space, nuclear, research, and civilian areas represents strong ties between government and business, but as always, the strongest bonds are formed by personal contacts between the two sectors. In this respect the most extensive interconnections are in defense. In numerous ways the big defense suppliers have developed close personal links to the civilian-military complex that has its center in the Pentagon.

Over the years contractors have hired ex-military officers for jobs ranging from president on down with a principal objective being to "maintain contact" with the services and with their Congressional patrons on Capitol Hill. Responding to an inquiry from

Senator William Proxmire, the Pentagon disclosed that as of 1969 there were some 2,072 retired military officers of the rank of colonel or Navy captain or above on the payrolls of the 100 biggest defense contractors (they do about two thirds of all military contract awards, equal to more than $30 billion in fiscal 1969). Lockheed, a highly ranked contractor, alone employed 210. Boeing, McDonnell Douglas, General Dynamics, and North American Rockwell each employed more than a hundred. Retired admirals and generals often head major defense firms, seeking contracts from their fellow West Point and Annapolis alumni who are still on active duty. The list is by no means limited to those who have served in uniform with the armed services. Former Army Secretary Frank Pace was at the helm of General Dynamics when it was the number one defense contractor. An ex-Navy Secretary, Dan Kimball, is president of Aerojet-General, which received defense orders worth $2.3 billion between 1961 and 1967. Retired Admiral William F. Raborn, who directed the CIA from 1965 to 1966, is also a high official of Aerojet-General. And when the Johnson Administration folded its tent in 1969, two key civilian Defense Department aides who had been intimately concerned with systems planning and procurement policy left to join Litton Industries, which had received nearly a half billion dollars in military contracts in 1968.

By no means, though, is this a one-way exchange of personnel. The contractors also provide key officials for government agencies. Just one example is John H. Rubel who left a post in 1961 with Hughes Aircraft to become deputy director of Research and Engineering in the Defense Department. Later, in 1963, he resigned and became a vice president of Litton Industries. Many of the Cabinet and sub-Cabinet officials named by President Nixon came direct from industry, often with the clear understanding that they would return to their former employer with bonuses intact. One such executive, Jerome Rosow, departed Standard Oil of New Jersey to become an Assistant Secretary of Labor, but he retained his right to collect Standard Oil bonuses and other fringe benefits and was reportedly given a special $50,000 bonus by the company to assist him in meeting expenses while with the government.

It would not be accurate to think that government-business exchanges of policy-making officers is confined to the defense sector. In education, for instance, Francis Keppel resigned as U.S. Commissioner of Education to become president of General Learning Corporation, a General Electric-Time, Inc. venture in learning systems. The opportunity was particularly attractive because the Congress had just provided for a major expansion in educational research which opened up $150 million a year in contracts for private firms.

Keppel was not the only high government official to join up with industrial firms seeking a bigger role in education. One of his top aides, John Naisbitt, became assistant to the president of Science Research Associates, a publishing and curriculum-producing firm affiliated with IBM. Robert N. Hills, who had worked for then-Assistant HEW Secretary Wilbur Cohen, took a post as director of government programs for Basic Systems, Inc., a Xerox subsidiary. A former HEW Deputy Assistant Secretary for Education, Edward L. Katzenbach, Jr., joined up with Raytheon to manage its newly formed education division. The flow of personnel has not been completely one way, however. R. Louis Bright moved from director of instructional technology at Westinghouse to head the U.S. Office of Education's research bureau. He was joined by Louis Hausman, an ex-vice president of the National Broadcasting Company, who became an assistant to then Federal Commissioner of Education Harold Howe.

One government official, George Donat, who held a top job in the Department of Commerce where he was concerned with commercial rights in inventions developed in the course of government-sponsored research, resigned to join Parke-Davis, the big Detroit drug firm. The number of former White House staff aides who have left public service to join or form Washington law firms which represent clients who must regularly deal with government agencies (the airlines are a good illustration) is too long to bother listing.

Drawing upon these personal contacts, government policy

makers increasingly seek out their counterparts in business to discuss problems and proposed programs. The extent to which this is done would surprise most people, yet many policies are adopted by major government agencies only after they had been reviewed with business spokesmen to a greater extent even than with key members of Congress. This is not to say that business always has its way or can exercise a veto over government action. It does not and cannot. But the significant thing is that its views are now more earnestly solicited, and at an earlier stage in the decision-making process, than at any time in the history of activist national Administration. One major reason is the new-found affinity between government and business policy makers who are coming more and more to share common experiences and confront common problems.

The Active Politics of Today's Business

An even closer relationship between government and business can be expected in the future as private firms become more deeply involved in large-scale civilian programs. The systems techniques of the nation's big companies can be put to valuable use in tackling the challenges of the cities, education, health care, and all the rest. This, though, will mean that corporate executives will have to grapple with what traditionally have been regarded as "political" matters, and in doing so they will inevitably have to take on some of the coloration of the politician or government bureaucrat. This will certainly bring into even closer contact what once were the separate worlds of government and industry. But industry, quite understandably, is unlikely to stop at this point in its new participation in the affairs of business. No less a figure than a former president of the National Association of Manufacturers, W. P. Gollander, has urged businessmen to see the need for "influencing the kind of decisions its government is making." Alcoa President John D. Harper, echoing similar comments made by former Ford Motor President Arjay Miller and other industry chieftains, has made it even clearer, urging that business be "realistic about government's role and make its views known, and make sure these views influence the action of the government. We must become participants rather than opponents."

In exerting "influence" over government policies and programs, big business resorts to many techniques, but none is of greater impact than direct financial and personal participation in the political process. In the past most company executives remained aloof from the "dirty game of politics" except for an occasional contribution to a party, usually the Republican. This passive attitude is now disappearing and a new, more aggressive, and more pragmatic political commitment is taking its place. Business's financial support of political parties and candidates has now become bipartisan. The old ideological ties that once bound industry to the Republican party have been severed and significant, though still modest, support is now provided to Democrats. This was especially evident during the Johnson years. Members of the President's Club, formed in 1964 and almost all of whose members are company executives or their advisers, contributed at least $4 million in support of the Johnson campaign. Of its 4,000 members, 532 were in California alone, home of the biggest defense-space contractors and the state which accounts for about a third of all contract awards. If allowance also is made for the sums which came from corporations whose lobbyists bought, with cash and usually anonymously (as far as the public is concerned at least), tickets at $25 to $1,000 per plate for luncheons and dinners, business picked up at least three fourths of the tab for President Johnson's election. Democratic Senators and Representatives (and their Republican colleagues) have like cause to be grateful.

In return for its support, big business has received appropriate recognition. Within days after his 1965 inauguration President Johnson held a private dinner for a group of top business leaders, most of whom were members of the Business Council. The Council, which rose to prominence under President Eisenhower and then fell into disfavor in the early days of the Kennedy Administration (ties were reestablished in September 1961), now receives a cordial greeting at the White House. Its roster is a veritable *Who's Who* of business. Of forty-five active members from manufacturing firms, thirty-five come from companies numbered in the largest 200 and twenty-five in the top 100. With sixty-two executives comprising its active membership, the Council meets regularly with top government officials in closed-door sessions in and near Washington. Cabinet members typically brief the Council about topics and with detailed information not generally accessible either to the public or to nonmembers. It can be used to bypass established lines of communication, as former Commerce Secretary John Connor discovered. When appointed to the cabinet he was told by President Johnson, "I want you to be my man with business." He soon found out, as *Washington Post* business editor Hobart Rowen reported, that when the President "really wanted to know what business was thinking, he would pick up the phone and call members of the Business Council." It is a cozy club, bringing together the top policy makers of government and business in an elitist environment that may be foreign to our traditional ways of making public policy but that is now coming to be an accepted way of life for the new partnership.

The Johnson Administration demonstrated that business, or at least big business, could get along amicably with a Democratic President, but it clearly signaled no permanent disaffection of the business community for the Republican party. In 1968 most corporate executives lined up behind Richard Nixon, giving him their votes and, more importantly, their contributions. A *New York Times* survey of the presidents of companies listed on the New York Stock Exchange indicated that 85 percent would vote for Nixon. Still, big business has shown its new flexibility in supporting political candidates and has indicated that it is no longer solidly frozen in its allegiance to the Republican party.

As business and government substitute their new coalition for their old suspicion and hostility, its greatest potential for development, and problems, will come as the partners join forces to cope with civilian problems—education, housing, medical care, job training—which historically have been regarded as being within the exclusive province of government.

CHAPTER 14

Business's New Frontier:
Social Problem Solving

By the mid-1970s social problem solving will be one of the biggest new industries in the United States. That is the considered judgment of many political observers and it is the basis for planning by the nation's technologically hep and most aggressive companies. What they contemplate is a transfer of the skills they have acquired in handling the enormous problems of defense and space exploration to civilian areas which now are beginning to receive the intensive public attention they have long been denied. Education, transportation, medical care, law enforcement, job training, pollution control, housing, city renewal, and even large-scale regional development represent the great new frontiers of business expansion. The potential is as large as the problems are complex; they will strain the capacities of any enterprise, however big and diverse its experience and breadth of vision.

What makes the challenge to business even more difficult is that these problems are intrinsically political in nature, necessitating substantial government involvement and compelling industrial firms to contest with issues that are beyond their established expertise. Education, to cite but one instance, is not simply a complex technical problem; it involves social considerations (who, for instance, is to be taught what with how much emphasis and in what way with what order of priority) that normally are resolved, not by experts, but in a public forum. Crossing the new industrial frontier means, therefore, not just tough challenges and immense market opportunities, but a basic change in the character of the problems with which business must deal. Whether business can cope with all of these demands, in an economically and politically acceptable manner, is an open question.

In our successful quest for private affluence we Americans have shortchanged the public sector, spending far more on our own homes, autos, and appliances than our schools, transportation facilities, law enforcement, and the collective amenities that can make life in our cities bearable. This sharp imbalance has left us with an immense burden of neglect which is now visibly encroaching on our individual lives. A good home means little if the air is polluted, a fine suburban residence loses much of its appeal without efficient transportation to and from work, and life in a metropolis can be frightening if the central city ghetto is likely to erupt in violence like a steam valve letting off the pressures of rotten housing, crime, disease, and despair. All of these realities have at last been sensed by most of the public and Congress has adopted programs, for the moment limited in funding and cautious in character, that promise far more attention to our long neglected civilian needs.

Determining how our resources should be mobilized to meet our public problems most efficiently presents an opportunity for business to make its contribution and to earn a sizable profit in the process. By their nature most of our civilian problems are tremendously complex. As an example, developing a good transportation system for a city or a country is a far bigger, more difficult task than anything ever faced by business. Governments have snipped away at it in piecemeal fashion, but hardly anyone thinks the present transport complex more than minimally adequate to meet our needs, and perhaps not even that. But to improve it substantially requires more than foresight or engineering skill. Transportation interacts with every other dimension of urban life—with land use, air pollution, employment, housing, and a host of other factors. In the same way a solution to the pollution of a river near a big city involves much more than better purification techniques and restrictions on waste disposal. It can affect industrial location and thus employment, and significantly change an entire metropolitan region's economic development. The same intricate pattern is also characteristic of education, where decisions concerning what is to be taught and in what way can influence the very substance of the society itself. All of the big civilian problems have this same feature—they are as intricate and intertwined as a watch, and their solution, or an approach to a solution, calls for the attention of and at the same time strenuously tests those accustomed to intricate problem analysis.

Systems Techniques and Civilian Problems

The big technically sophisticated contemporary corporation offers significant promise of applying its "systems analysis" capability to the delineation of possible solutions to large-scale social problems. The origins of "systems analysis" as a term and as a managerial concept can be traced back a good many years, but in its modern connotation it is most accurately associated with the massive defense-space undertakings launched by the Federal Government in the 1950s. Development of a family of intercontinental ballistic missiles such as the Polaris undersea weapons system and the Apollo space capsule demanded the preliminary refinement of the problems to be met and the integration of many specialists in perfecting a final product. Involved in each multiyear project were thousands of scientists and hundreds of companies whose individual contributions had to be skillfully coordinated under severe time constraint.

The success of these vast programs was a great engineering-managerial achievement and suggests that the same technique could be employed in grappling with even bigger, tougher social problems. When reduced to its essential ingredients and stripped of the public relations hoopla that always encrusts institutional accomplishments, systems analysis is nothing more than organized problem solving on a grand scale. Simon Ramo, vice chairman of TRW, Inc., and a pioneer in the field explains:

> All systems engineering is, is that to meet a problem, you should start by understanding the problem; you should look at alternative approaches; you should attempt to estimate the value of the various approaches; you should break it down into its pieces and insure that the pieces are put together to constitute a harmonious optimum ensemble. So for "systems engineering" read "logical solution of a problem."

Viewed in this way it would be fair to say, for example, that voice communication in the U.S. has been solved on a systems basis, but not transportation. A phone call can be made fast and efficiently between virtually any two points, fully exploiting available electronic technology. The same obviously cannot be said of intercity transportation. It is a helter-skelter assortment of badly related components, jet aircraft, taxis, buses, walking, that interrelate so as to accentuate the inefficiency of the whole. There is no coherent plan, anymore than there is in the field of medical care or pollution control. No one has systematically appraised the problem as a whole and devised alternative solutions.

Several large corporations—mostly those which have matured in the expansive worlds of defense and space—are starting to fill this gap, identifying and solving elephantine civilian problems. The most interesting efforts have come in California, where a number of big aerospace companies, working under contract with the state, have carried out systems studies in four areas: transportation, crime prevention, data handling, and waste management. Interestingly, and providing a further example of the new partnership at work, the state, recognizing its own skill limitations, hired another company, Systems Development Corporation, to monitor and evaluate the four special studies for which it had contracted. As part of the California effort North American Aviation made a long-term projection of the state's transportation needs and the best way of meeting them. Lockheed reviewed the data and information requirements of the state as well as its local governments. This project determined that a centralized information and retrieval system could far more effectively satisfy government demands in such time-consuming functions as the issuance of licenses and special permits. A ten-year, $100 million investment in an information system, said Lockheed, could save the state and its local governments more than $400 million in a year, mostly in personnel. In the field of crime prevention the Space-General Corporation estimated the costs of various sorts of criminal behavior and concluded that law enforcement agencies should place greater stress on higher-cost crimes (like check forgery, where the costs per criminal average $16,000) than on less costly crime. Finally, the Aerojet-General Corporation assessed waste management, identifying a dozen interrelated functions that can best be performed through some sort of intergovernmental cooperation.

Each of the California contractors has gone on to do similar work for other states and cities. Space-General is looking into California's entire social welfare system, Aerojet-General has a contract dealing with solid waste management in Fresno County, and North American is engaged in elaborate airport planning studies for airlines and airport management. While the California-sponsored studies triggered the entry of large aerospace firms into the field of social problem solving, many other companies have plunged in too, often on extraordinarily grand scale. Litton Industries has contracted with Greece to guide and hopefully accelerate its economic growth. The company expects that this effort in what it calls "nation-building" will lead to contracts with other developing countries and, for that matter, with whole international regions. TRW, Inc., has been asked by West Virginia to propose a comprehensive plan for that state's economic expansion. Its preliminary proposal calls for a large-scale program (including substantial Federal participation) designed to encourage the growth of cities in what are now rural areas. General Electric, through its TEMPO division, has also put in its hand, making a contract with Detroit to appraise the city's administrative organization and make recommendations for a thorough overhaul. Conclusions reached by the GE analysts indicated that drastic reorganization is needed, with agencies consolidated and restructured along functional lines. The RAND Corporation, founded right after the war to serve as an Air Force think tank, is carrying out a similar project for New York City.

To see what all of this can mean to one company, take the case of Lockheed. Up to now it has been engaged almost exclusively in defense work, playing a key role in the Polaris submarine-missile program. From 1961 through 1967 it received nearly $11 billion in defense contracts, making up almost 90 percent of its total sales. A company forecast completed in the sixties showed, however, that reliance on military work was extremely risky, an assessment that was fortified by the company's unhappy experiences in 1969 with the cancellation of the Cheyenne helicopter contract by the Defense Department and the disclosure of large cost overruns in its production of the C-5A military cargo plane. Reviewing its own systems and managerial capabilities Lockheed determined that it could best use its skills in the resolution of large problems calling for a systems approach. This brought it into direct contact with many of the nation's key social problems. One it identified, for example, was in medical care. By 1975 expenditures on health care in the U.S. are likely to approach $120 billion a year. Given the limited supply of skilled doctors, nurses, and medical personnel and the steeply rising cost of equipment, Lockheed concluded that there was a serious need for information systems that would make better use of people, machines, and hospitals. It suggested, as one specific possibility, that a computer center be established to serve all of the hospitals in the San Francisco area and that comparable regional facilities be set up in other areas. Working with the Mayo Clinic, Lockheed is studying many possible uses of the computer in hospital-medical care (direct doctor-to-computer communication could provide vast amounts of information about a patient and present alternative diagnoses and treatment possibilities).

Extending its work in the information systems field, Lockheed has contracts with the states of Alaska, Massachusetts, and California to develop large-scale information systems. The company is also moving into education, oceanography (it occupies a top position in the construction of deep-submergence vehicles), and housing (it has devised a special technique that speeds the construction of low-cost, prefabricated homes). Abroad, it has a contract to apply systems techniques in the analysis of the Sudan's transportation requirements. Lockheed, like a good many other large firms with systems experience, is obviously interested in branching out and moving into civilian fields that have long been neglected or viewed in a fragmented way that has frustrated sensible problem solving. Like the other defense contractors, however, Lockheed's degree of interest in civilian problem areas depends to a great extent on its prospects for obtaining future military work. There can be little doubt, as Bernard D. Nossiter pointed out in a series of articles in the *Washington Post,* that the defense companies would prefer to stick to that which they know best, armaments, and that their resource commitments reflect this bias. Still, though, the scale of civilian problems and the large commercial prospects they open up, coupled with the vagaries of post-Vietnam defense planning, strongly indicate that systems-oriented companies, particularly those that in the past have not been totally or very largely committed to defense work, will aggressively move into the area of big-scale civilian problem solving.

There are several social problem areas that are likely to receive the main thrust of government-business attention in the next decade. To gauge their potential and identify the problems that could emerge through this new involvement of industry in fields historically reserved largely for government, one—education—warrants close scrutiny.

Business and Education

Of the civilian fields attracting intense business interest, education is probably the biggest, the most consequential, and the severest test of industrial ability to meet its own demand for profit without conflicting with society's wishes in the training of youth. The sheer scale of the education market provides clear and ample explanation of its appeal to business. Today the nation's educational institutions, ranging from public and private elementary schools through the universities, spend about $50 billion a year for goods and services. By 1975 their spending will increase to

$70 billion (in 1968 dollars). Part of the explanation, of course, is rising enrollment. By 1975 some 63 million persons will be enrolled in school, up five million from 1967. With half this increase coming in college enrollment, higher education will account for 15 percent of total school enrollment (it's now 12 percent). Costs per pupil are also climbing, with projections calling for an increase from $532 per pupil in public schools in 1966 to $700 by 1975 (again, in 1968 dollars). Educational costs, therefore, are going up substantially. A major reason is that schools, at all levels of instruction, are beginning to spend much more on computers, closed-circuit TV systems, and on other electronic hardware and its associated materials. The old triumvirate of buildings, books, and teachers now has a fourth partner: electronics. Today schools are spending about $500 million a year on educational hardware. But by 1977 the figure will reach at least $5 billion and may soar as high as $10 billion.

Sensing the enormous market opportunities that lie ahead, many companies have moved into the education field. Makers of audiovisual equipment (motion pictures, projectors, records and tapes, slides and filmstrips, etc.) have expanded their offerings, tailoring them to meet more particularized learning situations. It is now possible in many schools for a student or teacher to dial a library and listen to or see a recording of information on a subject of his immediate interest. The student is thus freed from the lack of individuality in the classroom and put in a truly personal learning environment—with electronics in effect sitting on the other end of the proverbial log.

Important though the contributions of audiovisual systems and electronics learning aids have been to education, the greatest potential involvement of business will come through programmed instruction that will substitute electronics for the book. "It is possible," says one of the country's outstanding education authorities, Alice Rivlin, "that the present situation is not unlike that of Europe at the time printing was introduced." Just as printed materials replaced oral instruction, the prospect is that the computer and its assorted electronic helpmates will narrow greatly, if not actually replace, the role the book has played in education since the Middle Ages.

Cognizant of these prospects most of the big electronics companies have entered the education field, usually by acquiring a textbook publisher or some other firm already established in the trade. Raytheon had been one of the leaders, buying D. C. Heath for $40 million in 1966 (a year earlier it had acquired three smaller, specialized education equipment suppliers). Explaining the move, Raytheon president, Thomas L. Phillips, said:

> Busy educators should not have to assemble the various components and fragments of learning equipment from a multitude of sources. We will now be able to build an integrated capability—a systems approach.

Xerox has made similar moves for essentially the same reason. In 1962 it purchased Ann Arbor-based University Microfilms (giving it access to a competing medium for the presentation of instructional material) and then, in 1965, it acquired two other firms, Basic Systems (which was developing fundamentally new teaching techniques) and American Education Publications. In 1968 Xerox added Ginn and Company, the Boston textbook publisher, to its education domain, at a price of $120 million.

New families of firms, heavily electronic in orientation, have penetrated well into educational territory through the mergers, joint ventures, and other steps they have taken in the last half dozen years. What this can mean in terms of its actual impact on education in the United States is suggested by the recent experience of the Naval Academy at Annapolis in seeking bids and proposals for the development of comprehensive new courses in physics, economics, and leadership (called "management psychology" at the Academy). With an overall cost estimated at $10 million, the undertaking made available more money for a single educational research project than ever before. But, far more important, the contractors were commanded to come up with integrated, multimedia courses that would combine, in an optimal way, every possible teaching technique. The final product would be education; books, closed TV presentations, tapes, movies, and even individual live instructors would only be alternative means of achieving that objective. The Navy proposal made clear that "course content is not restricted to that presently available in books, films, programmed instruction, or any other media" and asked bidders to develop "the most effective possible materials, using existing materials only when no better ones can be prescribed." It was a revolutionary opportunity and the diverse members of the knowledge industry responded enthusiastically to the challenge. The forty prospective bidders included giant industrial electronics firms like IBM, General Learning (GE-Time), Litton, Xerox, and TRW as well as such smaller systems-electronic companies as Software Systems of Falls Church, Virginia, and the URS Corporation of San Mateo, California. An executive of one of the companies summed up why so many firms took such a great interest in the opportunity, saying "this is a real breakthrough in the field of instruction. . . . It is oriented to management techniques and is not tradition-bound." One can expect more situations like this in the near future, as part of a process that will shake up education just as it will also violently disturb the industrial status quo.

Big business thrusts into the education field, impressive though they have been, only serve to expose some fundamental unanswered questions to which answers must be provided before the knowledge industry can achieve its full potential. The questions are hardly new; they have befuddled man since he began to ponder his purpose. What should be taught? What is the purpose of education? What order of priorities should govern the teacher? How do the means and ends of education interact? In developing a course on economics, for example, as bidders were asked to do by the Naval Academy, what is to be taught, stressed, omitted? To none of these basic questions are there any unambiguous responses.

Even if each of us has an opinion, most people would agree that the ultimate answers are not to be dictated by equipment suppliers or educational administrators, but rather by the electorate, for the implications are simply too large to leave such sensitive matters to any elite. Business, therefore, is confronted by something of a dilemma. Systems-oriented firms can make a contribution to the development of better teaching aids and instructional packages, but it cannot make conclusive judgments about what is to be taught. If it ventures into this treacherous terrain, it opens itself to the prospect of sharp public criticism, yet if it tries to remain aloof it cannot bring to bear its full innovative talents. Here is a conflict that is common to virtually all of the civilian problems that business is anxious to confront.

The Many Problems of an Urbanized Society

Many other civilian problem areas hold out great opportunities in the immediate future for business. Pollution control is one. Expenditures here could reach $10 billion a year by the early 1970s as states, local units of government, and private firms—prodded by new regulations and attracted by Federal incentives—attempt to create the higher quality environment the public now demands. Today more than seven thousand communities, with a total population of more than fifty million, have serious air pollution problems. Some four hundred thousand tons of pollutants are expelled into the air each *day* over the United States, about half of them associated with auto emission. The cost—to property, to crops, and to human health (the emphysema death rate, believed to be associated with air pollution, is up more than twice in the last ten years)—is high and the cause is preventable. Requirements for the installation of emission control devices on new cars will help ease the problem, at an estimated cost of half a billion dollars a year in higher auto prices. Congress's passage of the Air Quality Act of 1967 provides $400 million for research and signals additional Federal grant assistance in the near future. The Department of Health, Education & Welfare is aiming at reducing plant stack emissions in 75 specified interstate areas by 90 percent by the early 1970s. That will require large expenditures by industry to meet tougher pollution standards (such outlays rose by 70 percent in 1967, compared with 1966, amounting to more than $700 million), but it will also open up a major new sales market as companies devise equipment and processes to reduce air contamination. Water pollution control may be an even bigger market. Presently fifty million Americans, served by nearly six thousand of the country's nineteen thousand municipal drinking water systems, drink water that does not meet Public Health Service standards. To rectify this deficiency and to insure the health of the population, not to mention industry's own need for purer water, an outlay of $5 billion a year will be required for improved city water treatment facilities alone. The Clean Water Restoration Act of 1966 increases Federal aid to $3.5 billion in the period 1968 to 1971; or more than four times the Federal assistance provided to states and municipalities from 1958 through 1967. It is calculated to increase local outlays by an additional $11 billion. Many billions of dollars in new equipment to purify wastes will have to be invested by industry.

Consider another dimension of environmental contamination, solid waste disposal, and what it can mean for those firms experienced in the systematic solution of big problems that have usually been thought of as public in character. Currently we dispose of 175 million tons of trash each year, or about 4.5 pounds per person each day. Within a decade each of us on the average will be discarding daily six pounds of trash. In all, the nation must dispose this year of 50 billion cans, 25 billion bottles, and more than six million cars. In doing so old techniques, like incineration, become unacceptable or impractical. Air pollution is one limitation. Too, many products cannot be burned since wastes are now mainly nondegradable inorganic substances. The result is that costs of disposal are skyrocketing. By one calculation it costs more to dispose of the Sunday *New York Times* than it does to buy it at the corner newsstand! With landfill becoming increasingly costly (New York City uses up two hundred acres a year) and with the proliferation of throwaway products, radically new disposal techniques are required. There are many ideas (transportation of waste to abandoned coal mines, use as fill to create airports in bodies of water, etc.), but the problem is of such magnitude that it represents a challenge as formidable as that involved in getting a man safely on the moon. What is also clear is that waste management is but one facet of a larger problem that also includes air and water pollution control and whose scale and complexity are accentuated by the unavoidable political overtones.

Whether it be something so grand as education or medical care or so ordinary as waste disposal and pollution control, the social problems of the United States present immense opportunities for industrial firms to take a part in improving the quality of our life at the same time they derive sales and profits from the undertaking. Certainly the problems are of vast scale, transcending even those of national defense and nuclear development, and call for the kind of elaborate organizations geared to rational analysis and systematic decision making that is characteristic of many of our technologically oriented corporations.

The Political Dimensions of Social Problems

The problems, though, are also inherently political in nature and are not susceptible "merely" to objective definition and resolution. They can be ultimately resolved only with public participation and it is this fact which means that business must accept government as a partner, working out accommodations as their efforts proceed. This sounds good in theory, but whether it can or will work in practice is open to serious question. The partners have different, legitimate objectives—one, profit, the other, political support—and it may be impossible for them to arrive at mutually acceptable understandings that do not unacceptably compromise at least one set of goals. Both participants in the government-business new partnership thus are obligated to walk an unfamiliar tightrope across a crevice whose dimensions and dangers have yet to be identified. Politicians are often compelled to dance on a delicately balanced strand of wire—it is part of their calling— but businessmen are rarely in such an exposed position. For them, therefore, the venture into social problem solving, with its large market potential and the lure of immense sales and profits, will be faced with strange new risks—with crosscurrents of criticism and compromise—to which acclimation may be terribly difficult. The severity of those strains and business's capacity to adjust to them will be tested most rigorously in meeting the complex problems of the cities—housing, job training, and civil rights.

CHAPTER 15

Business and the Urban Crisis

A hundred years ago the American frontier was in the West. Today it is in the cities. So large and so fundamental a challenge do they represent that their problems are leading to an unprecedented alliance between government and business that is the epitome of the new partnership. Politicians are earnestly soliciting the involvement of business in solving hard-core inner city problems, and businessmen are not only responding positively to these appeals, but are beginning to exercise considerable initiative in creating the conditions that will enable the private sector to play an expanding role in the urban economy. Despite this interest, however, it remains an open question whether business in fact can make a meaningful contribution on terms that reflect more than the usual role of business in satisfying wants in return for a profit. This is a fundamental and as yet unresolved issue, one that should be kept constantly in mind in this chapter's examination of business's new urban commitment.

The new-found mutuality of interest between government and business in tackling the problems of the cities reflects three factors.

First, it has become obvious that old ways of managing our cities, with reliance placed exclusively in government and the private sector standing off to the side, have failed—and failed so miserably that the ghetto dweller sees as much hope in violence and destruction as he does in promises of improvement. New approaches are urgently needed and the involvement of business, with its experience and profit orientation, looks as promising as any other alternative. This changed attitude now finds liberal politicians proposing a central role for business in the creation of better housing and jobs for slum residents. For people who grew up in the belief that the public and private sectors are and should be kept distinct that is a radical change indeed.

There is a second, closely related explanation. It stems from a practical realization that while the needs of the cities are enormous, the existing political system is unlikely to generate the multibillion-dollar appropriations that are required. Public programs for housing and job training, among others, have been only skimpily financed by Congress. Appropriations have fallen far short of the demand, leaving a gap that has not been significantly narrowed in recent years. Recognizing this, many liberals see in the prospect of closer cooperation with industry a practical way of enlarging our financial commitment to the resolution of urban problems.

Third, looking at the matter from the business side, it is evident that the private sector has radically revised its thinking about the desirability and practicality of participating in urban affairs. The reasons are many. One is that there is a burgeoning market in urban rejuvenation that holds promise of sales and profits for industry. Beyond this, however, is the urban crisis itself—a national upheaval that is impossible for anyone to avoid, especially those who reckon themselves as playing a significant role in influencing the course of national policy. The cancer of the cities eats away at the vitality of the economy, sapping the nation's strength and denying business—and the whole citizenry—the opportunity to exploit our resources. Urban slums make it even more difficult to give millions of Americans a chance to participate fully in our bounty. Businessmen now have recognized this fact and are beginning actively to do something about it.

Dimensions of the Urban Crisis

The confluence of these forces, bringing together business and government in an attack on the accumulated problems of the central cities, comes at a time when the situation has already assumed grave proportions. Not only must there be physical reconstruction of our cities, but improvements must be made in a way that will assure Black America the respect it has long been denied. Decades of neglect must be overcome quickly and it will not be easy, for while urbanization has proceeded intensively in the U.S., it has left the cores of our older cities bankrupt and blighted. In the postwar years our central cities have become progressively the province of the poor, the Negroes and other minority groups, the sick, and the unemployed and the undereducated. The white population, except for the very wealthy, has fled to suburbia. Between 1960 and 1968 the Negro population in central cities rose by 25 percent; the white population actually declined. Business has followed a similar pattern of emigration. Most new jobs created in urban areas in the last two decades have been located in the suburbs, often inaccessible to ghetto residents.

America's city slums show all the signs of their years of neglect. Unemployment is high. With the jobless rate for the U.S. as a whole now about 4 percent, unemployment in Harlem is twice this level and in the Hough section of Cleveland it is 16 percent, in Watts it is 12 percent, and in the slums of St. Louis 13 percent. Subemployment is even higher. It is estimated that in the Harlem and Bedford-Stuyvesant areas of New York fully a third of people with jobs are underemployed. Why is the slum employment record so bad? One reason is health. Nearly 10 percent of jobless slum residents are unable to work because of poor health—often tuberculosis. Another big factor is education. Only a third of the unemployed in city slums have a high school education. Of those who do graduate from high school (and only about a third of those who enter the ninth grade in Harlem public schools get this far), the average graduate has only about the equivalent of an eighth-grade education.

Making a bad situation worse is the rotten housing in our cities.

Nearly half of all Negroes who rent live in housing officially cate-
gorized as dilapidated. Conditions are not getting better. In 1960
some 18 percent of the housing in the slums of South Los Angeles
was judged "substandard." By 1965 that ratio was up to 34 percent. In the meanwhile average rents had gone up. Poor people
were paying out a larger share of their income to live in rapidly
deteriorating housing.

Whatever the standard, slums are costly. A study in Sacramento
showed that its blighted areas contained 20 percent of its population and contributed a slim 12 percent of its tax revenue. But
those same areas accounted for half its police and health budget
and for 25 percent of the costs of fire protection. More than 36
percent of the city's juvenile delinquency, 42 percent of its adult
crime, and 76 percent of its tuberculosis cases were attributable to
this city's slums. Ghetto costs to the community as a whole are
obviously large, but even more important they deny the nation the
contributions its residents could make—for their own good and
for that of the economy as a whole—if they could be put in productive work. With a fully employed worker today contributing
about $12,000 annually to the GNP, unemployment is as bad for
the country as it is for the jobless.

Unemployment and subemployment, an unhealthy environment,
poor educational opportunities, and rotten housing combine to
make the city slums socially and economically debilitating. Many
people have known that for a long time, yet efforts to eradicate
slum-breeding conditions to date have been a colossal failure. The
reason—whether it be skimpy funding or the deficiencies of established programs, with their principal reliance on government—is
less important than the result. Lack of accomplishment is a major
explanation for the new willingness of political leaders to involve
the private sector in the tough job of social problem solving. Take
housing as an example.

Housing

Adequate, decent housing for lower-income families is a goal
that has successfully eluded past government efforts. In fact, with

the construction of only fifty thousand new units of low-rent public housing a year, we have actually fallen further behind. Past efforts have manifestly been inadequate. One way to meet the need, of course, would be through expanded Federal spending—grants or loans for the actual construction of housing. A few years ago that would probably have been the favored course, certainly by leaders of the Democratic Party. Indeed, it had become almost a tenet of political faith that Democrats supported publicly built and operated housing for the poor while most Republicans insisted that the private market would provide all the housing that was really required.

Come 1968, however, and the old party ideologies gave way to the new partnership. Two factors help explain this shift in attitude. One stems from the growing recognition of the immense difficulty in inducing Congress to appropriate the requisite amounts of money; another is attributable to a declining lack of conviction that government-run programs are the most efficient way of dealing with the problem. Both forces were at work when, in his message to the Congress on "Houses and Cities," President Johnson outlined a program "summoning the talents and energies of private enterprise to the task of housing low-income families through the creation of a federally-chartered private, profit-making housing partnership." Specifically, he asked Congress to "authorize the formation of privately-funded partnerships that will join private capital with business skills to help close the low-income housing gap." Private funds—drawn mostly from industry—would provide the bulk of the capital and construction, and management would be the responsibility of private firms. To the extent necessary Federal subsidies would be provided to keep rents within the income reach of prospective residents, but the organizational initiative would come from investors, not the government.

The late Robert F. Kennedy, Senators Jacob Javits and Charles Percy, Hubert Humphrey, and Governor Nelson Rockefeller, proposed private-public arrangements bearing many significant resemblances to the program outlined in 1968 by President Johnson. All had a single ingredient in common: the desire to tap the resources of private capital and to place primary responsibility for organizing and carrying out a project in private hands. Profits would not only be allowed but would be anticipated, just as they would be in any real estate investment. Government would continue to be involved, but by subsidizing the impoverished tenant rather than the developer and perhaps, as in the idea advanced by Nelson Rockefeller calling for the creation of a state-chartered Public Urban Development Corporation, through exercise of the power of eminent domain.

In 1968 Congress adopted the essence of many of these proposals with the passage of the Housing and Urban Development Act. Title IX of that law creates a National Housing Corporation, which is to serve as the general partner, manager, and principal investor in low-income housing projects around the country. The corporation will get its initial capital of $200 million from corporations and will borrow an additional $4 billion with the aid of government loan guarantees. Working with local builders and real estate developers, the corporation can put up capital to finance as many as fifty thousand low-income housing units a year—as many as all that are now built yearly under existing public programs. The Housing Corporation, which has its origins in a proposal made by Edgar F. Kaiser, president of Kaiser Industries, while he was serving in 1967 as chairman of the White House Committee on Urban Housing, represents a hopeful way of tapping private capital and mobilizing industrial organizational techniques. It is especially interesting because it is not a charity or not-for-profit operation; with the tax benefits which can be realized through real estate partnerships, business investors in the Housing Corporation should realize highly respectable earnings. Adhering to the private-public approach to the housing problem the Nixon Administration inspired the formation of the National Corporation for Housing Partnerships. Headed by Carter Burgess, formerly the chief executive of American Machine & Foundry, the Corporation plans to raise $50 million from large companies and banks for investment in local housing partnerships. Those partnerships will also borrow money from other sources, with the assistance of government-guaranteed loans.

Plans for involving the private sector in the provision of lower-income housing on a cooperative basis with government have their parallels in other fields. A predecessor is Comsat, a strange type of institutional beast set up in 1962 under Federal law to launch, own, and operate communication satellites. Corporate in form, control of the Board of Directors is divided among members appointed by the President (and approved by the Senate), those chosen by communications carriers, and those elected by owners of publicly sold common stock. A similar arrangement has been used in establishing a Public Broadcasting Corporation, with the significant exception that it cannot sell securities to the public but must rely for funds on Congressional appropriations. Like Comsat, though, it is a hybrid, mixing public and private features to create an artificial being not susceptible to ready classification.

The new interest in slum housing has induced a number of big companies to try their hand at demonstrating what private business could do in meeting this vital national challenge and realize a profit to boot. The U.S. Gypsum Company acquired six dilapidated tenements in East Harlem and proceeded to experiment with ways of refurbishing them through the use of prefabricated units. The American Plywood Association put up $150,000 to renovate housing in the Hough area of Cleveland (Warner & Swasey, Clevite, Midland-Ross, and Republic Steel, among others, have also been active in Cleveland). Similarly, Armstrong Cork took over and rehabilitated a tenement in North Philadelphia. Putting aside the humanitarian feature, what all of these companies realize is that if the United States were to make available a million lower-income housing units a year, as some urge, it would open up a $10 billion plus market. To keep costs down and rapidly to construct or rehabilitate housing units, however, would require the development and adoption of new, mass production techniques that are as foreign to home building at the present time as the assembly line was to auto making before Henry Ford. The plans of Housing & Urban Development Secretary George Romney to create a mass-market housing market, big enough for assembly-line home production, recognizes this fact, and if it is implemented it can create a gigantic commercial opportunity for companies that have never wanted to get involved in the traditional construction industry. Reflecting this new interest, building materials producers are integrating forward to end-use markets through acquisition of home builders, as in the case of American Standard, Boise Cascade, and Texas Industries. Other big industrial firms—like Chrysler, ITT, and Occidental Petroleum—have also entered the building field through merger. All recognize that there may be validity in Secretary Romney's assertion that "meeting our housing needs can do in the future what railroad building did in the last century."

Job Training, Job Creation

The situation in job training and job creation closely parallels that in low-income housing. Realizing that grossly underfinanced government programs could not be expected to deal with the problem of hard-core unemployment any more effectively than with housing for the poor, liberals have sought a greater role for private firms in filling the need. Government-dominated efforts to train the unemployed and find them jobs, though tested in new ways in the sixties, proved to be grossly inadequate.

Recognizing this, liberal Democrats began offering proposals that might make private industry a larger participant in the job-creating effort. Robert F. Kennedy, joining with a number of Republican businessmen in New York, urged that Federal subsidies and tax credits be made available to firms willing to locate plants in slums like Harlem or Bedford-Stuyvesant and train and hire local residents. "To ignore the potential contribution of private enterprise," he said in his book *To Seek a Newer World,* "is to fight poverty with a single platoon while great armies are left to stand aside."

Taking a different approach but one equally reliant on the private sector for solving the hard-core unemployment problem, President Johnson put his Administration in partnership with business in a message on employment he addressed to Congress on January 23, 1968. He announced the formation of the National Alliance of Businessmen, headed by Henry Ford II and an executive committee composed of sixty well-known industrial chieftains, and proclaimed that it would assume responsibility for finding 100,000 jobs for the hard-core unemployed by July 1, 1969 and a total of 600,000 jobs by mid-1971. The Alliance would work with government in meeting these goals, but the responsibility would be that of business itself. Federal job-training assistance is available (government training costs per worker average about $3,000), but it was fully expected that the brunt of the burden of job training and assimilation into the work force would be borne predominantly by the business community. In the weeks following the President's announcement the Alliance formed regional committees and opened a national office. Pledges were sought from more than a thousand firms and by 1969 it was reported that 146,000 new jobs had been provided for the country's unemployed slum dwellers. Whether the effort will have lasting success is yet to be determined (58,000 of the 146,000 who got jobs under the program have quit or been terminated, and anti-inflation measures promise to have an even more severe impact), but the important thing is that the task of finding jobs for unemployed Americans—something which historically we would have assumed to be the responsibility of government itself, in accordance with the traditions of WPA— had been assigned to business *and* willingly accepted. The private sector had been put to work solving a national problem of a kind that would previously have been automatically labeled "public." The Alliance's role, and what it implies, is no temporary phenomenon; less than two months after taking office President Nixon offered his assurance that it had "the complete and unqualified support of the Administration."

It is not only with respect to housing and jobs that business has been brought into direct confrontation with the bitter realities of an America where thirty million people live in poverty. Private firms, like ITT, Litton, and Xerox, have operated job corps centers under contract with the government, aiming to make unemployed slum teen-agers productive members of society. Westinghouse was awarded a grant by the Office of Economic Opportunity to develop a total "battle plan" for an assault on a Baltimore slum area. In California OEO contracted with a private research group to explore ways in which private contractors could be substituted for public agencies in the administration of welfare programs. Each case reflects liberal acceptance that the participation of the private sector in social problem solving is not only not necessarily evil, but may actually mean a more efficient program—even with profit included.

Matching this attitude is a growing willingness of businessmen to immerse themselves in the dirty world of urban politics. Part of the reason is explicable as a reaction to the terrible violence that has gripped our cities. The eruptions which took place in the slums of many cities in the summers of 1966, 1967, and 1968—in Detroit, Newark, Watts, New York, Cleveland, and Washington—stimulated meaningful concern for the cities and a desire, shared by government officials and business leaders, to act. What emerged, as a consequence, were coalitions of corporate executives, church leaders, labor union officers, and government officials organized to focus public attention on the ghettos.

Business and the New Detroit

Perhaps the most significant steps came in Detroit. Shortly after the ghastly riots that caused $25 million in damage in July of 1967, executives of the city's major enterprises met with Mayor Jerome Cavanaugh. Included were the presidents of the Big Three auto producers; Joseph L. Hudson, Jr., chief executive of J. L. Hudson Co., Detroit's biggest department store; top officers from the local banks and utilities; Walter Reuther of the UAW and other union representatives; the presidents of Wayne State University and the University of Detroit; and a roster of other notables from what passes for the Detroit establishment. Styling itself the New Detroit Committee, the group accepted the Mayor's challenge to help rebuild Detroit "by mobilizing available resources in the private sector" and "by serving as a focal point for total community action." Nine months after its creation the Committee issued a progress report pointing to a few accomplishments (members for example, had supported passage of the state's new open occupancy law), but acknowledging that the difficulty and complexity of the problems it faced left it with a great many things unaccomplished. Everything that the Committee has done so far, concludes the *Wall*

Street Journal, "has fallen well within the boundaries of corporate prudence, self-interest and profit making." Business's actual contribution on the urban scene remains yet to be measured.

Limited though its successes have been, the New Detroit Committee helped provide the spark for other joint government-business-public efforts to dramatize and deal with unmet urban needs. In August of 1967 a group of national business executives (including Andrew Heiskell, of Time, Inc., Gerald L. Phillippe of General Electric, and J. Irwin Miller of Cummins Engine Company), as well as church, labor, and government leaders, assembled in Washington to form the Urban Coalition. In an almost radical statement of guiding principles the Coalition called upon the Federal Government to develop an emergency work program to provide jobs for the unemployed, pledged the support of private industry to provide creative job training and employment, and advocated the construction of a million housing units a year for lower-income families. Now headed by John Gardner, previously Secretary of Health, Education, and Welfare and earlier the president of the Carnegie Foundation, the Urban Coalition conceivably could become an articulate voice for business and other segments of the public in the support of government programs calculated to meet city problems. So far, however, the Coalition's potential remains largely that—potential, as yet unproven.

Business Ends, Public Needs: Do the Twain Meet?

Whether the challenge be housing, employment, pollution control, or any of a myriad of other large, difficult undertakings, the new political ideology—liberal and conservative, Democratic and Republican—is to involve business. What's more, business is not only accepting the challenge but embracing it positively—spurred on by the dual objectives of "doing good" for the community and making a profit. This new spirit—the spirit of coalition or partnership—constitutes a sharp break from older conceptions of the "proper" roles of the private and public sectors. It implicitly accepts big business as capable of executing "public" responsibilities (housing, welfare administration, education, job training, etc.) in a socially desirable way if united in partnership with government.

But can business educate, build, train, and perform the other tasks inherent in social problem solving in a democratically acceptable manner? Or is there something inherent in business's search for profit that yields results that run counter to the public good? Michael Harrington, the thoughtful neo-socialist and author of *Toward a Democratic Left,** insists that there is a basic conflict between business interests and the social welfare. Industry, he argues, suffers from a kind of incurable schizophrenia—what Walter Lippmann described as a situation in which "one part of the brain is intent on profits and another part of the same brain is intent on public service." Applying this diagnosis in the case of business's new involvement in the cities, Harrington concludes that even "when business methods are sincerely and honestly applied to urban problems, with every good intention, they still inevitably lead to antisocial results." His lesson: America cannot depend on business, but must build new institutions of "democratic planning" to get the kinds of programs needed so desperately to improve the quality of our life.

Harrington may move too quickly from the identification of a problem to a judgment about its inevitability, but there can be no doubt that the new involvement of private sector in social problems, like those of the cities, poses a grave dilemma for business. Often the problem to be faced requires profits to be forsaken, which contradicts the sine qua non of corporate existence or, if the quest for profit maximization is not compromised, the social need is only inadequately met. What industry is being asked to do, as in the case of job creation, is incur a cost it would not otherwise accept. Many of today's unemployed are lacking in education, work experience, and training. At the wage rates set by minimum wage laws or union contracts, they would not normally be employed on the very simple ground that their productivity is less than their cost. That may sound harsh (and in a way it is), but it reflects the kind of tough calculation that is at the root of a free enterprise system. But businesses are now being asked to accept such workers

* Macmillan, New York: 1968.

—to incur the costs involved on the ground that it will help solve a national problem. In the same way businesses are being encouraged to invest in urban low-income housing even if it will not yield a return on investment comparable to that which could be gotten elsewhere. The reason is the same as in the case of employment. Yet if a business firm accedes to such requests it deviates from its established profit-maximization objective and stockholders are left with lower earnings than they have an economic right to expect. After all, there is no more economic logic in expecting a corporation to make what amounts to a "contribution" to the society than there is for a plumber to charge a charity less than General Motors to repair a leaky faucet.

But if private business should not be expected to participate in social problem solving on a profitless basis, does not the presence of a profit motive intrinsically render the outcome antisocial? For Harrington, of course, the answer is yes. That response, though, merely reflects many socialist preconceptions about the legitimacy of profit and is not relevant whether we are talking about urban problems or the production of automobiles. However, while as a matter of theory it may make no difference whether Johns Manville Corporation makes an equivalent rate of profit on selling its products for use in the construction of a luxury apartment building overlooking Central Park or a low-income housing unit in Harlem, it is crucial to note that, based on actual experience, luxury apartments will be built by private investors, but not low-income housing for Harlem. That is a critical distinction. To close that gap —and it must and should be closed—requires either that industry forego profit (which is as unrealistic as it is economically self-defeating) or that government establish the appropriate institutional arrangements that will stimulate the needed kinds of construction. At the present time government and business together are groping for that arrangement, and it is considerably more important to realize that they have commenced the search than it is to note that they have yet to find the answers.

This quest must start with an understanding that if the new partnership of government and business is to confront, in any meaningful way, the large, difficult civilian problems of the United

States, government must play a large role. For years politicians of both parties have refused to deal with the grave civilian problems of America. Matters of defense and outer space have been given urgent attention, but not those of the cities or of the nation's poor. Now the prospect of forging a new partnership with business provides a fresh opportunity for government leaders to get at the hard core of our national ills by eliciting the large-scale participation of industry. At the same time, though, there is a serious risk, for the earnest new concern of business with the plight of the cities can be turned into an excuse by politicians for the avoidance of their responsibilities. This is a real danger.

If the potential of the new partnership is to be realized, on terms that are consistent with our other social objectives, government must make a major commitment and assume an aggressive posture. This is to ask more than is generally realized for if the problems of our cities, and the nation as a whole, are to be resolved, business cannot and should not be expected to go without a fair profit. But that means that government has to stand ready to make available, in one way or another, billions of dollars annually in recouping past, unmet debts. Politicians have to be ready to vote for bigger appropriations and not expect that business, in some magical way, will take care of things, free. It simply will not do so. Government is going to have to foot the bill, whether it is paid directly via appropriations or indirectly via subsidies (rent supplements, special tax treatment, interest-free obligations, etc.). Equally important, government must be more than an equal partner; it must provide clear, creative direction to business so that the final product will reflect, not merely the technical-economic judgment of company experts, but the democratically expressed desires of the community. Government cannot pass the buck to its business partner, nor can business reasonably expect that government will remain aloof from issues that vitally affect millions of people.

If, however, government plays as positive a role as this would suggest—providing substantial funds and considerable program direction—some segments of business may lose much of their interest in social problem solving, relinquishing their new status as a partner for their older role as a hired servant. Schools, low-income housing, and medical centers can, of course, be constructed by business under contract in accordance with traditional, strict government specifications. That's the way things were done in the past, but such an approach defines a relationship that has hardly worked well, as the plight of our urban ghettos so vividly illustrates. The truth is that government-dominated, government-monopolized programs have often been unimaginative, tardy, and fragmented, administrative nightmares. Most people now recognize this and are as anxious to experiment with new approaches as are businessmen to exploit the profit potential in dealing with the problems of housing, job training, education, medical care, and the associated affairs of urbanization. The tough challenge, and the one we have not yet faced, is to find an institutional mechanism that mobilizes private capital and unleashes the organizational skills and creativity of business, without at the same time prejudicing the larger public interest or abdicating overall program direction to private interests. Such an alliance, whatever its exact form— whether it be modeled on Comsat or some equally imaginative arrangement, inevitably must involve a great deal of compromise by business leaders no less than liberal and conservative politicians.

The old styles of business and the old ways of politics are clearly going to be fundamentally altered by the new partnership, and it is not yet possible to delineate the ultimate allocation of power or gauge the consequences for the general public. Certainly, though, we are in a new world, where business power is accepted as fact and there is broad agreement that it should be brought to bear on social problems that were previously reserved for government attention. The important thing is to recognize the basic and as yet unsettled questions posed by the emerging partnership of government and business and to confront the challenge of devising the means to harness them in a publicly responsive manner.

PART V

The
Internationalization
of Business

CHAPTER 16

Business and
the Emerging World Economy

Americans, more so than most, still think in nineteenth century, neo-mercantilist terms—as if the world were just a collection of individual countries and national economies linked by slim bands of trade. In continuing to speak of *U.S.* companies, *U.S.* workers, and *U.S.* goods as if that adjective still had meaning, we spotlight our own failure to appreciate what has been going on around the globe. Yet no changes in the affairs of business have been as significant or as important for purposes of public policy as the internationalization of corporate activity. Long strides have been taken in the last twenty-five years toward a genuine world economy and by the end of the century—probably much sooner—it will make no more sense to consider the United States a separate economy than it would Delaware, Iowa, or Oregon.

Adding emphasis to the significance of the trend to internationalization is the accelerating expansion of the world economy. Although U.S. output is increasing rapidly, it is still not growing as fast as the aggregate world economy. From 1948 down to date the combined output of all countries has increased at an annual average rate of about 6 percent, compared with 4 percent for the United States. While this might partly be explained in terms of the natural processes of postwar expansion in countries whose economies had nearly collapsed in the 1940–1945 period, the disparity in growth rates is likely to persist through the remainder of this century. From now to 2000 total world GNP is expected to expand almost five times, a fourth again more than the U.S. economy. Looking ahead it is apparent that while economic growth and the global population expansion will create vast market opportunities, business enterprises will be confronted with many unique conditions and compelled to devise new approaches. The national and regional economies of the world are developing at significantly different rates and will continue to display marked disparities in their relative standards of living. As business goes global it will have to adapt to these differences—differences that are as much political and cultural in their nature as economic. In doing so the businessman will be sailing an uncharted sea.

The fact is that business is internationalizing faster than the governments of the world and is forced to play the modern economic game by rules established at a time when there was no real world economy and national rules conformed reasonably well with the scope of the separate markets. That is no longer true and now business is in the vanguard of an economic one-worldism which is finding governments still pursuing their parochial sovereign interests. Their new international status will make life extremely difficult for businessmen, requiring that they often wear the robes of diplomats as much as salesmen.

To sense the full meaning of this political dimension to international business activity and to place the issues in proper perspective requires an examination of the economic parameters of the world in this the last third of the twentieth century. This chapter provides that essential economic backdrop, starting with an assessment of trends and market prospects in the developing nations and then turning to an appraisal of changes taking place in the industrialized world.

Rich Nations, Poor Nations: The Widening Gap

Today the world's three billion inhabitants annually produce goods and services valued at something approaching $2 trillion, with not far from half of this accounted for by the two hundred million Americans. By the end of the century world population will approximate seven billion and aggregate GNP will increase by five times (in real terms). U.S. economic expansion will not quite keep up with this pace—"only" quadrupling between now and 2000— and thus there will be a slight narrowing of the gulf that now exists between America and other countries. However, virtually all of this gain in wealth will be registered by the industrialized nations rather than by the poorer countries of the southern hemisphere and Asia. While the United States will relinquish some ground to Canada, Japan, and Euro-Russia, it will continue to be confronted by a world in which most people are hungry, if not starving, and getting poorer, in relative terms. For business these realities—widespread affluence and enormous economic expansion in the industrialized countries in a sea surrounded by billions of impoverished people— present special problems and unique challenges, calling for the exercise of considerable diplomacy as well as older-style economic skills.

The global economy of the future thus is largely a study in imbalance—in contrasts, if you prefer. Incomes will rise for just about everyone, but the rich will add to their wealth at a faster rate than the poor. The principal explanation is population. Take India as an example. In 1968 her GNP amounted to $45 billion, or less than $100 per capita (the comparable figure in the United States that year was $4,100). If the Indian GNP increases at 5 percent a year, by 2000 her annual aggregate output should approximate $215 billion. That, of course, would be an impressive acccomplishment, given the country's present position. However, India's population growth will literally devour most of this economic expansion. Some demographers anticipate that India's population will grow at a rate of nearly 2 percent a year (slower than the country has known in the recent past, but still much above the 1.5 percent rate that now prevails in the United States), nearly doubling her present five hundred million inhabitants in thirty years. If this happens, Indian per capita GNP in 2000—despite economic growth of 5 percent a year—will amount to $215. In the meantime U.S. output per person is likely to soar beyond $10,000. The dollar distance between the peoples of these two key world countries will have lengthened substantially, further fanning the fires of expectation and depressing the hopes of those in other lands that they can improve radically their own standard of living in a world dominated by democracy and free enterprise.

The Indian case is by no means exceptional. In most of the developing countries economic growth will be able to keep only a little ahead of population expansion. Given the present large absolute difference in the comparative economic condition of the industrialized and developing countries, the gap is bound to widen although their exact percentage proportions may narrow a hair. Table 7 sums up the key facts, postulating forecasts for rates of economic and population growth that fall in an intermediate range between the highest and lowest made by various prognosticators.

Aggravating further the plight of the poor countries are the worsening terms of trade. Prices of primary goods have been going down relative to the prices of the finished goods they must buy from the industrialized producers. Ghana, for example, points out that a machine that could be bought a few years back for ten tons of cocoa now costs the equivalent of twenty-five tons. Even the price of transportation has soared. Most of the world's ocean shipping is under the control of European ship conferences (a fancy word for "cartels") that often charge less to haul manufactured products to the lesser developed countries (LDC) than to carry raw materials to the factories of Europe and the United States. Too, the developing countries are finding that an increasing proportion of their capital must be diverted to the payment of interest on "aid" they were given in the past in the form of loans. Between now and 1980 India will have to raise $14 billion merely to service its debts.

As the industrialized countries develop new products and processes there is the further likelihood that they will need even fewer of the primary raw materials that are the foundation of the economies of the LDC. The shift to synthetics (noted in Chapter 10) already has had a severe impact on many poor countries. In the last half dozen years the earnings of the twelve rubber-producing countries fell by more than $4 billion, largely because of a shift

TABLE 7

Anticipated Economic Growth and Economic Expansion in Selected Principal Countries to Year 2000

Country	GNP (In billions of 1967 U.S. $)		Assumed growth rate 1968–2000 (in percent)	GNP per Capita (In 1967 U.S. $)		Population (millions)	
	1968	2000		1968	2000	1968	2000
U.S.A.	829	3,391	4.5	4,121	10,600	201	320
U.S.S.R.	380	1,809	5.0	1,610	5,170	236	350
Japan	130	620	5.0	1,283	5,000	101	125
West Germany	129	528	4.5	2,154	7,500	60	70
France	121	495	4.5	2,399	7,600	50	65
Communist China	91	433	5.0	118	340	770	1,270
United Kingdom	115	404	4.0	2,071	6,700	55	60
India	45	215	5.0	86	215	520	1,000
Italy	70	286	4.5	1,358	4,400	51	60
Canada	60	286	5.0	2,877	7,200	21	40

Source of data: United Nations; U.S. Department of State, Agency for International Development.

to rubber substitutes, notably rayon and nylon. Increasingly international trade consists of commerce between the industrialized countries rather than with the developing world. From 1950 to 1965, for example, world exports grew at an annual average rate of 7.4 percent. But the exports of developed countries to each other rose by 9.4 percent while the exports of LDC increased by only 4.5 percent. If petroleum shipments were excluded, the poorer countries' exports showed an annual increase of a mere 3.6 percent. This trend is continuing. According to the International Monetary Fund, exports of the industrial countries rose 9 percent in 1966 compared with 1965; LDC exports increased by only 7 percent. The rich countries are trading more and more with one another, isolating their poorer neighbors. In the process the rich are getting comparatively richer and the poor, poorer.

Business Prospects in the Developing World

Despite the fact that the citizens of those countries making up the LDC world are going to remain very poor in comparison with those of the affluent industrialized nations, their sheer numbers nonetheless make them a market of immense importance. Right now about two thirds of the 3.2 billion persons who live on this planet reside in the LDC. By the year 2000 at least three fourths, and perhaps 80 percent, of the world's seven billion population will live in Latin America, Asia, and Africa. Merely to satisfy their most elementary needs—for food, housing, clothing, and medical care—opens up markets whose size transcends anything within our commercial experience.

Consider, for example, what it would take to feed adequately the tens of millions of people in the developing countries. Right now their daily food intake falls three hundred calories short of a minimum acceptable standard; their protein consumption is deficient by at least a third. The simple expedient of food from surplus countries, like the United States and Canada, is impractical, for even if production could keep pace, the poor countries would not be able to pay for this volume of imports. Some better answer must be found and here business can play a key role —and a profitable one.

The biggest challenge is the problem of protein deficiency. Human caloric requirements can be satisfied with relative ease, since carbohydrates (starch and sugar) are found in many substances and are available at low cost, around three cents a pound. Protein is much more expensive as a food, costing about fifteen cents a pound. To cut the cost of protein and to make it more easily available in food form is a major technological problem— and one to which a number of companies are directing their talents, lured by a market measured in billions of customers. The Corn Products Company, for instance, is producing and selling an enriched, high-protein cornmeal product called Maizena. The Quaker Oats Company processes and distributes in Central America an all-vegetable protein formula known as Incaparina. Other companies are experimenting with fish flours, dried soybean milk powder, and similar high-protein substances. European and American oil companies have demonstrated that protein can be manufactured in edible form from a petroleum or natural gas base. Efforts, then, are underway and the potential sales are nearly limitless to those enterprises that can devise practical means to satisfy man's nutritional requirements. Each day, let it be recalled, there are an additional two hundred thousand mouths to feed.

The greatest potential business rewards are likely to go to those firms that can become self-contained agricultural empires— assuming complete responsibility for the production, processing, storage, and distribution of food supplies in developing foreign countries. So-called "agribusinesses" are already beginning to take shape, albeit slowly. Their success will depend, to a very considerable extent, on their ability to work out arrangements with local governments that meet their quasi-political needs, but do not unacceptably interfere with efficient managerial operations. Often this will mean some sort of shared undertaking in which the government, or perhaps local private capital, has a substantial stake in the ownership and control of the operation. The ultimate enterprise is likely to look rather strange by the typical standards of Western-style business, but this is something to which businessmen anxious to serve the markets where three fourths of the world's people will reside must become accustomed. In India, for example, American and European oil and chemical companies have joined in quasi-socialist enterprises to supply nitrogenous fertilizer. One of the basic ingredients for the fertilizer, ammonia, will be imported into India from U.S.-owned plants located in Iran, where that country's government shares ownership with American investors. This mixture of Western capital and know-how with indigenous socialistic government investment and control is certain to be a common future characteristic of corporate participation in the economies of the developing nations.

It is not just man's food needs, of course, that will create an urgent demand for the skills of business. Housing is of near equal importance. U.N. sources estimate that the world is now short by at least two hundred million dwelling units—and the situation worsens daily as people migrate from farm to city. About a third of the world's population now is located in cities of twenty thousand population and over; by the end of the century the figure will be close to 60 percent, signaling an increase in the urban population of three billion in the next three decades. To meet this housing demand it would take forty million new dwelling units each year to provide minimally decent shelter, but the present construction rate is closer to ten million, partly because of high costs and inefficient organization.

Based on the record it is evident that the developing countries will not be able to meet these housing demands on their own. Today, for example, in East Africa there are no factories producing any basic building components and in West Africa, despite vast forest reserves, only three countries have plywood factories and most wood (and other) products are imported. There is an obvious need for industrial know-how and Western capital, as some investors have recognized. The International Basic Economy Corporation, controlled by Rockefeller interests, is seeking to promote basic economic development in underdeveloped countries, on a profit-making basis, by investing in agriculture, food distribution, and housing. But its contribution, and that of similar endeavors, barely scratches the surface of the problem. The potential for profitable, truly large-scale business attention to these vast problems—and huge markets—is yet untapped.

The Changing Industrialized World Economy

The growth of the international economy and the widening gap between the rich and the poor countries will be accompanied by equally significant changes taking place within the industrialized world itself. Long accustomed to thinking of our domestic markets as economically preeminent, Americans are going to find that other parts of the developed world will narrow its lead, evening out the distribution of wealth among the affluent nations. There is little question that the U.S. will continue to have the single biggest economy, but the absolute margin of its superiority is definitely going to shrink. This is one important development to be anticipated. It means, among a lot of things, that foreign markets, already big and attractive, are going to exert an even greater magnetic appeal on business, generating a still more powerful impetus to corporate internationalization.

In previewing the growth of other national and regional economies, it is striking to note which groupings are likely to offer the biggest markets. Asked to take a guess most people would nominate the six-nation Common Market, perhaps EFTA (the European Free Trade Association, or Outer Seven) and maybe Japan. All represent good candidates. But, as Chart 6 shows, quite dramatically, the Russia-East European Communist bloc will have a larger economy by 1985 than the Common Market, EFTA, or Japan. It is particularly startling to realize just how important a position the Communist East will assume later in this century. In 1968 the U.S.S.R.'s GNP was about $380 billion, less than half that of the United States and about equal to that of the EEC. By 1985, however, annual Russian output will add up to nearly $800 billion and surpass that of the Common Market. There is a good reason, though, to consider the East European Communist countries along with Russia, as a kind of economic equivalent to the

CHART 6

Comparison of Projected Growth Rates for Economies of Selected Countries and Regions to 1975, 1985

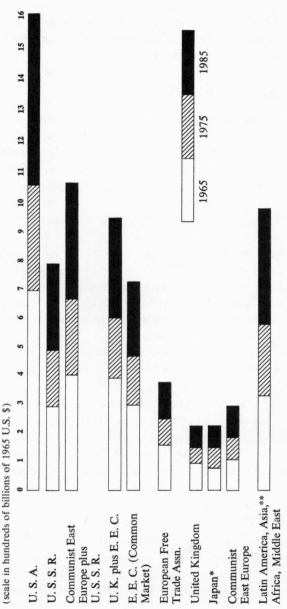

(scale in hundreds of billions of 1965 U.S. $)

* Assumes a 5 percent rate of growth to 1985.
** Except Japan and Mainland China.
Sources: United Nations; U.S. Agency for International Development; Herman Kahn & Anthony J. Wiener, *The Year 2000*, Macmillan, New York, 1967, table X.

Warsaw Pact. Not only is this compatible with Communist ideology, but, more importantly, it is consistent with reality, for the economies of the East European countries are closely interwoven with that of the U.S.S.R. If, then, the East European Red nations are lumped together with Russia, their aggregate GNP in 1985 will exceed $1 trillion, greater than England and the EEC combined.

The economic rise of East Europe and Russia, awesomely important as it is in the pragmatic world of business, should not becloud the fact that Western Europe nonetheless will be growing rapidly and assuming constantly greater importance vis-à-vis the United States. The United Kingdom and the Common Market will constitute a market approaching trillion-dollar status by 1985. Clearly, then, the businessman of today, peering into the future, must begin now to plan for active participation in the lush markets of Europe, West and East, or run the serious risk of falling far behind in the competitive race.

The Booming Communist Markets

While for the moment—due to a combination of factors, many political in nature—free world exports to Communist areas are not a large part of total world trade, the growth of the East Europe and Russian economies makes them prime sales targets in the future. Of present free world exports, less than 5 percent reflects sales to Russia, East Europe, and the Communist countries of Asia (East Europe and the U.S.S.R. alone account for about 4 percent). Small though trade with the Communist bloc still is, it is up sharply over the last few years. Although free world exports have doubled since 1955, trade with Communist areas quadrupled —rising from 2.5 percent of total trade to 4.7 percent in 1966. Similarly, imports from Communist areas have also increased sharply, climbing steadily year by year from 2 percent in 1952 to about 5 percent of free world imports. With free world-Communist two-way trade—exports and imports—now approximating $20 billion a year, and growing at 12 to 14 percent a year (over twice as fast as total world trade), it is of obvious economic consequence to Western business interests.

Significantly, however, it has been the companies of West Europe which have reaped most of the gains of increased Communist country trade. Direct U.S.-Communist trade, by comparison, has been insignificant in amount and retarded in growth. In 1967 American exports to all Communist countries together totaled $200 million or less than 1 percent of our aggregate foreign shipments. This was not even half of the exports to Communist areas by France, Italy, or England and barely a seventh of West German exports. For these countries shipments to East Europe, Russia, and China amount to as much as 7 percent of their total exports. Even more noticeable is the expansion in West Europe exports to Communist countries. In 1965, for example, England shipped $396 million worth of goods to Communist nations, but by 1967 these markets absorbed more than $587 million in British exports. Between 1947 and 1967 West European countries as a whole increased their exports to East Europe-Russia from $410 million to $3.3 billion. Significantly, most of the gain—nearly $2 billion— was attributable to purchases, not by Russia, but by the East European bloc.

Attracted by the booming markets of the Communist countries, U.S. business has moved to enter Eastern markets—cautiously and often secretively. The explanation for their interest is elementary: sales and profit opportunities. Italy provides an example. Fiat, the giant Italian complex, is building an auto plant for the Russians that will turn out six hundred thousands cars a year. Pirelli, another Italian firm, worked out a $50 million deal to make tires and rubber parts for the Fiats. Olivetti will supply Russia with much of its office equipment. Watching these missed opportunities, American firms have begun to look East, but U.S. law and politics have often necessitated indirect approaches to Communist bloc markets.

The United States restricts the sale of many goods, on the theory that an embargo will punish the Reds by denying them access to the advanced technology of the West. The hypothesis is fundamentally unsound and the embargo policy succeeds primarily only in denying U.S. firms a chance to make sales which Western European corporations make as a matter of business course. Perhaps

worse, it is hypocritical, for U.S. firms, supposedly barred or inhibited from selling products to the Reds, often resort to supplying
Red buyers from their European subsidiaries. IBM, as an instance,
sells much data-processing equipment to the East Europeans, but
practically none of it comes from the United States. Instead it is
produced and shipped from IBM plants on the continent. Trade
statistics record its sales as if they were made by a European
firm, not by an American company. Or take Caterpillar Tractor.
It has a plant at Grenoble, France, and supplies Communist purchasers from there rather than from its big factory complex in Pe-
oria, Illinois. Similarly, most of the equipment sold by Honeywell in
East Europe is manufactured in its West German plant. Significant
sales by U.S. firms are disguised in this manner, showing up in
trade accounts as exports of England, Germany, or France, when
in fact they are made by Americans. An even larger volume of
sales comes in the form of earnings received for the licensing of
technical know-how to Communist countries.

Despite extensive evasion of restrictions on Communist sales,
it is apparent that U.S. firms have been irrationally excluded from
rapidly expanding markets and severely impeded in their sales
efforts. This is bad economics and it is even worse politics, for
it has cut off East Europe and Russia from the influence of American ideology and contributed to an accentuation of the inward-
looking attitude which Russia has tried to inculcate in her satellites.
Recognizing this, President Johnson proposed the East-West Trade
Relations Act in an effort to build economic and diplomatic
bridges to the East. Formulated in cooperation with a group of
business leaders led by J. Irwin Miller of the Cummins Engine
Company, the legislation would have authorized the President
to use nondiscriminatory tariff treatment as a bargaining element
in negotiating commercial agreements with the Soviet Union and
the Communist countries of Eastern Europe. Unfortunately, despite
Administration and business support, the measure was not passed
by the Congress. Why? The answer is rooted in emotion and stems
basically from a fear that voting for a measure to permit fuller
contact with the Communist world might be publicly regarded as
pro-Red. It is a fear not without some reason. When Firestone

Tire proposed building a plant in Rumania, under active encouragement of the U.S. Government, the company was viciously attacked by Young Americans for Freedom, a right-wing political group. The company finally abandoned its plans and other firms —and politicians—took it as a general lesson. The result is that the U.S. continues to make it hard for American companies to participate fully and openly in what promises to be one of the biggest, fastest growing market regions in the world.

Problems of Economic Internationalization

With full acknowledgment of the sales opportunities presented by the LDC and the nations of East Europe and Russia, the problems of business accommodation to the special features of these markets can hardly be understated. The economic challenges are formidable, but the difficulties stemming from divergent cultural and political traditions are even more so. Their resolution will require the patience, ingenuity, and understanding of the diplomat as much as it will the skill of the engineer or the aggressiveness of the salesman. On every front—from manufacturing and distribution to merchandising and sales—the international enterprise of the future, eager to reach the billions of customers in East Europe and the southern hemisphere, is going to confront problems and be forced to pursue approaches that will be truly unique.

Many of the countries in these areas in which the modern company must sell its wares are socialist in outlook and in political orientation; they will restrict advertising, insist on shared ownership in plant facilities, demand that a substantial percentage of a product be manufactured locally, require that transactions be handled exclusively by a state trading organization; they will often lack hard currency and insist on barter arrangements; they will be distrustful, culturally sensitive, unpredictable, and tentative in their dealings. None of these hurdles are insurmountable, but they are uncommon and will force businessmen to adopt a style and attitude that is largely alien to that which has characterized trade up to now. In this complex process of accommodation corporate executives are going to be affected just as severely as company practices.

It would be a serious mistake, however, to think that business affairs in the older, supposedly more mature industrialized countries are not also going to continue to be burdened by national governmental policies that can seriously interfere with free trade. The old bogeyman of tariffs has been gotten under control, but the spread of customs unions ("common markets") promises to erect a new institutional impediment to free access to major markets. Such arrangements, best illustrated by the formation in 1958 of the European Economic Community, constitute an important—and foreboding—exception to the basic free-trade principle incorporated in the 1948 General Agreement on Tariffs & Trade. The key operative postulate of GATT was nondiscriminatory treatment—with tariffs applied equally to all countries, on a most favored nation basis. It has been a sound approach and has greatly helped foster international trade. Now, however, it is being attacked as countries form preferential groupings, eliminating or reducing duties among their members but maintaining high external customs barriers. The idea is being implemented in Africa and Latin America as well as Europe and, as it spreads, it could gravely impair the growth of the world economy. The threat is serious and some alert businessmen are diversifying their investments internationally to avert precisely this problem.

Customs unions cast a shadow on the future international economy, but a more immediate problem are the nontariff inhibitions on trade between countries. They assume various forms—quantitative restrictions, discriminatory customs valuation, burdensome (and inequitable) inspection practices, and border tax adjustments. National laws that supposedly set quality or product definitional standards can severely prejudice sellers in other countries.

Taxes, too, may have a differential impact: French road taxes, for instance, impose a levy of $200 on a Chrysler Imperial, only $18 on a French-made sedan. Beginning in 1968 German sales taxes were levied on a value-added basis for goods manufactured in the country (an auto manufacturer deducts the price of components before paying tax on the value of his cars), but on full value for imports (a U.S. auto maker pays tax on the gross market value of a car imported into Germany). This change in German law alone added 4 to 5 percent to the taxes paid by foreigners, but it did not increase the taxes of German firms. Americans complain bitterly and understandably about such practices, but their own house, let it be said, has a lot of glass in it. "Buy American" restrictions, limitations on the types of ships that can be used to haul U.S. Government-aided shipments, import quotas on foreign oil, and a host of other practices discriminate against foreign sellers.

Nontariff restrictions—like tariffs at an earlier day—must be resisted, not merely because they both inhibit trade and shield inefficiency from competitive forces but equally because of their insidious tendency to balkanize the world politically. Businessmen, no less than statesmen, have a large stake—and not just an economic one—in exerting their efforts to reduce all such encroachments on their freedom of operation. Politicians, too, must face up to their responsibility, recognizing that short-term measures, like the 1968 U.S. restrictions on overseas investment, are no substitute for policies that maximize the freedom of international trade.

If the enlightened elements of business and government do not exert their influence in this way, there is a very real risk that the United States could turn isolationist, hiding behind the protective cover of tariffs and quotas. Further shrinkage of the U.S. balance of payments trade surplus will only increase the probability that this kind of ostrich-like policy might be adopted. While the U.S. still runs a big trade surplus in the sale of high-technology capital goods like aircraft, electronic equipment, and machine tools, imports of semifinished goods (and even some finished goods) have been increasing sharply. Foreign steel now represents about 12 percent of domestic steel consumption.

Beset by foreign competition and uncertain that trade opportunities abroad will constitute a sufficient offsetting market, some American industrialists have sought tariff protection. In the 90th Congress more than seven hundred bills were introduced to provide quota or other protection for the steel, textile, and other industries. Most U.S. businessmen have wisely resisted this defensive approach to the new world of international competition, but the emotional demands for government help are likely to increase in volume and intensity if the U.S. merchandise surplus continues to shrink.

Hopefully businessmen will direct their attention—and that of government leaders—to more constructive areas of concern. Over the long pull, the U.S. can be a positive factor only if we are involved in the world. All things considered, that can be true only if our businesses both trade and invest multinationally. Most aggressive, farsighted American companies have grasped this point, but some, as in steel, have not and are trying to play the new international game by the old national rules. They can't win, but in the short run they can express their dissatisfaction in ways that will work against sound long-term economic and political interests and of all but the most backward segments of the American business community.

The New Business Internationalism

The awesome complexities of a changing world economy which have been reviewed in this chapter help make up the new international environment in which business must function. It is a strange and sometimes hostile environment, but the opportunities are nearly limitless for those companies wise and creative enough to participate as actively in the total global economy as they have in the Atlantic world.

Most American and many foreign enterprises have recognized this and have begun to get involved internationally—to such an extent that they are now true world economic citizens. Indeed, the modern multinational business corporation has become the most potent de facto political instrumentality of internationalism, of far greater practical consequence than the United Nations. It is supranational business, with its immense power and special political-economic features, that is the centerpiece of the next chapter.

CHAPTER 17

The Internationalization
of Business

"Either one is an international corporation or one is an empire, and I must tell you very frankly that I prefer the international corporation. It pays better."

—Caesar Rupf to Emperor Romulus in Friedrich Duerenmatt's
Romulus the Great

The opportunities presented by the booming world economy have been clearly recognized by American and foreign business interests. Partly through trade but primarily through multinational investment and operations, corporations are becoming genuine economic citizens of the world. This fact, with its obvious economic implications, presents even more critical political problems for it draws into serious question both the sufficiency and the relevance of existing legal arrangements to control, and service, corporations which have severed their ties with any single nation.

No longer is it accurate to think of most of our large corporations as "American." The oil companies, the big auto, drug, and chemical producers, and the makers of computers and electrical equipment, among many others, are so heavily committed to foreign markets that they have in fact lost their U.S. identity and assumed a multinational character. Just as regulation of business corporations by the states became outmoded sixty or so years ago as an integrated U.S. economy supplanted the local and regional markets which had characterized the nation in its first century, today the global scope of commercial activity by major

U.S. and foreign companies is rendering national regulation obsolete.

With firms like Standard Oil of New Jersey, Mobil Oil, Woolworth, National Cash Register, Burroughs, Colgate-Palmolive, Standard Oil of California, and Singer deriving more than half their income or earnings from "foreign" sales, and with a long list of others, including such familiar giants as Eastman Kodak, Pfizer, Caterpillar Tractor, International Harvester, Corn Products, and Minnesota Mining (MMM) making from 30 to 50 percent of their sales abroad, even these once-American companies are beginning to acknowledge openly—indeed with occasional enthusiasm and a frequent boast—their new supranational status. In explaining why it had changed its corporate name and trademark to Uniroyal, U.S. Rubber proclaimed that "it is now meeting the research and manufacturing needs of the whole polyglot world."

The expanding geographic scope of business operations, accentuated in the last several years by billions of dollars in overseas investments by American and foreign firms, typified by ITT, poses grave political and economic questions that are yet to be answered. The problems posed are by no means simple, but what must be grasped is that they are fundamentally *international* in character and cannot be understood or resolved if looked at in outmoded nationalistic terms.

The Diminishing Importance of Trade

What partly obscures our recognition of the evolution of the world economy is that we traditionally think about it in terms of trade—of exports and imports of goods. Viewed this way the growth of the global economy is significant enough, but it misses the more subtle, more powerful underlying economic currents and greatly understates the role of the United States in international commerce. Currently, we export over $33 billion a year in non-military goods and services and import somewhat less, leaving us with a significant though erratic and generally shrinking trade surplus.

While these data reveal sizable increases in trade during the postwar period—with exports up more than twice since 1948 and imports up about four times—they also suggest that our involvement in the economic affairs of the world is extremely limited. The figures show, for example, that U.S. exports amount to less than 4 per cent of the GNP—hardly big enough, it would seem, to show that the United States has become as fully immersed in the world economy as it has. For European countries, by contrast, trade represents a big proportion of their total economic activity—with exports in The Netherlands, for example, equaling almost a quarter of that country's GNP. Similarly, U.S. exports pale by comparison with total world trade, which now amounts to about $200 billion annually. Approached from the trade standpoint, American participation in the world economy looks very limited indeed and is hardly suggestive of a trend to internationalism.

Trade statistics, however, actually mask the realities of the new globalism in economics. The key fact is this: companies no longer operate in a single country, making goods and shipping them to purchasers in other parts of the world. Instead they establish plants in a number of countries and supply their customers from the lowest-cost location. Just as an auto producer locates factories in those parts of the country best calculated to meet market demands rather than shipping its new cars from a single plant in Detroit, so too does it establish production facilities around the world rather than ship finished cars from our shores. From a business standpoint this makes perfectly good economic sense, but it also means that there is less trade in exports from the United States.

Business Foreign Investment

American business has, of course, been directly engaged in foreign markets for many years (Henry Ford began producing cars at a plant in Manchester, England, in 1911), but since the end of the war—and especially since the mid-1950s—there has been a great outrush as U.S. firms—literally by the thousands—

have made permanent commitments in foreign markets. So powerful has been this impetus to invest abroad that it actually differs in kind from earlier overseas business activity.

Since 1955 U.S. direct business investment abroad has skyrocketed from $19 billion to more than $65 billion. At the recent rate, the value of our foreign direct investments increases by an average of about $10 million a *day*. Table 8 presents a detailed statistical picture for 1967, when total U.S. investment amounted to $60 billion. It shows that U.S. external investment has been very heavily concentrated in a few geographic areas, most notably in Canada and Western Europe. Also important to note is that a very large percentage of present business investment abroad is now in manufacturing, taking the form of the construction or acquisition of factories, distribution centers, and office buildings—the ingredients necessary for staking out and developing a permanent position of influence in foreign markets. In 1969 American companies spent an estimated $12 billion on new plant and equipment in foreign countries. As a result the familiar names of domestic corporations—usually the big and long-established, but often the small and new as well—can be seen today in dozens of countries, particularly in and around the Atlantic Community.

This new surge of investment does not merely involve the purchase of a stake in overseas markets, such as is the case when investors buy stock in a foreign corporation. That has taken place too, of course. Today Americans own about $15 billion worth of securities in overseas firms—double their position in 1960 and five times the amount held at the end of the war. Direct investment, by comparison, is not only bigger in dollar terms but is of greater long-term consequence since it involves a permanent commitment and actual control of the physical means of production and distribution.

Just as our companies have greatly expanded their investment abroad, so too have foreigners sharply increased their holdings in this country. There is, though, a basic difference. While considerable direct foreign investment here is made by octopi like Shell and Unilever, about two thirds of all long-term foreign capital in the United States is in corporate stock and bonds—the bulk of it from Western Europe (especially Swiss and British interests) and Canada.

To get a better picture of the character and significance of overseas investment in the last few years, consider the activity in Western Europe of the fifty largest U.S. manufacturers. In all, these fifty firms took nearly five hundred separate steps to expand their position, especially within the Common Market, in the eleven-year span 1958–1969. They formed joint ventures, acquired foreign firms, set up subsidiaries, established additional plants, and entered into hundreds of licensing arrangements (mostly involving the use of patents in high-technology areas).

Of these various moves the mergers are the most important because they removed foreign competitors at the same time they expanded the position of big American companies in the Atlantic market. GE, for example, bought a major Swiss-French-German maker of household appliances for $43 million, Goodyear enlarged its position in the German tire market through merger, Dow acquired nine European chemical manufacturers (it also has set up its own Swiss bank to take care of its European financial needs), and Celanese and several other firms followed the merger route to gain a bigger share of rapidly expanding West European plastics and synthetic fiber markets. Schlitz took control of a large Belgian brewer. All of the major American oil companies made acquisitions, buying up everything from refiners and petroleum distributors to petrochemical specialists. Chrysler was especially active, purchasing auto companies in England (Rootes Motors), France (Simca), Mexico, South Africa, and the Netherlands, as well as in Spain.

One major result of this floodtide of foreign mergers and the accompanying outrush of capital for investment abroad is that our companies now typically supply customers abroad from factories situated overseas rather than via export from domestic facilities. In 1950 foreign sales by U.S. firms totaled approximately $37 billion. Of this, a third was supplied by exports from these shores. Today, by contrast, only about a sixth of our estimated $200 billion in foreign sales is supplied by exports, with the rest coming from plants located in other countries. Since 1950 U.S. busi-

TABLE 8
U.S. Direct Investments Abroad, by Area and Industry
($ in millions)

	MINING		PETROLEUM		MANUFACTURING		PUBLIC UTILITIES		TRADE		TOTAL	
	1950	1967	1950	1967	1950	1967	1950	1967	1950	1967	1950	1967
Canada	334	2,337	418	3,819	1,897	8,083	284	506	240	1,032	3,579	18,069
Latin American Republics	628	1,218	1,233	2,917	780	3,301	927	614	242	1,207	4,445	10,213
Other Western Hemisphere	38	431	70	585	1	271	15	51	3	92	131	1,708
Europe, total	31	61	426	4,404	932	9,781	27	78	186	2,055	1,733	17,882
Common Market	3	19	210	2,063	317	4,964	10	49	49	851	637	8,405
Other Europe	28	42	216	2,341	615	4,817	17	29	137	1,204	1,096	9,477
Africa	64	398	124	1,232	55	369	3	3	24	148	287	2,277
Asia, total	21	43	769	2,599	60	986	52	76	49	321	1,001	4,282
Middle East	10	3	666	1,607	1	59	2	6	3	19	692	1,748
Far East	11	40	103	992	59	927	51	69	46	303	309	2,533
Oceania	12	322	110	592	107	1,332		2	18	139	256	2,515
International shipping companies			240	1,264			116	968			356	2,321
All areas, total	1,129	4,810	3,390	17,410	3,831	24,124	1,425	2,387	762	4,995	11,788	59,267

Source: Department of Commerce.

Note: Totals may not add due to rounding.

ness investment abroad has climbed at 10 percent a year; our exports have increased only 7 percent a year. In all, between 1958 and 1968 American manufacturers increased their overseas capacity 471 percent, compared with 72 percent at home. To an increasing extent, U.S. companies supply foreign markets from foreign facilities. International production, *not* trade, is the key to understanding the contemporary economic situation. What's more, U.S. firms often supply the "home" market from plants located beyond our borders. Burroughs, for example, reportedly makes *all* its small, desktop office equipment abroad, mostly in Scotland, and ships it to the United States. Many American electrical equipment companies produce components or complete ready-to-use radios and similar items, in Hong Kong, Formosa, or Korea.

Oligopoly Around the World

In shifting production abroad, U.S. companies have been shrewdly using their resources to gain dominant positions overseas roughly equivalent to those they have acquired in this country. Autos provide a good example. Long in firm control of the domestic scene, the Big Three—General Motors, Ford, and Chrysler—have invested hundreds of millions of dollars in expanding their foreign plants and acquired dozens of auto and auto parts companies. The result is that in all of the European auto markets they now hold sizable shares. In England, Ford (which in 1961 paid out $360 million to acquire the remaining interest in its U.K. subsidiary) and GM challenge British Motors, and are not far ahead of Chrysler, which bought its way in by acquiring control of Rootes Motors, once a major independent factor in Britain (and, indeed, in America). In the big German auto market, GM's Opel and Ford's Taunus contend aggressively with Volkswagen. A new $100 million plant built by GM at Antwerp and a vast new Ford plant located in the Saarland will make these companies, along with Chrysler, even larger factors in European car sales. One major consequence of all these moves is that Ford at present makes 40 percent of its cars outside the U.S., Chrysler over 30 percent, and GM 25 percent.

Through Chrysler's acquisition of Simca and Rootes, Ford's assumption of total control of its English subsidiary, and through direct expansion, the Big Three American auto makers have carved out a position in the world auto market that reflects the same basic characteristic that distinguishes the auto industry at home—namely, oligopoly. It is true, of course, that a few of the biggest foreign auto companies have taken steps to enlarge their own positions with the consequence that a half dozen giant corporations now dominate the global trade in passenger cars. Nonetheless, the U.S. firms are far and away the leaders—with bigger sales and profits and far greater assets. There is a comparable situation in a number of other basic industries where a few international companies, competing with one another around the world, account for most of an industry's sales. In terms of sales Chart 7 shows the relative size of the biggest companies in selected industries, with the number one firm in each case being U.S.

Two features in this graphic array stand out. First for these industries and for a number of others of equal consequence, the predominant structural pattern is one of oligopoly. In each a few firms—a few international firms, to be more specific—are dominant. Second, despite the oligopolistic feature of these industries, the big U.S. corporations are usually far bigger than their rivals. Table 9 offers additional pertinent data. It is this fact which has sent shudders of fear through Europe and triggered mergers in a mad race to achieve greater size in a search for something approaching more equality with their rivals from across the Atlantic. Today the gross sales revenue of the top twenty or so American companies is equal to Britain's GNP. Belgium's budget could be financed from the profits of just America's top four firms. Of the world's companies with sales of $285 million or more in 1968, 60 percent are American-based. Indeed the United States had nearly six times as many firms in this size class as any other single country.

Relative to their American rivals, even the biggest European companies generally look like midgets. Among the world's companies U.S. businesses are on the average five times larger than the leading British or German corporations, and ten times larger

CHART 7

Comparative Size of World Corporations, Selected Industries *

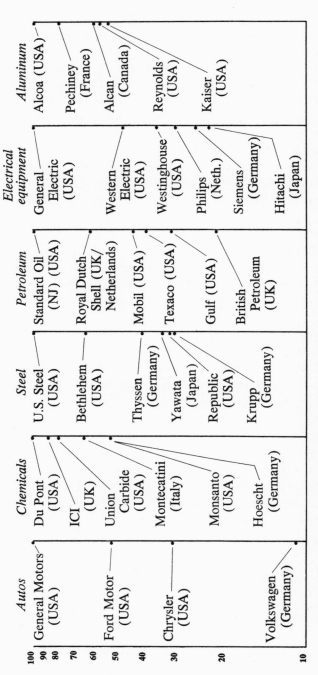

* Chart shows comparative firm sizes, by 1967 sales, of the largest firms in each industry. The leading firm is set at 100; figures, on a log scale, show relative size of others in terms of sales.

TABLE 9

World's Twenty Biggest Industrial Corporations, 1968

(ranked by sales; $ in millions)

Rank	Corporation	Country of Principal Affiliation	Sales	Assets	Net Income (after-tax)	Employees
1	General Motors	U.S.A.	$22,755	$14,010	$1,732	757,231
2	Standard Oil (NJ)	U.S.A.	14,091	16,786	1,277	151,000
3	Ford Motor	U.S.A.	14,075	8,953	627	415,000
4	Royal Dutch/Shell	U.K./Netherlands	9,216	14,303	935	171,000
5	General Electric	U.S.A.	8,382	5,744	357	400,000
6	Chrysler	U.S.A.	7,445	4,398	291	231,089
7	IBM	U.S.A.	6,889	6,743	871	241,974
8	Mobil Oil	U.S.A.	6,221	6,872	428	78,300
9	Unilever	U.K.	5,534	3,432	206	312,000
10	Texaco	U.S.A.	5,460	8,687	836	78,475
11	Gulf Oil	U.S.A.	4,559	7,498	626	60,300
12	U.S. Steel	U.S.A.	4,537	6,391	254	201,017
13	ITT	U.S.A.	4,067	4,022	192	293,000
14	Western Electric	U.S.A.	4,031	2,722	192	176,970
15	Standard Oil (Calif.)	U.S.A.	3,635	5,770	452	47,885
16	McDonnell Douglas	U.S.A.	3,609	1,335	95	124,740
17	Du Pont	U.S.A.	3,481	3,289	372	114,100
18	Shell Oil	U.S.A.	3,317	4,230	312	39,080
19	Westinghouse	U.S.A.	3,296	2,271	135	138,000
20	Boeing	U.S.A.	3,274	2,186	83	142,400

Source of Data: *Fortune's* 1969 surveys.

than the French companies. Based on the 1968 experience Belgium's largest concern would not even rank among the top 100 U.S. industrial companies in terms of sales; France's would be number forty-six; Germany's would place only number twenty-three; and Italy's number thirty-four. When grouped by industries the comparison is even more striking.

In 1968 U.S. Steel's profits were seven times greater than those of August Thyssen-Hutte, Germany's biggest steel producer. Du Pont's profits are nearly twice those of Imperial Chemical Industries and three times greater than those of Farbenfabrikan Bayer. Similarly, General Electric towers above Philips, Siemens, and Hitachi, the biggest foreign producers of electrical equipment. Goodyear's profits are bigger than those of the European Big Three—Dunlop, Pirelli, and Michelin—*combined*. General Motors' sales are almost eight times those of Volkswagen and are bigger than the Gross National Product of the Netherlands and well over a hundred other countries. Indeed, the aggregate sales of VW, Fiat, Daimler-Benz, British Motors, and Renault are equal to only three fourths of Ford Motors' sales, which in turn are only about two thirds those of G.M.

The American Business Invasion of Europe

Seeing the spread of American business power across the ocean, Europeans have issued a clarion call not unlike that sent forth by Patrick Henry, John Adams, and the rest of their revolutionary coterie 180 years ago. The most stirring and perhaps the most eloquent declaration has come from the French journalist Jean Jacques Servan-Schreiber, who says in his *The American Challenge* * that "the third industrial power, after the U.S. and the Soviet Union, could easily be in 15 years not Europe but American industry in Europe." Across the channel British Prime Minister Harold Wilson made much the same point, declaring that "there is no future for Europe or for Britain if we allow American business and American industry so to dominate the strategic growth

* Atheneum, New York: 1968.

industries of our individual countries, so that they, and not we, are able to determine the pace and direction of Europe's industrial advance. . . ." This attitude of challenge—perhaps the better word is fright or the fear of conquest—was summed up as well as anyone by the French politician Gaston Defferre, who warned that "Europe will be colonized by the United States unless we decide to pool our resources in order to create industrial firms comparable in size to the American ones."

While the full measure of American corporate strength may never be brought to bear on the European market (General Motors obviously must tend to many other areas), the mere existence of such awesome power is itself worrisome. If General Electric can operate its foreign divisions at a loss, as it did in 1965, the threat to smaller companies is not merely hypothetical. As many Europeans see it, American entry calls for the merger of their firms to form bigger business units that can meet the goliaths and exploit the advantages of the Common Market. Governments on the Continent, particularly France, have read the signs and initiated steps to inspire mergers, and across the Channel the Labour Government has created an official agency to encourage consolidation of British companies.

Slow to start, the merger process in Europe and Japan has moved into high gear. In many ways it is as significant as that which swept the United States in the early 1900s. Dozens of major mergers have been announced and more are being discussed. In Italy, the marriage of Montecatini and Edison united the two companies that account for 80 percent of its chemical and petrochemical output. The 1968 merger of British Motor Holdings with Leyland created the sixth largest auto producer in the world. At just about the same time that British Motor and Leyland affiliated, in Germany Volkswagen and Auto Union (maker of the DKW) joined forces; together they will offer cars in all price ranges, just like GM, Ford, and Chrysler. Later, in an arrangement that took effect in 1969, after extensive negotiations with the French government, Fiat, the dominant Italian car maker, and Citroën, the second largest French auto producer, entered into far-ranging cooperation agreements and formed a joint management committee. And as these consolidations were taking place in Europe, major mergers were being completed in Japan, with the overt encouragement of the government. Four such mergers were concluded by 1969 and it is generally anticipated that Japan's ten passenger car makers will be reduced to three or four major groups by the very early 1970s.

Although mergers among auto manufacturers have attracted considerable public attention, European steel has been distinguished by more mergers than any other industry. With the consolidation of Hoescht, Dortmund-Hoerder, and Holland's Hoogovens, a steelmaker with capacity of about nine million tons has been formed, putting it on a plane with Germany's Thyssen-Hutte (itself created only in 1964 and now working in close cooperation with Krupp). Meanwhile France's first- and fifth-largest steel producers, Usinor and Lorrain-Escaut, and its second- and third-largest, De Wendel and Sidelor, have combined. These and other mergers on the Continent have ended most national competition in the steel industry in West Germany, France, and the Benelux countries. A similar picture emerges in Japan. There, despite the opposition of the government's Fair Trade Commission, the country's two largest steel companies, Yawata and Fuji, are eager to merge. That consolidation would make the resulting firm the second biggest steel company in the world, larger even than Bethlehem Steel or the British Steel Corporation. It is certainly anomalous that America, which professes more loudly than any other country its firm dedication to competition and which broke up the German and Japanese steel giants during the postwar occupation, is now used as an example by the Europeans for the oligopolization of their major industries.

While the European protest against American investment may simply be, as the Atlanticist Pierre Uri has said, "the new rebirth of old-time protectionism," the French, in particular, look upon the U.S. business invasion as little more than a modern form of economic imperialism. This fear helped explain de Gaulle's concern for preservation of sovereignty and underscores what to some appears to be little more than French obstinacy.

In aggregate terms U.S. investment in Europe is not especially large, but since most of it is in a few basic, growth-oriented industries it has posed a distinct threat to local independence. American industry in France, for instance, accounts for only about 7 percent of value added in the private sector of the economy. However, in specific industries the U.S. share is huge. Nearly all of the computers, office machinery, photographic equipment, and synthetic rubber, and the bulk of agricultural equipment and oil and a large percentage of the prepared food, textiles, and cosmetics sold in France are American made. The situation is much the same in Germany, where more than three fourths of American investment is concentrated in autos (and other transportation equipment), oil, chemicals, and electrical equipment (largely computers). As the French and Germans see it, then, some of their most important industries are increasingly dominated from across the Atlantic, putting them at the mercy of companies beyond their effective control.

The sixteen hundred American-owned companies in England account for more than 10 percent of the country's industrial output and for nearly a fifth of its exports. By 1980, and perhaps sooner, U.S. businesses are likely to produce 20 percent of British manufactures. Right now American companies are the biggest suppliers in English markets for goods ranging from typewriters, automobiles, and agricultural implements to drugs, prepared foods, and razor blades.

In the European view, the most serious consequences of American investment stem from our control of those industries widely regarded as shapers of the future. In electronics, notably computers, we are far ahead of the rest of the world, a fact which can mean that other countries will fall steadily farther behind in economic and technological development. By striking up affiliations with major American electronics companies, the biggest French, German and Italian companies—Machines-Bull, Siemens, and Olivetti —have gained limited access to U.S. know-how. The consolidation in 1968 of ICT and English Electric Computers, with the strong encouragement and active financial backing of the British Government, represented the United Kingdom's catch-up effort. Nonetheless in spite of such moves a great gap persists between American and European technical competence in electronics, one that is not likely to be closed as long as the Federal Government continues to pour billions of dollars into research carried out by private industry. As discussed in Chapter 9, about 60 percent of R&D conducted in the United States is supported by government funds and two thirds of the work itself is carried out by industry. By contrast, France spends less than a tenth as much on research. Even more important than their greater support of research, U.S. firms have proven their superior ability to translate laboratory discoveries into salable products. It is this talent, whatever its exact causes, which especially awes most sophisticated European economic analysts.

Big Business, Worldwide

The flood of mergers and consolidations that has taken place in Europe and Japan in the last half dozen years is part of a worldwide trend to industrial concentration. The United States has unquestionably and after a fashion typically led the way—with bigger mergers, more diversification, and the formation of larger corporations. But other countries are now falling in step, hurrying to catch up. As this process unfolds it requires no unusual foresight to see that the entire industrialized world will soon be characterized by as high a degree of concentration as now prevails in the United States. A good guess is that by 1980 three hundred large corporations will control 75 percent of all the world's manufacturing assets.

The transition from a world economy in which thousands of companies competed with each other to one in which three hundred giant firms dominate the scene is of nearly immeasurable public consequence, presenting on a global scale all of the issues identified in Part I of this book. What is even more striking, however, is the internationalization of business. The big American companies have become true multinational enterprises, and the large European and Japanese firms are not far behind. Within a decade every firm of consequence will operate extensively in twenty or more countries, guided by efficiency and the quest for profit and paying little but formal attention to national boundaries.

"What is taking shape, slowly and tentatively but nevertheless unmistakably," said *Fortune* in an editorial, "is 'one world' of business, a world in which business will truly know no frontiers, in which the paramount rule governing the movement of goods and money will be the rule of the market." That fact—that crucially important fact—has not yet been grasped by the governments of the world. They are still dealing with business in terms of national laws and national policies at a time when business has shrugged off its national robes and put on new supranational trappings. What clearly is needed are new ways for the world's governments to relate to business on business's new multinational terms. That calls for novel systems of law and distinctive institutions. Nothing less will suffice.

CHAPTER 18

The Political Dimensions
of Corporate Supranationalism

"The international corporation operates in a kind of governmental vacuum . . . it is constantly exposed to the danger of expropriations, discriminatory legislation and the hatred and opprobrium of the people whom on the whole it serves. It seems to be one of the unfortunate facts of society that being merely useful is a poor source either of prestige or of legitimacy."

—*Kenneth E. Boulding*

With the hyperdiversification and internationalization of corporate operations that have taken place in the past two decades, business has assumed a scale and mode of behavior that gives today's larger enterprises the essential trappings of a political state. In fact, dozens of firms are involved more deeply in global affairs than are most countries. Today the sun *does* set on the British empire, but not on the likes of Standard Oil, IBM, General Motors, Royal Dutch Shell, and Unilever. The wide scope of concern of the U.S.A., the U.S.S.R., and perhaps Great Britain puts them in the same league, but for most countries international economic involvement is little more than a matter of import-export trade relationships with other countries. For the United States—and similarly for GM, IBM, and ICI—there are substantial fixed commitments in many countries. In practical terms this means that the world corporation, like the big nation-state, possesses special characteristics requiring recognition and special treatment.

ITT tells much of the story in its own words, proclaiming that "well over half of [its] worldwide research and development in telecommunications and electronics is done in Europe by Europeans." The company, generally thought of as "American," embraces over 150 associated firms, employing 300,000 people (more than half "foreign"), and carries on research, manufacturing, sales or service in fifty-seven countries, with sales outlets in sixty-two more. A company with world commitments, such as ITT, not only dramatizes the multinational dimensions of contemporary business, but underscores the need to treat such a firm in international terms. To pretend that ITT is just an American firm, or that Unilever is just a British enterprise, or that Shell is Dutch is absurd—a fiction good neither for these firms' own long-term interests or for the citizens of any of the several countries whose economies are affected by their operations.

Today all of the functional characteristics of modern business have become transnational, subsuming nations and demanding suitable institutional and legal treatment. Yet as almost always seems to be the case, legal policy is several decades behind the evolution of business and technology. There is, as George W. Ball has said, a "lack of phasing" between business realities and existing legal and political institutions. Almost every aspect of contemporary business activity has been internationalized, but the rules by which executives must conduct the affairs of their companies are still as nationalistic in scope, outlook, and character as they were in the nineteenth century.

The Worldwide Web of Business

To better grasp this disharmony consider the case of a fairly typical but hypothetical major international corporation. We can just call it Apex. Headquartered in New York City, Apex has a dozen corporate subsidiaries chartered in other countries and substantial direct investments in twenty nations, mostly in Europe. Its annual worldwide sales, a third to customers outside the United States, amount to $1 billion. Roughly that same proportion of its production is in its European and Latin American plants and this year a third of the company's investment in new plant and equipment will be abroad. Profits generated outside the U.S. provide 35 percent of its current $100 million net after-tax yearly earnings.

Forty-five thousand of its seventy thousand workers are citizens of other countries. At least 10 percent of Apex's stockholders are foreigners; the real number may be twice this if account could be taken of clandestine foreign stock ownership.

To get a closer impression of Apex's operations, imagine that we were to spend a few days accompanying the firm's president and observing his activities. About a fifth of his time is spent visiting Apex's foreign offices and talking with his coterie of overseas vice presidents (several are Oxford-Cambridge alumni, two graduated from the Ecole de Technique, one came from Muenster in Germany). Even when not traveling outside the U.S. the Apex president rarely finds that a day passes when he does not discuss issues over the phone with his international managers. In addition, there is a steady inflow of information which is assimilated by the Apex computerized management control system, which links together all of the Apex offices, wherever located around the world. Thumbing through the statistical summary which is updated and placed on the desk of the Apex president each morning, one would find data reviewing the performance of the factories at Chicago, Liverpool, and Antwerp, the sales centers at Frankfurt and Los Angeles, the regional headquarters in London and Tokyo, and the distribution centers at Milan and Cleveland.

Looking in the Apex president's appointment book we spot the following entries scheduled for the next few weeks:

- Meeting in Paris to discuss opening of new sales office in Budapest to handle East European contacts.
- Two-day session in London to meet with regional vice presidents and six special consultants to appraise proposed investment in a joint government-owned fertilizer facility in India.
- Conference in Brussels to reach a conclusion about the location of a major new plant on the Continent to replace the outmoded Apex facility in France. One group within the company favors a location in Belgium; another group favors a site in France, partly out of a desire to avoid coming into the disfavor of the French Government.
- Meeting in Zurich with representatives of European bankers

to complete details on the placement of a $25 million issue of bonds. The securities will be sold in Europe, thus avoiding any conflict with U.S. capital outflow restrictions.

• Discussions in Tokyo with officials of the Japanese Government to consider prospects for the establishment in that country of a factory to serve Asian markets. These discussions have been going on for many months and have yielded no measurable progress. On the way back from Tokyo preliminary conversations will be held on Formosa and in South Korea to explore possible investments as a substitute for location in Japan.

We could browse further through the Apex president's schedule of upcoming appointments—or we could examine the calendar of commitments of the chief executive of any large corporation—and find all sorts of evidence that documents the degree to which the modern business firm is increasingly caught up in the currents of world commerce. Whatever aspect of corporate operations is examined, this same interpretation is unavoidable. Equipped with the means of modern communications and transportation, fueled with funds generated by highly efficient international capital markets, and attracted by the sales and profit opportunities of a world in which the population grows at a rate of two hundred thousand people a day and in which the total GNP already exceeds $2 trillion, the big corporations of North America, Europe, and Japan are now active participants in the global economy. As noted earlier, and as was shown in detail in Table 9 American companies had invested $60 billion outside the U.S. in 1967. Their current holdings exceed $65 billion. U.S. financial institutions, led by the banks (most notably the Bank of America, Chase Manhattan, and First National City) and the insurance companies, have foreign assets of more than $25 billion. But it is not merely U.S. business that is active internationally. The British, for example, have nearly $17 billion in direct foreign investments. The activities of English banks, insurers, and real estate syndicates are of special consequence.

International business activities form a veritable web of interconnections. To show what this can mean, contemplate something seemingly as simple as a supertanker that hauls crude oil from the

Middle East to a refinery in Belgium. Built in Japan on behalf of a group of California investors, it is financed by a syndicate of New York banks and is chartered on a long-term basis to a Dutch oil company. The ship itself flies a Panamanian flag, is manned by a Hong Kong-Chinese crew under a German master, and is insured by Lloyds of London. What is "the" nationality of such a ship—American, Dutch, Panamanian? The question itself is naive and there can really be no answer, for the ship is in essence nothing but a piece of floating international property—stateless, in one sense, or multinational, in another. It typifies the character of contemporary business.

In no single area—finance, communications, transportation, management, or operations—is the large corporation free from international entanglements. Take science as a case in point. For the big American drug makers, electronics manufacturers, and oil companies, substantial research is conducted in laboratories located outside the U.S. IBM has a major scientific facility on the south coast of France and ITT carries out advanced research in several European countries. Standard Oil of New Jersey has six research centers in Europe (the staff of its Brussels center is drawn from fifteen countries). But even if research is done at home, the scientists doing the work often are Europeans or immigrants from other lands. Indeed, in 1967 alone more than ten thousand scientists and engineers came to the U.S. for employment, commonly with private companies. Wherever and by whomever scientific research is carried out, the results are swiftly transmitted around the globe, through patent applications, technical conferences, or any of the tens of thousands of specialized periodicals and journals which freely circulate throughout the advanced industrialized countries.

The Diplomacy of International Business

The internationalization of business, in all its forms, is a development of transcendent economic importance, but the political and diplomatic overtones are of no less consequence. In a period when the world is still divided along national lines that reflect different ideologies and stages of development (East versus West, China versus just about everyone else, the poor of the southern hemisphere versus the rich of the north), business has become, quite without design, the most powerful supranational force in the world. The multinational companies have become the outriders—the advance men, so to speak—of internationalism. Indeed their activities involve the exercise of far greater power than is possessed by more than a very few countries. The decisions of a billion-dollar international corporation to invest or not invest, to alter prices, to curtail or expand production, to shift from natural to synthetic raw materials, to automate or not to automate a plant, or to bring a new product on the market, can have serious effects on any country, big or small. This is the true exercise of power and it can often be far more important than a decision of the government of the United States, England, or France.

The ceremonial relationships between nation-states or the verbal fireworks in the U.N. General Assembly may seem impressive, but typically they are more formal than substantive in nature. This, though, is not true of business activities. The opening of a new mine or the establishment of an assembly plant can mean hundreds of jobs, a needed product (like fertilizer or a high-protein food substance), or revenue for the state (the Kaiser Corporation's decision in 1961 to process bauxite in Ghana was viewed by that country as the key to its economic future). By contrast, a mutual aid pact with the United States is far less helpful and may impose costs and create serious internal difficulties for the host country.

Governments—even rich ones like the U.S.A.—often speak in grand terms, but business backs up its declarations with the commitment of resources. Since the end of World War II, to cite a good illustration, the U.S. has advanced only about $1.5 billion to the major international lending institutions (the World Bank is one) for investment in other countries. During that same period business has increased its direct foreign investment by almost $50 billion! It is rather obvious that business, not government, has put up the capital and made the choices that play the principal role in shaping the world economy. In the face of this evidence it is only realistic to regard the globe-circling corporations as what they are: immensely powerful political states. The big corporations have become the colonizers of the twentieth century, and the chief colonizers, because of their vast wealth and technological superiority, will be the large American companies. Their "army" consists not of men bearing arms, but engineers and executives equipped with vast amounts of capital and organizational know-how. Their embassies are their factories, mines, and sales offices. The only thing they usually lack is a flag.

Although the international corporations are a powerful force in shaping the economics and politics of the world, they are also in the vanguard of change and often are inclined or compelled to pursue policies which lack the explicit approval or even the acquiescence of the governments of the nation they affect. In many ways they resemble the British charter trading companies of the seventeenth and eighteenth centuries, for they too are venturing into unexplored terrain. The matter of trade with the Communist countries is one example. Despite the chilliness which still characterizes East-West relations, many companies are establishing intimate economic ties with the Communist countries of East Europe and with Russia itself. If bridges are to be built to the East, it is quite evident that they are likely to be constructed, not by government, but primarily by business.

Much the same is also true of the underdeveloped countries. By and large, they are distrustful of the United States and the other rich countries of the West and fear that government aid, often military in nature, is designed not so much to hasten their growth as it is to lessen their independence. Whether one agrees with their attitude or not is quite unimportant; it exists and will contaminate their relations for many years to come with the industrialized world. It is, though, essential that these poorer nations develop their economies, increase their output and wealth, and improve the lot of their citizens. To accomplish these ends, however, requires capital, organization, and experienced manpower—precisely the resources which the big companies of North America and Europe possess in great abundance. If, then, the LDC are to "take off" economically they must work out mutually acceptable arrangements with the capitalists who manage the industrial empires—the very same capitalists whom the politicians of Asia, Africa, and

Latin America are prone to castigate as "robber barons" and "monopolists."

Given this ideological orientation one's first reaction may be to conclude that it is unrealistic to think that the corporate capitalists of the North could ever deal effectively with those who govern the developing lands of the East and the South. In fact, however, they have been able to devise ways—quite unorthodox at times—that enable them to work together for their mutual advantage. It is indeed quite remarkable to find profit-seeking U.S., Canadian, Japanese, and European corporations simultaneously working in reasonable harmony with the apartheid government of South Africa, the Communist powers of East Europe and Russia, the diverse nationalist (and often socialist) governments of the developing countries of Africa and Asia, assorted military dictatorships, and the inscrutable Indians. The explanation, of course, is the old one— that each has something to offer and something to gain. For the corporations there are valuable resources and growing markets; for the countries there is capital, revenue, and the prospect of acceleration in their development.

Business's Foreign Entanglements

The interplay that takes place between the international oil companies and the nationalist regimes of the Middle East and North Africa tell us a great deal about business's foreign policy. Altogether Iran, Iraq, Saudi Arabia, Kuwait, Abu Dhabi, Libya, and Algeria produce some twelve million barrels of oil daily, or nearly 40 percent of the free world's total output. Western Europe obtains 75 percent of its oil needs from this region, Japan 90 percent. With oil supplying more than half the world's energy requirements, the Middle East-North Africa area occupies a critical place in world affairs. Its significance will not shrink in the future either. By 1980 it is estimated that the world will need fifty-five million barrels of oil a day. In the 1970s alone the world will consume more oil than has been produced so far in the history of the petroleum industry. While new sources may be found, the Middle East-North Africa area has greater known reserves—more easily accessible and at a lower cost, too—than anywhere else. Right now those reserves amount to almost three hundred billion barrels; that is eight times those of the U.S. and twelve times those of South America. Indeed, Kuwait and Saudi Arabia each has oil reserves as large as those of the United States and South America combined.

In gaining access to the reserves of the Middle East, American and European oil companies have dealt with the various countries in the manner of representatives of nation-states and have created a web of contracts so tangled that it is a body of law in itself. Pursuant to these contracts the oil companies pay to the governments involved about $3 billion a year in taxes and royalties. American oil interests alone have invested approximately $3 billion in pipelines and the assorted paraphernalia of oil extraction and shipment (this figure makes no allowance for the tankers used to move the oil to refineries). The British and Dutch, among others, have invested at least an equivalent amount. For companies like Standard of New Jersey, Gulf, Standard of California, and Texaco, their investments and reserves in the Middle East are crucial to their survival. More than half of Mobil's worldwide oil production is from the Middle East. In all, U.S. oil company profits from production in this region are estimated at more than a billion dollars a year. The financial significance of the Middle East to the major oil companies is readily apparent, but so also is the flow of royalties crucial to the development of the Middle East countries. Oil revenues, for example, make up nearly 80 percent of the total income of Saudi Arabia. Iran gets $750 million, a sum that about matches its annual economic development budget.

However one views it, the United States—not to overlook the countries of Europe—has an enormous stake in the Middle East, but, it is vital to note, it is one that has been created and is defined by private companies rather than the "normal" processes of governmental diplomacy. By no means, of course, is the Middle East oil situation distinctive, even if it involves a greater investment and a highly sensitive resource. In South Africa, where the local government's color policies are officially viewed with disdain by the United States, American companies have an investment of nearly a billion dollars, almost five times what it was in 1960. Some three hundred U.S. firms operate in South Africa. General Motors manufactures Chevrolet, Vauxhall, and Opel cars at Port Elizabeth. Chrysler opened a $48 million assembly plant at Pretoria in 1965. International Harvester, Singer, Burlington, and Pfizer (along with most of the big drug companies) have manufacturing facilities in the Union. Just as in the Middle East, the United States has a huge economic position in South Africa—and, again, it is one that has been created by business, for its own quite understandable profit-seeking purposes.

Globally minded American companies are not only active as investors in the Middle East, South Africa, and in other developing countries, but they are also providing technical advice to these countries. In Greece, for instance, Litton Industries has a twelve-year contract with the government calling for it to analyze the economic potential of Crete and the Western Peloponnesos and to attract investment in opportunities it finds. Litton's initial plan calls for the investment of $850 million by 1978, an amount that exceeds total Greek public and private investment in recent years. From Litton's standpoint, and perhaps that of Greece itself, the contract is a good one. The company will receive its costs plus 11 percent, along with finder's fees. The arrangement, however, has come under sharp attack from those who oppose the military regime which took power in Greece in 1967. They allege that Litton's arrangement carries with it the tacit approval by the United States Government of the Greek military oligarchy. Litton insists it is acting completely "on its own," but its role is so great that, as the London *Economist* put it, it amounts to "running the whole program itself with the Greek government as a sort of junior partner." Caught in the cross-currents of criticism, Litton finds itself embarrassed for taking on a job—economic development in a poor country—that seems both in its own interest and consistent with the declared political objectives of the United States.

The role of American business in the Middle East, South Africa, East Europe, and Greece—and in other parts of the world—carries with it a number of important implications. They are really more political than economic in nature, reflecting the breadth of business's growing international responsibilities. First, the big multi-

CHART 8
General Motors Worldwide

VAUXHALL MOTORS LIMITED
Luton, England (Plants in 3 cities)

Design and manufacture of Vauxhall Viva, Victor and Viscount passenger cars, Bedford commercial vehicles

ADAM OPEL A.G.
Russelsheim am Main, Federal Republic of Germany (Plants in 3 cities)

Design and manufacture of Opel Kadett, Olympia, Rekord, Commodore, Kapitan, Admiral and Diplomat passenger cars, light commercial vehicles

EUCLID (GREAT BRITAIN) LIMITED
Motherwell, Scotland (Plants in 2 cities)

Manufacture of Euclid off-highway earthmoving equipment

GENERAL MOTORS LIMITED
London, England (Plants in 4 cities)

Manufacture of Frigidaire products and automotive components; import of GM products

GENERAL MOTORS (FRANCE)
Gennevilliers (Seine), France

Manufacture of automotive components; import of GM products

GENERAL MOTORS STRASBOURG S.A.
Strasbourg, France

Automatic transmission plant under construction

GENERAL MOTORS DE PORTUGAL, LIMITADA
Lisbon and Azambuja, Portugal

Assembly of imported

GENERAL MOTORS (NORWAY) A/S
Oslo, Norway

Import of GM products

GENERAL MOTORS CONTINENTAL
Antwerp, Belgium; Rotterdam, Netherlands

Assembly of imported vehicles; import of GM products

SUOMEN GENERAL MOTORS OY.
Helsinki, Finland

Import of GM products

GENERAL MOTORS NORDISKA A.B.
Stockholm, Sweden

Import of GM products

GENERAL MOTORS INTERNATIONAL A/S
Copenhagen, Denmark

Assembly of imported vehicles; import of GM products

GENERAL MOTORS GMBH
Berlin, Federal Republic of Germany

Manufacture of engine bearings

GENERAL MOTORS DEUTSCHLAND GMBH
Wiesbaden, Federal Republic of Germany

Import of GM products

GENERAL MOTORS AUSTRIA GES.M.B.H.
Vienna, Austria

Import of GM products

GENERAL MOTORS SUISSE S.A.
Bienne, Switzerland

Assembly of imported vehicles; import of GM products

GENERAL MOTORS ITALIA S.P.A.
Milan, Italy

Import of GM products

FINLAND

SWEDEN

NORWAY

DENMARK

NETHERLANDS

WEST BERLIN

FEDERAL REPUBLIC OF GERMANY

BELGIUM

GREAT BRITAIN

AUSTRIA

SWITZERLAND

FRANCE

ITALY

PORTUGAL

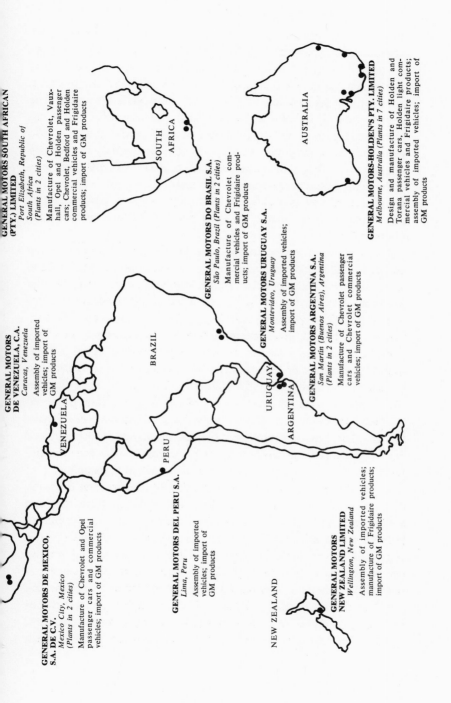

GENERAL MOTORS DE MEXICO, S.A. DE C.V.
Mexico City, Mexico
(Plants in 2 cities)

Manufacture of Chevrolet and Opel passenger cars and commercial vehicles; import of GM products

GENERAL MOTORS DEL PERU S.A.
Lima, Peru

Assembly of imported vehicles; import of GM products

GENERAL MOTORS NEW ZEALAND LIMITED
Wellington, New Zealand

Assembly of imported vehicles; manufacture of Frigidaire products; import of GM products

GENERAL MOTORS DE VENEZUELA, C.A.
Caracas, Venezuela

Assembly of imported vehicles; import of GM products

GENERAL MOTORS DO BRASIL S.A.
São Paulo, Brazil (Plants in 2 cities)

Manufacture of Chevrolet commercial vehicles and Frigidaire products; import of GM products

GENERAL MOTORS URUGUAY S.A.
Montevideo, Uruguay

Assembly of imported vehicles; import of GM products

GENERAL MOTORS ARGENTINA S.A.
San Martin (Buenos Aires), Argentina
(Plants in 2 cities)

Manufacture of Chevrolet passenger cars and Chevrolet commercial vehicles; import of GM products

GENERAL MOTORS SOUTH AFRICAN (PTY.) LIMITED
Port Elizabeth, Republic of South Africa
(Plants in 2 cities)

Manufacture of Chevrolet, Vauxhall, Opel and Holden passenger cars; Chevrolet, Bedford and Holden commercial vehicles and Frigidaire products; import of GM products

GENERAL MOTORS-HOLDEN'S PTY. LIMITED
Melbourne, Australia (Plants in 7 cities)

Design and manufacture of Holden and Torana passenger cars, Holden light commercial vehicles and Frigidaire products; assembly of imported vehicles; import of GM products national corporations, mostly but not exclusively American, are spearheading the world's political and economic development. They are generating most of the capital investment and making the key operational decisions that will shape, not just the international economy, but the political affairs of the late twentieth century. The United Nations, the World Bank, and the governments of the industrialized nations will play a part in guiding the course of the world, but, with the notable exception of their capacity to instigate or quell wars, they will occupy a place that is distinctly subsidiary to the great global corporations. The reason is simple: business has the resources and is willing to use them, whereas government is either unwilling or unable to exert the force that can mold tomorrow's world.

This leads to a second implication. With business serving as the unofficial outrider of internationalism, it will continue markedly to influence government policies. In the Middle East, for example, the enormous investments of the United States and European oil companies makes it virtually mandatory for the American, British, Dutch, and French governments to exert their diplomacy in a way that shelters those investments from expropriation. The U.S.-inspired overthrow of Mossadegh, the American intervention in Lebanon, and Britain's 1956 military campaign in Suez demonstrate that the industrialized powers of the West are fully prepared to defend their interests in the Middle East. It deserves reemphasis, though, that those interests were created by private investment and that the governments are acting as protectors of the business-defined status quo more than as independent initiators of policy.

Even where business commitments do not lead to such dramatic government action as has taken place in the Middle East, they can compromise and circumscribe the freedom of government to pursue policies which might otherwise appear desirable. Off and on it is suggested, as an instance, that the United States should impose severe economic sanctions on South Africa. But how realistic is this when American companies have an investment approaching a billion dollars in that country and when English and other European firms have an even larger stake in its economic vitality?

While the international activities of the American and European industrial colossi will often anticipate and shape government policy, the fact that they typically lack explicit government sanction means, for a third lesson, that business nonetheless will often be taking risks than can lead to embarrassment, public criticism, or, worse, uncompensated expropriation or other loss. Being in the forefront of internationalism, as it is, has its advantages but it also puts business sufficiently beyond the zone in which government can or will take protective action. Even in the Middle East, where the United States and other governments are quite willing to exert their power to protect investments, the oil companies are continually subject to threats by local governments that create a climate of uncertainty. Understandings with developing nations, however firmly enscribed in formal contracts, are always being "redefined." Even in the industrialized world there are changes in governmental attitudes, new regulations, or subtle hints that vitally affect business operations. In many of these situations firms cannot look to their "home" governments for more than pro forma expressions of sympathy; reflecting their powerful but nonetheless independent political and economic status, they must deal with these matters on their own. To a very considerable degree business is functioning in a legal and diplomatic no-man's-land, where it must conduct its affairs and strive to advance its objectives without the benefit of the elaborate scheme of law that is part and parcel of operations within a single country. Being supranational has its advantages, for it can spell freedom from regulation, but it also has its drawbacks, for it can deprive business of the support that government normally provides its citizens.

National Regulation and International Business: Square Pegs, Round Holes

While many American and foreign corporations have assumed a new supranational status, which gives them enormous economic power and ascribes to them a unique political status, they also remain subject to the laws of the countries in which they operate and whose internal and external commerce they affect. For an American company active in twenty-five countries, this quite literally means that it must comply with the commands of as many governments. The result is the legal equivalent of the babble of tongues. Sometimes the rules which the various countries set down are complementary, but more commonly they are outright contradictory. The result is that the multinational company is constantly being pushed and pulled, frequently in different directions. The situation is much as if a motorist were to pull up to an intersection and find himself confronted by a battery of signals—some red, some green, others yellow, some flashing, some suddenly alternating from one color to another—controlled by policemen with equal authority to make an arrest and impose a sentence. Kafkaesque, for sure, but this is a fair approximation of the state of affairs in which business now finds itself. The fact that the global corporations have been able to find their way through this maze is more a tribute to managerial skill and legal artistry than it is to rationality.

For one thing the fractured character of present-day national regulation impairs efficient business operations. Patents are a good case in point. Today, technology is international. Big companies conduct research in several countries. A German employee in a U.S. drug manufacturer's English laboratory may discover a new compound that will lead to production in a French factory and sales in 75 other countries. To protect that invention, however, requires that the same drug company must seek patents in every country in which it wants to safeguard its interest. This is a cumbersome, costly, and an administrative monstrosity that contradicts the inherently international nature of contemporary science. Reflecting this, more than 95 percent of the patents taken out in Canada are obtained by foreigners, more than half those in England and France, over a quarter of those in the United States. The absurd thing is that the preponderance of these patents covers exactly the same inventions!

The efforts of individual countries to deal with international business enterprises can do more than require duplicative effort, which, after all, is only inefficient. Indeed, things can be much worse, leading to a situation in which neither the governments nor the businesses involved sustain an advantage. Antitrust is an outstanding example. International law tells us that a country can exercise jurisdiction over conduct that it considers reprehensible, even if it takes place outside its borders and even if the parties involved are not its citizens. This is the principle of extraterritoriality and it can best be appreciated with an illustration. Suppose, for example, that officers of an American chemical company sit down in a London club with the executives of a British competitor and agree that the British firm will not sell in the U.S. and the American firm will not sell in England. Both sides may be happy about the arrangement, but not for long. Such an understanding is a clear violation of U.S. antitrust law and if the culprits—English as well as American—are apprehended, they can very well be prosecuted and fined. Why? The arrangement restrains the trade of the United States; in a legal sense no more need be said. The fact that the contract was negotiated beyond our borders is irrelevant.

The principle of extraterritoriality, which has reached its zenith in antitrust, can produce plenty of nasty conflicts. What the courts of the United States may view with disdain may be looked upon with favor, or at least with equanimity, by the courts of another country. In one famous case involving du Pont, an American court ruled that some contracts it had entered into with Imperial Chemical Industries were violative of our antitrust laws and decreed that they were unenforceable. But ICI was promptly told by a British court to abide by those contracts or risk the enmity of the Crown. This same point can arise in other situations. While the United States strongly disapproves of cartel practices, other countries think that they may be all right in some cases. Price-fixing, for one example, is not universally condemned, and market-sharing practices are an honorable way of life in Japan. What, therefore, is banned in the United States may be lawful in other lands—indeed, sometimes encouraged and occasionally compelled. For an American company, operating internationally, the effect can be that of our motorist who is faced simultaneously with red, green, and yellow lights. Does he stop, proceed, or what? Most world-oriented firms go ahead, but at reduced speed and uncertain of the consequences.

To put the matter in its proper context, however, it must also be recognized that the overlapping jurisdiction of many countries can leave cracks in which the clever business can walk, avoiding the harshest thrusts of the nations whose interest it affects. Antitrust, once more, is a good case in point. As noted in Chapter 12, the U.S. antitrust laws forbid mergers between rival firms on the ground that competition will be lessened. But today the market for many products is bigger than the United States. An acquisition of a principal foreign firm by one of its American competitors can just as directly affect trade as would the purchase of another American firm.

A few years ago, for example, Reynolds Aluminum, one of the Big Four in the U.S. industry, acquired British Aluminum, then (as now) the biggest English producer, which was about to enter the American aluminum market. The consequence was that the entry of an important competitor was blocked (and at the same time Reynolds gained a dominant position in the British aluminum market). On the face of it such an acquisition appears made to order for antitrust prosecution. In fact, though, nothing happened; the United States Government stood silently by. The explanation is not very difficult: this merger involved substantial properties in two countries and the United States was hesitant to act for fear that the British would be chagrined. Conversely the British also were reluctant to protest on the ground that this might anger their American friends. While this is not always the case—the U.S. challenge in 1969 of British Petroleum's merger with Standard Oil of Ohio, which led to high-level protests from the British Government grounded in misplaced claims that America was merely trying to protect its domestic market from foreign competition, is one of a comparatively few exceptions—typically there is inaction and acquiescence in the case of cross-border mergers.

International companies simply do not fit the legal holes which individual countries long ago carved out in formulating their economic policy. France found this out when it tried to check inflationary pressures by curtailing business investment. The effort was largely nullified because foreign firms with operations in France merely borrowed capital outside the country or were provided funds by their parents or subsidiaries. Government policy makers in all nations are discovering that decisions made outside their borders vitally affect their affairs, but that there is often little they can do about it as a practical matter without provoking a chain of diplomatic incidents.

Further complicating the matter is international stock ownership. It is becoming increasingly difficult for a country to take "drastic" measures, on the old parochial basis, when its own citizens own a sizable number of shares in foreign corporations. The biggest computer company in France is IBM; Frenchmen know this and buy its stock. The same is true of Esso in Germany, General Motors in England, and Royal Dutch Shell in the United States (20 percent of that Netherlands firm's stock is owned by Americans). This trend to multinational ownership is only accentuated by the operations of mutual funds like Fund of Funds. The roots of the big world companies run deep and extend far, and no single country can pull up even a part of them without risking serious adverse domestic and international political and economic consequences.

Whether it be antitrust, corporate financial reporting standards, labor relations, accounting rules, securities issuances, taxes, currency restrictions, investment limitations, or any of a variety of commercial practices, we have a state of affairs in world business that is distinguished by overlapping, frequently inconsistent, yet sometimes inadequate national regulations. On the one hand, business is hampered by contradictory and ambiguous commands; on the other hand, the public suffers when governments are unable or ill equipped to deal with questionable business behavior. There is, then, a manifest lack of harmony, which can only be remedied through some means of international cooperation. Governments have to learn to work together if they are to create the conditions that are sensibly related to the needs and challenges of multinational business. Their failure to do so will, in the long run, be good for no one. The global corporations will continue to be hobbled by a multiplicity of oft-inconsistent national regulations that do not assure the citizenry of the world any meaningful protection from the improper use of the power these great corporate empires will continue to amass. No one wins, everyone loses from a perpetuation of the haphazard, patchwork-quilt legal arrangements that now apply to international business.

An International Approach to International Business

Business has gone international, the countries of the world have not. That is the problem in a nutshell. Coming up with a solution, however, is a far more difficult task, for it must involve the co-operation of nations which are jealous of their sovereignty, suspicious of one another's intentions, and unalike in cultural and political orientation. Still, though, the advantages are sufficient, for countries and companies alike, to make substantial progress a realistic possibility.

The European Economic Community suggests what can be accomplished, if only slowly and with considerable difficulty. Its six member countries, recognizing that they have more to gain than lose through cooperation, have agreed on many common rules for important areas of business activity, like antitrust, and have taken preliminary steps toward the establishment of a comprehensive body of law governing such vital corporate activities as mergers and consolidations. The very real progress recorded by the EEC shows what other international political groupings might be able to accomplish. Organizations like the Organization for Economic Cooperation and Development (with twenty-one members, including all the principal Western industrialized nations), the European Free Trade Association (the so-called Outer Seven, led by England), and even such larger and less cohesive bodies as the General Agreement on Tariffs and Trade and the United Nations Committee on Trade and Development afford institutional settings in which the matter of world business policy can be considered.

Progress in these larger political groupings is certain to be much slower than in a more closely knit organization like the EEC, but the challenges presented by the big world corporations are becoming so obvious and so significant that not even the humblest developing nation can afford to treat them as other than rival political states, whose power and special needs must be attended to. The industrialized countries, led by the members of the Common Market, have begun to face the problem, if only slowly and hesitatingly. Their growing awareness parallels the recognition by the multinational corporations themselves that they have more to gain than relinquish by being able to operate within and be protected by a set of agreed-upon rules that are reasonably clear and substantially consistent and that provide protection from such untoward events as uncompensated expropriation.

Whether it be by multilateral international treaty or the adoption of a uniform business law, or by some less formal and more unconventional approach, the prospect is that in the next few years a sizable number of countries will jointly begin to evolve a code of legal principles to govern the international corporations. Discussions of the problem, already taking place, can be expected initially to lead to exchanges of information and other exploratory undertakings. Later, as the character of the problem becomes clearer and as the mutuality of their interests is established, more formal arrangements—perhaps dealing with just a single problem, like patents, antitrust, or expropriation—will be developed. Progress will be slow and uneven; there will be setbacks; novel approaches will have to be devised. But there must be forward movement, for the international corporations are just too big, too important, to be left on their own. It is in everyone's best interest if the pace of movement is quickened, but this requires a scarce ingredient—far-sighted statesmanship on the part of both corporate officials and political leaders, particularly in the United States and Europe. And the prerequisite to statesmanship is realism—an accurate understanding of what is actually going on in the worlds of business.

Conclusion

CHAPTER 19

Business, Government, and the Public

"The first responsibility of leadership is to gain mastery over events."

—Richard M. Nixon
September 19, 1968

In their size, extent of diversification, the breadth of their constituencies, technological prowess, and sweep of their internationalism, the worlds of business are being fundamentally transformed and the entire society is being radically affected as a consequence. Call it a silent revolution, or whatever characterization you wish, but make no mistake: what is taking place in business presents a basic challenge to all of our established ways of thinking about the relationships of government to what was once the private sector of the economy. At root, it is a test of democracy itself.

If "government"—meaning those people denominated as politicians who are elected by and who claim to serve the public—is "to gain mastery over events," a thorough reexamination of our whole range of public policies is essential. Just as business is changing its ways, so too must government. If it doesn't, the surging forces of private business—with their power, wealth, scientific know-how, and managerial skills—are going to shape the future of our civilization.

In overhauling our public policies as they pertain to business,

289

the first step is to free ourselves from the mythology and incantations that confuse and prevent rational discussion of the issues. That admonition applies equally to politicians, journalists, academicians, and businessmen. The notion that we can deal with business—its challenges and its needs—by speaking out in the manner of a Babbitt, or, conversely, by leveling populist-like verbal broadsides at "big business" and lamenting its high profits or supposed inhumaneness, must be coldly dismissed. We must refine our discussion and get on with that confrontation with reality of which John F. Kennedy spoke in 1962.

Much of what has been said in the preceding chapters no doubt will annoy a good many readers. The liberals—the advocates of a "tough" antitrust policy, for example—will be angry because there is too little unqualified criticism of business. Corporate executives, on the other hand, and those who identify themselves as business sympathizers, will likewise be disturbed because they will find passages that are critical and make plain that there is a role for government in protecting the public from the abusive exercise of concentrated private economic power. For many in government, especially in the Congress, there will also be unhappiness; for those in elective office always like to think they understand what is going on and convey the impression that their actions are timely and relevant to the needs of those they serve. Nor will those be content who anticipate a quick diagnosis and a simple remedy. To understand today's business and to come to grips with its challenges is perforce to question most of our traditional beliefs and much of what we have been doing. Facts often shock us because they knock the props out from under our assumptions and force us to consider taking a new, uncharted course.

The Contours of Change

The earlier chapters in this book reveal much about the changing character of business's place in the American and in the world economy. No attempt will be made here at summarization, but a few main points can be quickly restated. Perhaps most striking is that the big corporations—of which 100 dominate American manufacturing, making a third of the sales and capturing half the profits—are getting even larger, but in special ways. Through merger and investment of their fabulous earnings (the annual after-tax profits of the ten top U.S. industrial firms now exceed $7 billion), these giant enterprises are sprawling out across the economic landscape, extending their operations throughout the world and plunging into unrelated product fields. Expansion, merger, internationalization, and diversification: these are four outstanding features of contemporary big business.

At the same time that the largest corporations are getting even larger, shifts in their control are taking place. Individual shareholders are investing more and more of their savings indirectly, through mutual and pension funds. This is putting greater effective power in the banks and other financial institutions; more clearly than ever before, control of our biggest firms is coming into the hands of a duo composed of their immediate management and the representatives of a relatively few financial concerns.

As our industrial firms get bigger and diversify more extensively, the economic environment in which they function is also changing. While we have not yet concluded the industrial era (manufacturing still accounts for a third of our GNP), it is equally clear that the most rapidly growing areas of the economy are the service and government sectors. Education, health care, and research, along with the diverse functions associated with the qualitative improvement of life in an urbanized society, promise to supplant goods production as the economy's main propulsive force. Significantly, these suppliers of software are nonprofit in orientation and thus are not susceptible to appraisal in the same terms established for profit-seeking enterprises. Just as universities and nonprofit institutions form part of business's new external environment, so too do changes within the corporate workforce alter its internal environment. The growing number of highly skilled technical personnel and professional managers cloud the once-clear line between workers and executives, creating severe tensions within the corporate hierarchy.

The rapid pace of technological change, complemented by the steady growth and changing composition of the economy, continually modify the sphere within which business must function. Merely to keep pace compels a company to run, and run fast. By 1975 our GNP will have crossed the trillion dollar mark (in present dollars); by the end of the century it will have exceeded $3 trillion (again, in today's dollars). But just to run is not enough; one must know where. Technology is altering the mix of goods, killing off old industries and creating new ones. What this means for the public, in the way of new products and processes (in medicine, synthetics, and communications), is as important as it is for the companies struggling to keep in tune with the scientific revolution.

One final feature must be recalled: the new partnership of government and business. Once hostile, the public and private sectors have now formed tentative but nonetheless serious alliances. Business is now tackling some of the toughest problems facing the country, problems once thought to be within the exclusive province of governmental concern. Although no one can predict the ultimate consequences of this association with any degree of confidence, it marks a significant shift in public policy for it substitutes an implicit acceptance of the legitimacy of big business for the suspicion and distrust that once distinguished their relationship.

This brief review of the far-reaching changes taking place in the worlds of business should be sufficient to demonstrate just how important it is to equip ourselves to identify, anticipate, and assess their political and economic effects. While most firms have wisely oriented themselves to the future, devoting substantial resources to a refined forecast of technological and economic trends, this practical approach is without parallel in government. The Congress, in particular, is severely limited in its prognosticative capacity; it makes no effort to look into the future on any systematic basis and cannot, therefore, anticipate or plan for the changes that technologically acclimated business will help produce. It is the weaknesses of government in dealing with business that require the most careful attention in considering the policy implications of the changing worlds of business.

A Positive Role for Government

Business's immense power can be exercised in such a way as to advance or derogate the public interest; there is nothing inherently good or evil about the manner of its use, but it is the legitimate responsibility of government to insure that it is properly employed. However, given business's wealth, its internationalism, technological prowess, and managerial skills, government must assert itself aggressively if it is to maintain a minimally acceptable degree of influence over events.

While big business calls for big government, it is not the old, negative type of "policeman" government in which industrial firms were merely told what not to do. Our effort must be redirected along more positive lines, so that, often in the context of the new alliance with government, business power is harnessed for socially constructive purposes.

This, of course, is not to say that many existing negative legal prohibitions should be abandoned; cartel-like practices (price-fixing, bid rigging, and the rest) must still be forbidden, to cite but one example. Nor is it to suggest that government must become deeply involved in every aspect of business affairs; most of the decisions made by even the largest corporation are still its own concern because they do not conflict with, and usually advance, the general welfare. Yet government must be aware of what business is doing and plans to do; it cannot allow the immense power held by industrial corporations to be exercised completely unilaterally. What General Motors, or Standard Oil, IBM, Du Pont, ITT, or Unilever, or Pfizer, do, here or abroad, is of great public consequence.

But is the American system of government up to the challenge? Can it equip and condition itself to deal with business in the intelligent, sophisticated manner that this would imply? A realist cannot be other than pessimistic. Although the Federal Government has learned reasonably well how to manage aggregate demand so as to maintain a rate of growth that approximates full employment, it has not proven its ability to manage private economic power. Indeed few people in politics understand what the big companies are doing, sense the social and political implications of their technology, or appreciate the range of their international activities.

If this state of ignorance is perpetuated, the big industrial corporations will pretty much shape tomorrow's world, in their own image and without the guidance that democratic government should provide. They have enormous power and will use it, not out of any preconceived imperialistic desires of the sort that worried Karl Marx, but to further their own goals. Government can only make its voice felt if it is alert to what they are doing and is prepared to intervene, where necessary. The new administration that took office in January 1969 will hardly be the "master over events" if it does not recognize this point.

Thoughts on Government Reform

If government were to play a larger role in guiding the exercise of business power, there would have to be a modernization of its institutional apparatus, especially in Congress. The plain truth is that Congress is not presently equipped to cope with change at all, certainly not of the scale and complexity that characterizes the business community. It is responsive, not predictive. It lacks any significant capacity to define or assess scientific and technical events. It is insular in its outlook and, as an institution, knows little of business's place in the world economy. This is a pretty severe indictment, but it is disturbingly accurate.

Organized in about the same way as it was in the last century, the Congress continues to locate most of its practical power in committees that view their job as consisting principally of reacting, in the manner of judges, to programs advanced by outsiders, notably those in the White House and in the executive departments. Since the Senate and House committees are not organized along functional lines, a major problem usually involves a multiplicity of jurisdictions. This diffusion of responsibility makes studied assessment of critical issues virtually impossible. Making it even worse is the lack of meaningful staff advice, for Congress over the years has refused to spend money for the support that would enlighten its understanding of the difficult matters that confront the nation. It spends far more for auditing past actions than it does to discover what it should be doing; it looks over its institutional shoulder more than it looks ahead. The sort of staff assistance that is routinely available to a corporate chief executive, the President, or a Cabinet officer simply does not exist in the Congress. Bringing Congress into the twentieth century is the first order of business if government is to come to terms with business power. What it would take is a restructuring of the committee system along functional lines; a major increase in staff support; and the creation of a suitably equipped, quasi-independent Congressional staff agency that could advise the Congress in depth about future policy problems, including those stemming from business operations.

Congressional modernization is essential, but there must be other changes in the way the government relates to today's business world. Fundamentally, our existing system of law and the organizational structure of the Federal Government fail to relate efficiently and comprehensively to the power of industry. Incongruities abound. A company's false advertising claim can be suppressed, but not a substantial price increase it proposes to make. A company may be forbidden to sell its wares behind the Iron Curtain because it supposedly would work against U.S. political interests; but its investment in South Africa or the support of a Latin American military dictatorship where it has a factory are beyond the purview of government policy, even though they may be equally at odds with American diplomacy. If an enterprise fails to publish a complete statement of its finances, it can be severely sanctioned; but if its management sets up a pension fund, appoints the fund managers, invests the earnings in its own stock, and gains absolute control of the firm, government's interest is desultory.

Not only is existing government policy ill-tuned to the exercise of business power, but it is often completely unaware of what industry is going to do—even when there is a big public interest in the outcome. New products and processes are treated as closely guarded "internal" matters by most corporations, even though their sudden introduction into the market may adversely affect the public or impose a large social cost. The marketing of detergents, for example, created a serious problem because many water treatment facilities were not capable of dealing with their chemical properties. The problem ultimately was resolved but only with great difficulty and at huge public expense; adequate foreknowledge could have made it much easier. Many products are introduced only to be found hazardous later; radiation hazards in certain electrical appliances are but one example. Advances in medicine and microbiology, surveyed in Chapter 10, suggest many similar, and yet far more complex, social problems. Similarly, the institution of a new mechanical or chemical process may impose serious social costs through air or water contamination. In all of these cases, full awareness of what business planned to do could have permitted industry and government to have worked together far more constructively and to have adjusted the timing and conditions in which the product or process was introduced, with less public disruption.

The point is not that government should be unreservedly empowered to keep business from changing its prices, curtailing its investments, or interfering arbitrarily with its innovations. Rather it is only to recognize that what business, with all its power, can do has such a large impact on the society that government must be aware of, and anticipate, its principal courses of action. Otherwise, it is merely the servant of the corporation, following along behind, trying to adapt and "make do." Only by exposing business plans and activities far more fully to public review can government deal as an equal with the corporations which its laws permit to exist. Existing Federal legislation takes only limited account of this need for reviewability. It is negative in orientation and focuses more on the detection and suppression of abusive practices than on a continuing cooperative examination of corporate activities and plans that could detrimentally affect the public.

To broaden the scope of governmental involvement and to generate the kinds of information essential to intelligent response calls for a basic overhaul of existing Federal legislation and a reorientation of the functions of several government agencies. The basic aim must be to create the institutional circumstances that can permit government and business to treat one another as allies associated in a common endeavor rather than as foes. Certain features of this partnership have already been established, as Chapters 12–15 have shown.

The partnership notion must be extended further, however, if its full potential for public advantage is to be realized. What is needed is considerably closer continuing cooperation between government and business along the whole frontier of business contacts with the public, not just where business feels it is beneficial to its own interests. Whether it be a matter of price, merger, investment, or product innovation, there is no reason why a public agency should not be able to review and discuss in advance with a major company what its plans are and assess what special problems, if any, their execution might pose to the public. Whether it be the economic consequences of a price increase, the safety of a new product, or the diplomatic consequences of foreign investment, there should be sufficient rapport between the parties so that the issues can be discussed on a timely basis. Often this would lead to a resolution of the matter on mutually acceptable terms, without the disturbance that might result without prior consultation. If this approach is to have meaning it must not be a random endeavor, however. Summoning steel or auto executives to the White House to "persuade" them to abrogate a price increase is no substitute for the sort of regular contact between the industry and government that gives each participant an awareness of the other's plans and problems. What must be developed are the institutional means that will permit the private and the public sectors to coordinate more effectively and more comprehensively, and over a longer time horizon, their objectives and requirements and to consider them in terms of their respective responsibilities—the one being guided by the public interest, the other by profit.

Closer communication between business and government can have large benefits, for industry no less than for the public. Problems that might become serious can, in this way, be anticipated and reduced to manageable proportions. It should be clear, however, that big business and big government often will find simply that they disagree. A corporation will feel that a price increase is essential; government will conclude that it is inflationary. In such a conflict the outcome is unambiguous: one side or the other gives ground, and the public wins or loses. Presently the Federal Government lacks the means effectively to assert the public interest. If the dominant firms in an industry resolutely insist on raising their price, there is now usually no legal way to stop them. This is unacceptable and measures must be incorporated in law that authorize the President to suspend a price increase just as he now can obtain an injunction to suspend a labor dispute. Coupled with formal, public review procedures and with invocation of criteria similar to those incorporated in past years in the wage-price guidelines (such criteria could be adopted annually by Congress, giving them the force of law), prices (and wages) could thus be brought within the range of effective public control whenever the processes of improved government-industry consultation fail to yield an acceptable resolution of their differences.

Would all of this mean a constriction on business freedom? Yes. Would it mean an increase in government power? Unquestionably. But the alternative is to leave business essentially unchecked and to make the public subservient. If you like democracy, that should be repugnant.

Government must also assume a more aggressive posture if it is to be other than a silent and uninfluential partner in the new alliances that it is forming with business. Bringing to bear business's managerial and technical skills on problems such as housing, job training, and health care has considerable promise. However, government's constitution of the new partnership will not automatically yield the results it purports to seek (*e.g.,* low-income housing) unless it is prepared to put in substantial public funds and to participate actively in program planning. Michael Harrington is probably right in saying that many of the things we now seek in making America a better and more just society (jobs for the underskilled, decent housing for the poor, clean air and pure water) are not "sound business investments." Formation of alliances with business will not change this fact; what will change it is public spending (direct, through dollar outlays, or indirect through tax subsidies). More government spending on civilian problems, more active government involvement: both must be ingredients in the new partnership if it is to serve public needs.

This, like the earlier plea for extensive public review of business actions and business plans, means a larger role for government than most people have contemplated. It may also be politically unacceptable because it contradicts the myth that less government is what the country needs. There may be hope, however, because, in spite of our declared belief that the less government the better, government (Federal, state, local) is accounting for a rising share of the nation's employment and economic activity. Whether this hope can be translated into something more than that depends, as it usually does, on the perception and willingness of political leaders (and business leaders, too) to grasp the seriousness of the problem and to debate thoughtfully a course of action—far-reaching though it is—like that outlined here.

The Risks of Inaction

What if our political leaders do not rise to the challenge and government continues to remain passively deferential in its relationships to the vibrant worlds of business? The answer is that with their wealth, financial incentives, managerial skill, and technological competence, big corporations are going to pretty much shape the future of our world. This, to repeat, is not to imply that business will be guided by any conscious desire to subjugate people or nations. It is only to recognize that business is economically powerful, aggressive in using its wealth, and farsighted in the furtherance of its objectives—all laudable and understandable qualities. While its interests do not always coincide with what the public requires, it will work its will unless government acts as a positive counterbalance. Implicit abdication by government will leave business with a vast area of discretion within which to do as it pleases.

The failure of government to meet the challenge of business power is, in the final analysis, a risk to democracy itself. It is not difficult to foresee a polarization of society that could eventually destroy the sense of confidence in the ability of government to govern. There is a real fear that people will tend to gravitate into two groups. In one will be the well-off, highly educated, technical specialists—in business, the universities, the major government agencies, and in the nonprofit software establishments—who are in tune with the changing worlds of an economy dominated by the forces reviewed in this book (science, systems management, internationalism). They will not be without their complaints, of course; they may protest, often heatedly, about government policy (the Vietnam war is a good example of what is likely to mobilize their anger), or the lack of freedom in a highly organized world. On the whole, however, they will be pretty much content with their lot.

At the other pole will be a mixed group of malcontents. Their ranks will include a large number of legislators, out of touch with a world they seem unable to control; most small businessmen, bypassed by a highly technical industrial order; the poor, under-educated minority groups, mostly but not entirely in the cities, who find themselves cut off from access to the techno-affluent world that engulfs them; and a small group of ideologically rigid liberals (perhaps anarchists would be a better word) who do not like the concentration of power in private hands but who cynically concede they cannot do much about it. For this latter group frustration will be the common bond. Their frustration may very well become so acute that, for quite divergent reasons, they may be willing to exert their not inconsiderable power to destroy the political system as we now know it and start again, from dust if need be.

This is not a pleasant prospect, but its ugliness should not divert us from recognizing that it is a very real possibility if government does not come to grips with the reality of business power. Democracy must assert itself, but it can do so only if thoughtful men in politics and industry recognize the size of the stakes and devise procedures for accommodating private power to public purpose that are efficiently related to the politics and economics of the changing worlds of business.

Index

International Business Machines (IBM), 11, 103, 210, 245, 266, 283
International Telephone & Telegraph (ITT), 42–43, 86, 91, 222, 223, 251, 266, 267
internationalism, business, 8, 32
  new, 249, 250–265
  See also supranationalism
internationalization
  of business, 233, 234, 269
  economic, 246
  of finance, 59–62
investment
  business, 123–124
  capital, 119, 120, 122, 123, 278
  housing, 124
  international, 59, 60, 61
  overseas, 21, 248, 251, 252–256, 262–263, 267, 269, 271, 278
  See also finance
Investors Overseas Services (IOS), 61

Javits, Jacob, housing proposals by, 219
job creation, 222–224, 226
job training, 222–224
Johnson, Lyndon B., 187, 200
  attitude of, toward steel industry, 182
  business-government alliance encouraged by, 187, 200
  housing program of, 219
Johnson Administration
  antitrust during, 176, 178
  big business and the, 200
  economic expansion during, 190

Kahn, Bruce (quoted), 99
Kaiser, Edgar F., 220
Katz, Dr. Harold (quoted), 102–103
Katzenbach, Edward L., 197
Keezer, Dexter, research expenditures forecast by, 133–134

Kefauver, Estes, 11
Kennedy, John F., 290
  quoted, 10
  steel industry confrontation by, 182
Kennedy, Robert F.
  housing proposals by, 219
  quoted, 222
Kennedy Administration
  antitrust during, 176
  economic expansion during, 190
Keppel, Francis, 197
Kimball, Dan, 196

labor unions
  decline of, 84–88
  power of, 184
Ling, James, 45, 46
Ling-Temco-Vought (LTV), 5, 12, 45–47
Lippmann, Walter (quoted), 226
Litton Industries, 5, 44, 91, 92, 97, 196, 205, 223, 275
Lockheed, 191, 196, 204, 205, 206, 207
long-term planning, 9, 114, 116

McLaren, Richard W., 177
McLuhan, Marshall (quoted), 3, 143
management
  changing status of, 90–92, 291
  divisions within, 93–94
  policy making and, 89
  power of, 53–54, 65, 68
  See also executives
man-hours, increase in, 116–117, 118, 120
manufacturing, forecast concerning, 161–162, 264
Masefield, John (quoted), 99
materials, new, 155–156
Maytag, L. B., 98
Means, Gardiner, 54
medical care, 77–78, 206
medical research, 151–153

The Author

RICHARD BARBER has taught at the Yale Law School and formerly served as counsel for the Senate Anti-Trust Subcommittee. Mr. Barber makes his home in Washington, D.C.